New Media and Digital Pedagogy

Studies in New Media

Series Editor: John Allen Hendricks,
Stephen F. Austin State University

This series aims to advance the theoretical and practical understanding of the emergence, adoption, and influence of new technologies. It provides a venue to explore how new media technologies are changing the media landscape in the twenty-first century.

Titles in Series:

The Twenty-First-Century Media Industry: Economic and Managerial Implications in the Age of New Media, edited by John Allen Hendricks
Blogging: How Our Private Thoughts Went Public, by Kristin Roeschenthaler Wolfe
Beyond New Media: Discourse and Critique in a Polymediated Age, edited by Art Herbig, Andrew F. Herrmann, and Adam W. Tyma
Communicating User Experience: Applying Local Strategies Research to Digital Media Design, edited by Trudy Milburn
Navigating New Media Networks: Understanding and Managing Communication Challenges in a Networked Society, by Bree McEwan
Globalization's Impact on Cultural Identity Formation: Queer Diasporic Males in Cyberspace, by Ahmet Atay
Social Media: Culture and Identity, edited by Kehbuma Langmia and Tia Tyree
Swipe Right for Love: The Impact of Social Media in Modern Romantic Relationships, edited by Narissra M. Punyanunt-Carter and Jason S. Wrench
The Evolution and Social Impact of Video Game Economics, edited by Casey B. Hart
New Media and Digital Pedagogy: Enhancing the Twenty-First-Century Classroom, edited by Michael G. Strawser

New Media and Digital Pedagogy

Enhancing the Twenty-First-Century Classroom

Edited by Michael G. Strawser

LEXINGTON BOOKS
Lanham • Boulder • New York • London

Published by Lexington Books
An imprint of The Rowman & Littlefield Publishing Group, Inc.
4501 Forbes Boulevard, Suite 200, Lanham, Maryland 20706
www.rowman.com

Unit A, Whitacre Mews, 26-34 Stannary Street, London SE11 4AB

British Library Cataloguing in Publication Information Available

Library of Congress Cataloging-in-Publication Data Available

ISBN 978-1-4985-4851-9 (cloth)
ISBN 978-1-4985-4853-3 (pbk.)
ISBN 978-1-4985-4852-6 (electronic)

Contents

Chapter One

New Media and the Twenty-First-Century Classroom

A Research and Instructional Imperative

Michael G. Strawser, Phillip E. Wagner, and Crystal Simons

AN OPPORTUNITY

In 1963, James Brown and James Thornton highlighted what has become a cyclical discussion in higher education. They said:

> Opportunities to explore and further develop the instructional potentials of the new media are numerous, and they are ripe. We have good models which invite further study, refinement, and application. The space age is no time to be timid about using the modern technology in higher education.

Decades later, these sentiments still ring true.

The arguments for or against new media use and application are ample, especially in education contexts, yet academic practitioners, scholars, and instructors must remember that despite constant fears of new technologies, the evolving theoretical and practical implications of new media necessitates consistent exploration.

Higher education institutions, as catalysts and adopters of new media technologies, are worthy avenues to consider when inspecting the modern new media landscape. It is true that new media as a twenty-first-century classroom imperative has dramatic implications for the modern classroom environment and, as a result, researchers must continually examine the presence and educational relevance of new media technology. As new media emerge, and instructors adopt various digital technologies as instructional resources, the influence of these new instruments must be analyzed and assessed.

A HOLISTIC OVERVIEW

In order to preview the current educational context, and function as a roadmap, this chapter will serve as an overview, and a call, to research and implement a variety of new media in the twenty-first-century classroom. As an overview to the remainder of the text, this chapter will set the stage for the theoretical, practical, and instructional implications of new media on higher education. Additionally, this chapter will present a summary of the overall vision and mission of this book and present a synopsis of each corresponding chapter.

BACKGROUND AND HISTORICAL CONTEXT

The actual phrase "new media" can be referred to as an all-encompassing descriptor that has, primarily, twenty-first century connections to the Internet and web-based applications. However, new media as a field of study and as a pedagogical interest is not unique to the twenty-first century. Twentieth-century scholars were interested in the rise and relevance of new media technologies as well (McLuhan, 1964), and a discussion of new media would be incomplete without first recognizing that media is always new, constantly evolving, and rarely stoic and stagnant. While current perspectives and discussions on information and communication technologies stem from a web-based outlook, new media discussions and research-based initiatives have presented themselves for generations.

New media, or computer and communication technologies, also implicitly contains elements of production, distribution, and application (Chen, Wu, and Wang, 2011; Lin, Li, Deng, and Lee, 2013). Defining new media is difficult and Lin et al. (2013) wisely diagnose the conceptual problems as stemming from two perspectives. Specifically, researchers may classify new media by discussing technical characteristics while others focus on the sociocultural characteristics of new media (Anderson and Balsamo, 2008; Lin et al., 2013; Pungente, Duncan, and Andersen, 2005). This divergence of opinion, even at the foundational stage of defining and classifying new media, presents a conversational and conceptual dilemma.

Harrison and Barthel (2009) remind us that the urge for communication scholars to study and create media content is not historically new; rather, the desire is almost an embedded aspect of our disciplinary distinction. The transition from analog broadcasts and personal computers to digital technologies and online publications signals a revolution and media evolution.

Unfortunately, new media scholars and practitioners face the challenging task of constantly keeping up with the latest technologies. In an ever-evolving media ecosystem, the speed and frequency of new resources (e.g., books, publications, even the media tools and platforms themselves) create a landscape ripe for opportunity and, at times, frustration. Researchers, like those who focus on information and communication technologies, are not the only exasperated population. Instructors, trying to navigate the shifting new media scene, are also routinely excited and at times exacerbated.

Instructors often teach as they have been taught, many under the pretext of lecture. As such, they are often ill-prepared to utilize, or even think through, new media and digital components in their own classrooms. However, with the ever-increasing college audience that now includes an overwhelming number of digital natives, a conversant and working knowledge of new media and digital pedagogy is imperative.

Therefore, this book will address the influence of new media on instruction, higher education, and pedagogy. This book will not serve as a "catch-all" naming various resources that could be used in the classroom, rather this work examines the practical and theoretical implications of new media and the influence of new media on education. In an effort to create a timeless work that will not fade with the passing of new media technologies, chapter authors have addressed topics that discuss the role, use, and implications of new media. For the purposes of this chapter, the emphasis is primarily on the changing landscape and the creation of a foundational lens and framework for thinking through and navigating higher education in a digital and new media driven context.

THEORETICAL UNDERSTANDING

While much has been written on the applied use of new media in the classroom, this text explores the adoption and influence of new media and digital pedagogy from a theoretical context. The mediatization, one umbrella term used to classify media and communication research, of the classroom and the impending implications on student learning are substantial. Scholars recognize the need to build, and refer to, new media theory in light of advancing technologies, pedagogy, and theoretical tenets of the past (e.g., agenda setting, constructivism, media richness, etc.). The task for the twenty-first-century educator, and maybe more so the twenty-first-century educator-researcher, is to navigate foundational media theory and apply these theories in new and innovative ways.

Authors in this volume discuss new media and digital pedagogy from a variety of theoretical approaches and learning paradigms appropriate for an educational context. While we recognize that there is not one wide-ranging theoretical umbrella that categorizes all new media and digital pedagogy, researchers have astutely developed frameworks that capture the importance and necessity of new media concepts. The authors in this text wisely reflect on theories that firmly root their topics in a historical conversation and a future direction. Thus, tried and true educational theories like Kolb's Experiential Learning Theory and Constructivism are navigated side by side with recent theories like the Information and Communication Technologies–Technological Pedagogical Content Knowledge Model and the Instructional Beliefs Model, both recent theoretical developments for understanding the influence of technology and new media in the twenty-first-century classroom. These theories come together to make sense of the current climate of higher education.

ADOPTION

Perhaps one of the chief reasons faculty are hesitant to adopt new media in the classroom has less to do with *unfamiliarity* (of technology and/or media) and, in fact, centers on *familiarity*. Indeed, in an era where faculty are increasingly overworked and underpaid, pedagogical revision (such as incorporating new media) requires effort; effort requires time and energy—elements often lost in the shuffle of research, teaching, engagement, and service obligations faculty are required to meet. Thus, many return to and/or regurgitate their courses using a familiar format, with familiar content, in a familiar mode of delivery. Consequently, there is a divide among "media engaged" faculty and "traditional" faculty, characterized by heated conversations on the utility of new media in the classroom.

Many of these conversations center around ideas of new media as a frivolous toy; a mere trinket of engagement that will pass with students' ever-waning interest. Yet as noted above—media is always new and always being developed. Failing to harness the powerful potential of new media in the classroom because of fear of its frivolity and/or mortality demonstrates a static orientation to teaching and learning. In response, Kolb (2008) urges a shift in thinking about new media from "toys to tools," and sees digital means (such as smartphones) as a "Swiss Army Knife–type data-collection tool" (para. 3; see also Philip and Garcia, 2013). Be the entrance mechanical (as with smartphones, tablets, and smart boards) or delivery based (as with web applications, Internet-enabled learning, microblogging, or a host of other digitally enhanced learning modalities), the pervasiveness of new media has restructured our understanding of what it means to communicate, learn, and *be* in the modern era. Thus, dismissing new media as a frivolity is not a luxury faculty teaching in the digital age can afford—nor should they want to. In fact, there are innumerable benefits for wholeheartedly embracing new media in the learning environment, particularly in higher education. Entire works could be dedicated to declaring the benefits of embracing new media in the context of teaching and learning. For sake of clarity, let's briefly explore three: benefits to the student, benefits to the workforce, and benefits to the university.

First, we cannot deny the value of new media in helping inspire students to take ownership of the learning process. The typical portrayal of the college classroom in mainstream Hollywood films reveals rows of students sitting in a lecture hall, bored to tears listening to a lecturer addressing them ad nauseam. Though exaggerated to elicit laughs, this portrayal is perhaps not too far removed from the "traditional" lecture style of learning that many of us experienced firsthand during our university experience. Of no surprise, data reveals that this method is ineffective, and students in these traditional large lecture courses are up to 1.5 times more likely to fail than students in courses that involve active learning methods (Freeman et al., 2013). McLoughlin and Lee (2010) note, "digital-age students want an active learning experience that is social, participatory, and supported by rich media" (p. 28). According to the Educause Center for Applied Research (2010), this holds true, with over 67 percent of students reporting that mediated learning is important to their academic success.

There are a host of benefits to students when their instructor uses new media in their pedagogy. Using these means promotes a more student-centered design (Greenhow, 2011), partly because they facilitate and demand learner-led control throughout the entire learning process (Dron, 2007). Mediated learning focuses heavily—if not depends—on user creation of materials, emphasizing higher order action in Bloom's taxonomy (Agichtein, Castillo, Donato, Gionis, and Mishne, 2008). As Heath and colleagues (2005) note, the integration of digital means can also significantly boost students' confidence in their ability to master course content, perhaps because it stretches the boundaries of traditional teaching and learning and invites constant application of the "real world" to course content (Traxler, 2007). Indeed, the integration of new media in the classroom helps bridge a divide between the classroom and whatever else lies "out there" beyond the four walls that have typically separated the learning process.

Closely related then, we must look at the benefit that new media has on the community and the university. Though an often lambasted and misconstrued framing of what higher education is supposed to be, the fact remains that a large portion of the population sees the university experience as simply the necessary first step in securing a job. As legislative bodies (i.e., boards of regents, state legislatures, accreditation agencies, and external stakeholders) have turned a critical eye to the entire university experience, colleges and universities are having to prove to a much greater extent the ways in which they are preparing their students for success in the "real world." Liberal arts faculty, especially, are bewildered by the careless dismissal of their ancient traditions in pursuit of students gaining employment. Yet, new media offers a means of demonstrating that faculty are preparing their students with the skills they need in the "real world" (i.e., their career) while also staying true to the academic content at play.

According to NACE's (2016) most recent job outlook survey, some of the most sought after skill sets employers are looking for include the ability to work in a team (78.9 percent), written communication skills (70.2 percent), problem-solving skills (70.2 percent), technical skills (59.6 percent), and computer skills (55.3 percent). As much of the scholarship cited above already reveals, these skills are embedded throughout media-engaged learning. The digital landscape of learning is collaborative by nature; a space wherein individuals transcend the boundaries of time and space to contribute to the knowledge creation process. Through the use of digitally engaged learning mechanisms, faculty can demonstrate the development of sought-after skill sets in their students, even if their content falls outside of the landscape of courses typically thought of as "job preparation" courses (i.e., courses in the major field). New media provides a benefit to both faculty and the community, then. Faculty possess a means of communicating their commitment to developing career-readiness in students while future employers (i.e., the community) benefit from graduates who are practiced, engaged, and finessed in the art of digital communication and embody the corresponding skill sets they have developed through the process.

Of course, this cursory overview does not fully examine the innumerable and tangible benefits of new media in the teaching and learning process. So, too, does it forgo true exploration of the many concerns and calamities that come with the adoption of these mechanisms. The purpose is to demonstrate that this work is for all of us—early adopters, naysayers, skeptics, and the apathetic. Higher education has always been a catalyst for long-lasting social reform and innovation. Yet through growth comes growing pains. This work acknowledges those pains without losing sight of the *potentials* that are linked with them. The remainder of this volume provides greater theoretical and practical insight on the role of new media in higher education.

CHAPTER OVERVIEWS

Following this chapter, this work will focus on the theoretical and practical implications of new media and digital pedagogy on higher education. The faculty model of education, traditional modalities, uniform practices, and routine lectures, has evolved. Higher education, once a bastion for traditional instruction, has begun a transition to media-based teaching. The transformed pedagogical paradigm, from traditional to digital, represents an opportunity for instructional enhancement. The second chapter, "Instructional Enhancement: New Media as a Paradigm Shift," beautifully positioned by Marjorie Buckner and Mary Norman, explores the historical basis of the transition to new media classroom initiatives and will identify patterns and trends in new media instructional progression. Additionally, the second chapter presents a background and chronology for how and why new media emerged in the classroom context and discusses the development of new media in higher education.

Chapter three, written by Jason Martin and Jason Zahrndt, "Media and Digital Literacy: A Framework for Instructional Strategy," primarily delves into the issues of media and digital literacy. Media and digital literacy, in the new media age, has become a desirable and necessary skill for the twenty-first-century learner. The ability to construct, share, and collaborate with "experts" and public intellectuals has become commonplace in our social space. New information and social networking platforms are constantly emerging. As such, students must be prepared to evaluate media consumption and critically analyze media-driven messages. Therefore, the third chapter positions media and digital literacy as frameworks for long-lasting instructional strategy. While it is important that instructors communicate with students about unique new technologies, a structure for critical analysis of message intake is also crucial for the intellectual and lifelong development of the modern student.

The twenty-first-century faculty member, along with the twenty-first-century student, faces a challenging task. For the modern educator, content must be relevant, experiential, and engaging for the twenty-first-century learner. To remain viable, universities need to identify creative new ways to address these challenges through innovative pedagogical methods including new media technologies. Unfortunately, new media use and implementation may not come naturally to current faculty. To combat this issue, universities should develop relevant and applicable faculty development programs to train instructors how to effectively use new media and design digital-friendly courses. Thus, in chapter four, "Faculty Development in the Digital Age: Training Instructors in New Media Pedagogy," Russell Carpenter provides an overview of the necessary changes to faculty development as new media technologies continue to evolve. A charge to implement faculty-centered development that centers on new media and digital pedagogy will be discussed, and throughout this chapter, new media training initiatives, topics, and procedures will be propositioned.

Faculty members must address new media and digital pedagogy but cannot do so in a vacuum that ignores traditional facets of classroom climate.

For example, community and collaboration are important facets of the modern classroom. Learning space, virtual and physical, can have a significant impact on learning, and the emphasis on learning spaces that focus on principles and activities that facilitate learning and the role of technology in creating an effective learning environment is an important area of focus for instructors and researchers alike. To answer such challenges, Nigel Haarstad wrote chapter five, "Learning Interfaces: Collaboration and Learning Space in the Digital Age," to examine the ability of new media to function as a facilitator of collaborative community and the necessity for digital platforms to enhance student learning. The intersection of new media and learning management systems and new media and collaborative technologies will be dissected. Learning space has become a prominent avenue for instructional and educational research and the influence of new media must be examined as a vehicle for creating and sustaining an effective learning environment.

Chapter six, "Accessibility and New Media Technologies," crafted by Beth Case, positions classroom accessibility and equal access as pillars of successful new media use and application. As the population of students with disabilities continues to increase in higher education institutions, instructors should utilize, effectively, new media technologies. Instructors should recognize challenges faced by students with disabilities and strategically implement a classroom climate that engages students across the spectrum using new media and digital pedagogy. Therefore, this chapter will address the current landscape of accommodation challenges, discuss the potential of new media technology (technologies) as the classroom equalizer, and position new media pedagogy and digital tools as sound pedagogy perspective for equality in the higher education classroom.

In chapter seven, "Gamification and the New Media Imperative," Clay Ewing shifts from the institutionally philosophical and theoretical to the relevance and necessity of foundational new media tools and applications. Gamification has become a popular form of instructional strategy to engage digital natives. While it is true that K–12 schools typically engage in game-based enterprises, higher education classrooms have begun to transition to game-based and modified instruction. The current status of gamification in higher education and the impact of this course design on student learning, and instructor-student and student-student relationships, will be deliberated. Multiplayer, augmented reality, virtual reality, user-created content, and role-playing games are firmly situated in mainstream popular culture and have been utilized to effectively encourage creative design and identity management, document and reflect on student learning, and inspire class discussion from a variety of perspectives. To address this new reality, this chapter will explore the progression of gamification and the future of game-based learning in higher education.

Gamification is just one strategy for new media use in higher education. While new media is not confined to web-based applications, it is important to consider the impact of the Internet on the current state of new media classroom use. "The Internet of Things and Wearable Technology as a Classroom Resource," chapter eight, with foresight by Heather Hether, Joe Martin, and Andrew Cole, scans the current landscape of interconnectivity and wearable technology. It is expected that by the year 2020, 20–50 billion devices will be part of the IoT network. The growth of online and blended courses, and the use of digital technologies in the traditional classroom, have attributed to the advancement of networked devices in the world of education. Smart technology and integrated devices create a networked learning context for unlimited possibilities. Similar to devices that use IoT, wearable technology (like virtual reality headsets, augmented reality mechanisms, etc.) has the potential to significantly impact the college classroom. Thus, in an effort to diagram IoT and wearable technology in the classroom, this chapter becomes an important conversation catalyst.

While the mission of this text is not to list tools and applications that may become obsolete, it is important to describe what is available, in the present, for instructor and institutional use. Thus, chapter nine, "Current Tools and Trends of New Media, Digital Pedagogy, and Instructional Technology," by Renee Kaufmann, Nicholas Tatum, and Kody Frey, accomplishes a broad-based theoretical and practical overview of what is present and accounted for in new media instruction. The understanding and knowledge of current tools and trends are important, and instructors, graduate students, and education professionals need to know what is available for current implementation. This chapter includes various descriptions of new media applications and potential ways to use each application in the classroom with a heavy emphasis on the theory behind current tools.

The final chapter will look to the future by exploring what new media possibilities "are next" and where will digital pedagogy opportunities present themselves in the next decade and beyond. While the content may be conjecture, there are tools that exist but have yet to take a prominent position in the classroom environment. Drones, holograms, artificial intelligence, international high-speed web access, and other evolving technologies have capabilities beyond our current imaginations, and the content in this section will serve as a platform into the next phase of new media instructional technology. To conclude this work, chapter ten, "The Next Phase: New Media and the Inevitable Transition," written by Shawn Apostel, explores unique initiatives and experimental technology and presents the reader with a discussion that transitions us beyond our current proficiencies.

Each of these chapters explore relevant twenty-first-century themes and present arguments for a more foundational understanding of new media and digital pedagogy—not as an instructional preference, but as a necessity.

CONCLUSION

This chapter began with a quote, or maybe more so a call to action, to explore and develop the instructional potential of new media and digital pedagogy. As James Brown and James Thornton remind us, words written in 1963 that still ring true today, we have models, and theories, that invite further study, refinement, and application—we must not be timid about using modern technology in higher education. Thus, this volume recognizes and reinforces higher education institutions as catalysts and adopters of new media technologies. The contributors to this volume also know that new media as a twenty-first-century classroom imperative has dramatic implications for the modern classroom environment, and, as a result, educators and researchers alike must examine new media and the adoption and influence of new technologies. May we, as scholar-practitioners, recognize that the climate is ripe for purposeful classroom innovation that is theory driven, student centered, and purposeful.

REFERENCES

Agichtein, E., Castillo, C., Donato, D., Gionis, A., and Mishne, G. (2008). Finding high quality content in social media. *Proceedings of the International Conference on Web Search and Web Data Mining,* New York, NY (Retrieved November 27, 2016, from http://www.mathcs.emory.edu/~eugene/papers/wsdm2008quality.pdf).

Anderson, S., and Balsamo, A. (2008). A pedagogy for original Synners. In T. McPherson (Ed.), *Digital youth, innovation, and the unexpected* (pp. 241–259). Cambridge, MA: The MIT Press.

Brown, J. W., and Thornton Jr., J. W. (1963). *New media in higher education.* Washington, DC: Association for Higher Education.

Chen, D.-T., Wu, J., and Wang, Y.-M. (2011). Unpacking new media literacy. *Journal on Systemics, Cybernetics and Informatics, 9*(2), 84–88.

Dron, J. (2007). Designing the undesignable: Social software and control. *Educational Technology and Society, 10,* 60–71.

Educause Center for Applied Research (2010). *ECAR study of undergraduate students and information technology.* Louisville, CO: Educause Center for Applied Research (Retrieved November 20, 2016, from http://net.educause.edu/ir/library/pdf/ERS1208/ERS1208.pdf).

Freeman, S., Eddy, S. L., McDonough, M., Smith, M. K., Okoroafor, N., Jordt, H., and Wenderoth, M. P. (2013). Active learning increases student performance in science, engineering, and mathematics. *Proceedings of the National Academy of Sciences of the United States of America, 111,* 8410–8415.

Greenhow, C. (2011). Youth, learning, and social media. *Journal of Educational Computing Research, 45,* 139–146.

Heath, B. P., Herman, R. L., Lugo, G. G., Reeves, J. H., Vetter, R. J., and Ward, C. R. (2005). Project numina: Enhancing student learning with handheld computers. *IEEE Computer Society, 38,* 46–52.

Kolb, L. (2008). *Toys to tolls: Connecting student cell phones to education.* Washington, DC: International Society for Technology in Education.

Lin, T.-B., Li, J.-Y., Deng, F., and Lee, L. (2013). Understanding new media literacy: An explorative theoretical framework. *Educational Technology & Society, 16* (4), 160–170.

McLoughlin, C., and Lee, M. J. W. (2010). Personalized and self regulated learning in the web 2.0 era: International exemplars of innovative pedagogy using social software. *Australian Journal of Educational Technology, 26,* 28–43.

McLuhan, M. (1964). *Understanding media: The extensions of man.* Toronto: McGraw Hill.

National Association of Colleges and Employers (NACE). (2016). *Job Outlook 2016.* Bethlehem, PA: NACE.

Philip, T. M., and Garcia, A. D. (2013). The importance of still teaching the iGeneration: New technologies and the centrality of pedagogy. *Harvard Educational Review, 83,* 300–319.

Pungente, J. J., Duncan, B., and Anderson, N. (2005). The Canadian experience: Leading the way. In G. Schwarz and P. U. Brown (Eds.), *Media literacy: Transforming curriculum and teaching* (pp. 140–160). Malden, MA: Blackwell Publishing.

Traxler, J. (2007). Distance education and mobile learning: Catching up, taking stock. *Distance Education, 31,* 129–138.

Chapter Two

Instructional Enhancement

New Media as a Paradigm Shift

Marjorie M. Buckner and Mary S. Norman

INSTRUCTIONAL STRATEGIES AND LEARNING PARADIGMS

Teachers in higher education use a variety of strategies to engage and educate students. Books such as *What the Best College Teachers Do*, *McKeachie's Teaching Tips*, or *Teaching at Its Best* offer advice about lessons, activities, and overarching ideas on learning. Historically, instructors in higher education have relied heavily on lecture or the Socratic method in order to foster learning. Murray and Murray (1992) identify lecture as "the most common mode of instruction in higher education" (p. 109). Yet, instructional strategies have diversified as additional theories of learning and instruction are posited and technology and media arc introduced to the classroom. For example, instructors use popular social media platforms (e.g., Facebook and Twitter) and video conferencing to facilitate learning (see Frisby, Kaufmann, and Beck, 2016; Hosek, 2016; Kaufmann and Frisby, 2013; Madden, Winkler, Fraustino, and Janoske, 2016). Such pedagogical practices draw on more contemporary learning theories like Kolb's (1984) experiential learning theory, which describes learning as a continuous process of engagement, observation, experience, and reflection.

Experiential and participative learning now infuses many of the recent developments in technology and media. This shift in our understanding of "the nature of learning, relationships involved, the principles that underpin those relationships and the structural and cultural dynamics responsible for causes and effects of what happens (Denzin and Lincoln, 2000)" (Kivunja, 2014, p. 82) with regard to learning suggests a new learning paradigm. Learning paradigms are integral to making sense of learning and teaching processes and practices. A new media learning paradigm considers media advancements and technological innovations as integral to how college students learn and pedagogical strategies. Theories such as the framework for twenty-first-century learning (Framework, n.d.), job readiness with twenty-first-century skills (Trilling and Fadel, 2009), and connectivism (Siemens, 2004) embrace the influence of new media.

This chapter outlines various learning paradigm shifts and postulates the usefulness of a new media learning paradigm. First, this chapter will present a historical overview of learning paradigms that have informed the instructional choices educators make and the influence of new media in changing these paradigms. Next, the chapter will explicate how educators can enact this new paradigm and re-consider previous learning paradigms in light of new media. Then, we will discuss how instructors may adopt this new media into their classroom in addition to student and faculty experiences with new media. Finally, the chapter will posit the influence a new media learning paradigm will have on higher education practices and learning theory development.

BACKGROUND AND HISTORICAL CONTEXT

Digital literacy grounds new media learning and teaching paradigm and theory. However, prior to digital literacy, other forms of literacy served as a foundation for the learning and teaching paradigms and literacy. As Edgar (2012) states, "Recitation literacy was postulated to effectuate knowledge. This knowledge gained through recitation of facts, literacy in the form of reading and writing, and knowledge of spoken language (Latin, Greek, and German) was equated with learning" (p. 2). Social, cultural, economic, and political forces, coupled with scientific advancements regarding the learning process, propelled theory development and paradigm shifts that fit with the various literacy needs and expectations of learning and teaching (Edgar, 2012). This section traces some of the learning paradigms and representative theories as they have developed across time.

Learning Paradigms

A host of learning and instructional paradigms preceded the new media paradigm. Each paradigm encompasses a variety of learning theories that have informed instructional practice for decades. By understanding the learning theories and paradigms that have informed higher education to date, we are better able to make sense of the need for the development of a new media paradigm and the ways a new media paradigm may shape college and university instruction. Kivunja (2014) outlines four primary learning paradigms that have informed education—transmission paradigm, behaviorist paradigm, cognitivist paradigm, and constructivism. To this discussion, we have included the design-based paradigm, and we present a new media paradigm.

Transmission Paradigm

The transmission paradigm posits that learning occurs when information is communicated directly from the teacher to the learner (Kivunja, 2014; Monroe, 1925). Reflective of Shannon's (1948) theory of communication in which a message is communicated from a sender to a receiver, the transmission paradigm negates feedback between the instructor and learner and designates roles such that the instructor only provides instruction and the learner only receives instruction. Without acknowledging a feedback loop, engaging students through questions or discussion, conducting formative assessment, or responding to student reactions is not possible. Thus, clarifying information or adjusting lessons to ensure student learning does not occur. Further, by designating strict roles, the instructor and student are rigidly ascribed behaviors and norms for their performances in the classroom and learning process. Not only is this unrealistic, but this limitation further restricts the interactions between the educator and students. Scholars and educators recognize the inadequacy of this paradigm in accurately portraying the learning process, though this paradigm continues to inform pedagogical choices. Moreover, the instructional strategies derived from this paradigm (e.g., lecture) may benefit students when operating through a different paradigm.

Behaviorist Paradigm

Behaviorists believe that learning occurs when a student is presented with a stimulus that incites a response. Theories reflective of the behaviorist paradigm emphasize the instructor's role of inducing learning. For example, Ivan Pavlov introduced classical conditioning in which a particular action serves as a stimulus for a behavior. Over time, the stimulus of the bell elicits a particular response, and a behavior is said to be learned (Edgar, 2012). Another behaviorist, B. F. Skinner, also believed that a stimulus could affect individual behaviors. Skinner's theory, known as operant conditioning, introduced categorized stimuli as reinforcers or punishers, which could be positive or negative. By reinforcing a behavior or punishing a behavior, a behavior would increase or decrease (Edgar, 2012). Though originally conceived as learning, the stimulus-response and reinforcement beliefs lacked inclusion of uniquely human characteristics such as ideas and feelings that influence learning (Bigge and Shermis, 1999; Gredler, 2005; Schunk, 2004).

Cognitivist Paradigm

Rather than believing the learning occurred in response to a stimulus, cognitivists posited that learning occurred through an active and engaged mind. Individuals' minds develop over time and produce complex schemas to understand the world around them. Jean Piaget conjectured that individuals' cognitive abilities developed throughout the lifespan via stages. Though Piaget's theory paired closely with age and biological development, William Perry's (1970, 1981) scheme of cognitive development does not. Instead Perry's stages of learning focus on the progression of student attitudes and beliefs about knowledge, education, and learning. The cognitivist paradigm focuses on individuals' abilities to process information and how these may change over time such that their learning is improved and they are capable of understanding, synthesizing, and producing progressively abstract and complex ideas. This paradigm emphasizes cognition and influenced educators to devise instructional activities and materials that match students' abilities and preferences. Yet, theories reflective of this paradigm do not consider the effect of outside forces such as society that may affect student learning.

Constructivism

Constructivism considers interactions with others as integral to learning. That is, knowledge is created through social exchange (Vygotsky, 1978) rather than dependent on an expert for transmission, adapting a behavior as response to a stimulus, or developed through cognitive processes. Both Lev Vygotsky's social development theory and Albert Bandura's social learning theory reflect this paradigm. Constructivism extends cognitivism to consider social and cultural factors that affect learning (Edgar, 2012). Yet, these paradigms fail to address practical problems in an actionable way (The Design-Based Research Collective, 2003).

Design-based Paradigm

Design-based research and theories seek to resolve gaps between educational theory and practice (The Design-Based Research Collective, 2003). Within this framework, scholars consider "the whole range of designed innovations: artifacts as well as less concrete aspects such as activity structures, institutions, scaffolds, and curricula" (pp. 5–6). Design-based research unites researchers and educators to consider the broader learning environment in addition to learning and teaching interventions to devise and enact theoretically sound, contextually salient, and practical education methods. What the design-based paradigm fails to address is the specific influence of new media on teaching and learning.

A NEW MEDIA LEARNING PARADIGM

Continuous advancements and technological innovations demarcate new media. With interactive capabilities, the use of web-based or Internet platforms, and an extensive variety of functions including entertainment to productivity, new media shapes how we locate, share, evaluate, value, and create information. Moreover, new media is distinctly situated within the twenty-first century and, therefore, closely tied to theorizing about skills needed and resources available to ensure student learning and success (Trilling and Fadel, 2009). Recognizing the need for students to develop knowledge and skills that position students for success in the twenty-first century, P21, the Partnership for 21st Century Learning, developed a framework for twenty-first-century learning that lists "information, media, and technology skills" as an essential component to preparing students for success in the twenty-first century (Framework, n.d.; Our History, n.d.). P21 explains that "[being] effective in the 21st century [requires] citizens and workers . . . to create, evaluate, and effectively utilize information, media, and technology" (Framework, n.d., para. 9). Echoed by Chehayl (2010) in her book review of Trilling and Fadel's (2009) book, *21st Century Skills: Learning for Life in Our Times*, that describes the P21 initiative and advocates for adoption and integration of the P21 framework, "the problems of today can only be solved when pedagogical and curricular practice embraces all facets of the Digital Age and provides students with the pedagogical experiences they need to manage their digital world" (Chehayl, 2010, p. 100).

The P21 framework fulfills the gaps of previous learning paradigms by specifically naming new media as important content and process related to learning. It also demonstrates an important shift to thinking about new media as a central component of learning. Other theories, however, go one step further—positioning new media as the foundation of learning rather than a component.

Connectivism (Siemens, 2004) positions new media as the underpinning of a new media learning paradigm. This is not to suggest that other theories are not suitable for a new media learning paradigm; rather, locating new media as the cornerstone of a new media learning paradigm reveals the salience of new media to learning and a modern approach to bridging new media and learning. Connectivism (Siemens, 2004) departs from the twenty-first-century views of learning so as to locate new media as the foundation that undergirds the approach. Connectivism suggests that knowledge and learning is networked and exists in "environments of shifting core elements—not entirely under the control of the individual" (p. 4). Interestingly, this theory postulates that knowledge may exist outside of an individual and "the connections that enable us to learn more are more important than our current state of knowing" (Siemens, 2004, p. 4). Thus, connectivism emphasizes the role and process of new media as embedded and part of the learning process.

Both the P21 framework and connectivism illustrate a paradigm shift in how we understand and approach learning. The P21 framework situates new media as a separate component that may inform or shape a learning paradigm, whereas connectivism situates new media as the foundation of a learning paradigm. Though these theories approach new media differently, both emphasize new media as an important, contributing factor in learning. Because of their inclusion and focus on new media, both constitute a new media learning paradigm. Changing our learning paradigm to include new media requires us to consider how theories within this paradigm may inform how we make sense of learning and how we adopt this paradigm into our instructional strategies and practices.

THEORETICAL UNDERSTANDING

Based on the theories discussed as exemplars of the new media learning paradigm, instructors may use and implement new media differently than they have previously. That is, the ideas posited in new media learning paradigm theories may empower instructors to move beyond applying new media to traditional learning paradigms and consider new media as both content and process central to learning. This section explores three approaches that may enrich the learning process and considers ways of integrating new media and traditional learning paradigms and theories in a way that poises new media as an important and central focus to curriculum and the learning process.

The new media learning paradigm advances theorizing about the learning process in light of media advancements and technology innovations. Because new media shapes the messages, channels, and interactivity available to college and university instructors and students, theories related to this paradigm must provide insight and generate scholarship and practice related to new media and learning. Specifically, the new media learning paradigm suggests that new media may inform the learning process in three distinct ways: (a) instructional media, (b) media in instruction, and (c) mediated instruction. In other words, media may serve as the teacher, as content or an example, and as the process.

These three approaches to integrating new media and learning reflect the P21 framework and connectivism. The framework for twenty-first-century learning (Framework, n.d.) positions new media as one component of the framework and argues for including new media as content in course curricula (i.e., media in instruction) and as a process for learning (i.e., mediated instruction). This framework also separates digital literacy as a separate set of knowledge and skills, emphasizing the use of new media as content and process. In fact, Trilling and Fadel (2009) recommend students "use technology as a tool" (p. 71). Kivunja (2014) also advocates "[embedding] digital technologies in teaching, learning, and assessment" (p. 106). These ideas reflect new media's influence on higher education as what should be taught in courses (i.e., content) and suggest an experiential approach that may involve new media as the site of learning (i.e., process).

Connectivism (Siemens, 2004), however, posits new media as the teacher (i.e., instructional media) in addition to content and process. The principles of connectivism demonstrate how new media serves as content, channel, and interactivity. Connectivism also introduces potential and knowledge management as learning. The approach suggested by connectivism is complementary, yet different, from the approaches suggested by the P21 framework. Importantly, both theories embrace the new media learning paradigm and specify how instructors in higher education may conceptualize new media to best integrate new media into their teaching and curriculum.

Instructional Media

Instructional media, or media designed to deliver instructional messages and facilitate learning absent of a present instructor, affords institutions and students of higher education a number of prospects. Simulations and virtual worlds, for example, enhance education for students by providing scenarios that require advanced skills such as critical thinking in addition to digital, media, and information literacy. This media may be used to augment classroom instruction or operate independent of a traditional learning environment.

Media in Instruction

Media in instruction characterizes the integration of media in instruction. Examples of media in instruction may include building a social media page for students to ask questions, showing a movie clip in class, or assigning students various media sources to evaluate for credibility. Beyond providing examples of course concepts, media in instruction requires students to exercise multiple literacy skills and technology proficiencies. Media in instruction may also be used to spark discussion, integrate humor into the classroom, or generate connections in the class.

Mediated Instruction

Mediated instruction constitutes teaching through new media. Assigning a group project that requires students to use Google Hangouts to complete the project, posting a video-recorded lecture to a learning management system, or facilitating a discussion through a discussion board feature are instances of mediated instruction. With the rise of online and e-learning courses, mediated instruction is often used to connect with distance learners.

Instructional media, media in instruction, and mediated instruction integrate new media and learning; yet, all three practices highlight different aspects of theories aligning with the new media learning paradigm and necessitate different instructional strategies and materials. Despite the media advancements and technological innovations that inform the development of a new learning paradigm and theory, learning paradigms and theories previously used to inform education are not to be discarded. Rather, they remain an important influence in higher education.

Using Old Theories in New Ways

Importantly, adopting new media and engaging in this paradigm shift does not require individuals to abandon beliefs previously held about learning and teaching. Rather, theories and learning paradigms that have informed our past can still inform course design and instructional practices in practical and meaningful ways. For example, an instructor may draw on constructivism to construct a lesson in which a group discussion is part of the process. Or, an instructor may provide a varying degree of instruction of course assignments that reflect a cognitivist's view of students' learning stages. Thus, using old learning paradigms can be enacted in mediated and traditional classrooms and may or may not align with some aspect of a new media learning paradigm. To position the first example (i.e., student group discussion) within a new media learning paradigm, the instructor may require students to use a new technology to have the discussion and ask students to reflect on the process of working together in addition to the lesson. In the second example (i.e., staged learning across assignments), the instructor may use a virtual world for the students to progress through the learning process. Though using old theories in new ways provides instructors with perhaps a more comfortable avenue to gradually shift towards a new media learning paradigm, we must consider tactics and strategies for adopting the new media learning paradigm with an outright change. That is, how do we jump into a new media learning paradigm in a way that is authentic to the paradigm and reflective of the unique features this paradigm offers? The next section explores additional ways of adopting the new media learning paradigm in terms of instructional strategies and materials.

ADOPTION

Methods

Depending on the classroom environment, the new media learning paradigm may be adopted differently into pedagogy decisions and the learning process in higher education. Hence, we have demonstrated how educators in colleges and universities may adopt this paradigm for three common classroom environments—the traditional, hybrid, and online classroom environment. A traditional classroom environment includes face-to-face instruction in which students and the instructor meet in the same room at designated times and days. A hybrid classroom combines face-to-face, in-person instruction with online, mediated instruction. For example, the class may meet once a week in a classroom at the college then participate in online discussions held on a learning management system. An online classroom involves synchronous or asynchronous mediated instruction and learning processes.

Traditional Classroom

The classroom setting that will show the most remarkable difference by inclusion of new media is the traditional classroom setting. Hybrid and online classrooms already utilize digital space and the inclusion of new media may not feel as radical to instructors or students. In the traditional classroom setting, student response systems, class management systems, and media examples may inform pedagogy in traditional classrooms.

Student response systems offer instructors real-time feedback through polling. Student response systems can use supplied or student-owned clickers. However new media poll applications operate through programs available through subscription services found online. A benefit to these apps is they eliminate the need for department or student purchase of a clicker device, but more importantly they utilize a tool students already are familiar with, their smartphones. Polls can be created and the responses can be shown in real time either publicly or for the instructors use only. Polls can help the instructor to receive feedback on concepts that need review or to gauge interest in an upcoming event or speaker on campus. Instructors like using student response systems because it increases engagement in large classroom settings and students like the veil of anonymity that the system provides (Heaslip, Donovan, and Cullen, 2014). Additionally, student response systems can also assist in the pressure to conform and provide a platform for shy students to be involved (Stowell, Oldham, and Bennett, 2010).

Class management systems serve multiple purposes and facilitate communication and course administration for instructors and students. These systems can house the syllabus, grades, and assigned readings, but have discussion board and testing options that can be incorporated in real time.

Bringing class management systems into physical classrooms helps to make the connection between content covered in the classroom and resources (e.g., assignments, readings) available in the online system. Class management systems have the capability to serve as a virtual classroom for distance learning; however, many of the tools available can be incorporated into the traditional classroom. For example, reading quizzes created and administered in a digital class management system can save instructors and students time, may encourage students to arrive to class on time, and facilitates automatic grading (which may fulfill students' desire for immediate feedback). Analytics offered through the course management system also allow for the instructor to have a class breakdown per question and then instruction can stem from the quiz. Additionally, class management systems track student access to documents, which instructors can use to monitor student performance since repeated effort to access documents results in higher performance (Spivey and McMillan, 2013).

The final suggestion for including new media in the classroom is to include videos to illustrate key concepts or provide examples. A classroom is comprised of a variety of learning styles and providing visual content can help students to connect concepts and solidify their learning. YouTube calls on students to evaluate the quality, source, and message through summaries, critiques, or offering recommendations (Carrington, 2015).

Hybrid Classroom

Similar to a traditional classroom, a hybrid modality can maintain accountability and connection through the use of new media. A hybrid classroom is one in which the majority of instruction in the form or readings, lectures, and even assessments occurs outside of the physical classroom. Structuring class in this way allows for more experiential and application-based learning. Using technology in a hybrid classroom holds students accountable to required readings and lectures through the use of online quizzes or contributions to a blog or discussion board. New media can maintain a connection between student and teacher and student and peer even when learning is self-directed.

Within the hybrid learning paradigm, it is crucial that students receive support in their learning efforts. Video lectures or instructor responses to common mistakes permit the student to learn at their own pace while maintaining connection to the instructor. Difficult material can also be reviewed by the students numerous times. Creating online lectures can be time consuming for the instructor, but once created, they can be used in future courses. To ensure that students are viewing online lectures, assessments of comprehension can be used.

Online classroom management systems allow for writing prompts to be distributed and collected online, allowing valuable class time free for summarizing, debriefing, clarifying key concepts. Students are looking to acquire group work skills like brainstorming and pitching, but these skills take time and feedback from instructors. By pushing more of the traditional class work, like lectures and quizzes, outside of the traditional classroom, valuable time can be allocated to experiential learning.

Online Classroom

The applications of new media in the online classroom mimic the applications for hybrid and traditional classrooms, but online classrooms rely more heavily on new media.

A key difference in online classroom's use of new media, as compared to traditional and hybrid classrooms, is that there is more opportunity for student-supplied examples. Students can supply content through video uploads, case studies, or artifacts. These student-generated examples allow students to research, vet, and submit what they find memorable or useful for the class, all of which help them to move from understanding to applying and critiquing (Carrington, 2015). All of this can be incorporated into discussion boards, group work, or blog posts. This not only takes pressure off the instructor needing to supply all of the examples, it also puts students into an active learning roll whereby they perform the search and submission.

One challenge of the fully online classroom is the physical isolation from other students as well as the instructor. However, online classrooms need not be isolating. While it is true that some planning might be needed, online students have the ability to conduct group work through the use of new media. Online class management systems allow the instructor to create groups that operate as an online chat room for groups. Groups can participate in video conferencing calls to coordinate parts of a project. Using video conferencing may allow students to acquire new skills needed in a future occupation (Garner and Buckner, 2012). Simultaneous collaboration is available through mainstream online programs to facilitate presentations, reports, or spreadsheets. Collective documents also allow for transparency for group members because all work occurs in a visually open environment. This cuts down on the common group pitfalls of working in isolation and compiling at the conclusion.

STUDENT AND FACULTY EXPERIENCES

Importantly, when determining how to adopt the new media learning paradigm and choosing instructional strategies and course designs informed by the paradigm, instructors should also consider the perceived experience they and their students will have.

Student Experiences

Benefits

A new media learning paradigm can be enlightening and useful in the twenty-first-century classroom. In particular, student benefits include access, cost, appeal to various learning styles, tool familiarity, and convenience.

- Access—Student access to course materials occurs through technology and tools they already own. A 2013 study of a university sample found that 99.5 percent of students owned a mobile phone and 85 percent reported owning a smartphone (Emanuel, 2013). For this reason, the act of engaging in learning can feel more natural because learning happens where students already live digitally.
- Cost—New media platforms that license access to course material for the semester eliminates the need for hardware purchases such as clickers. Some textbooks have online or software versions of their products that are the primary means of education with a supplemental physical textbook as a purchase option.
- Learning Styles—New media can help instructors appeal to a variety of learning styles by offering content as text, audio, visual content, learning checks, prompts, and quizzes. For example, publisher-provided content may be paired with a physical textbook and could incorporate online versions of the text in an audio format.
- Interaction—New media levels the playing field for students who are shy or wary of participating in traditional class discussions (Stowell et al., 2010). Students have the ability to interact with peers and instructors and in some cases anonymously in online discussion groups.
- Tool Familiarity—Many college campuses use the same online classroom management systems campus-wide. This allows for a shallow learning curve, because once a student has used the platform in one course, the experience will be visually similar with the same capabilities. This allows students to focus in on the content of the course without the frustration of user error. Alt (2015) found that a mediator between academic motivation and engagement with social media is the fear of missing out. Instructors can use this motivation to their advantage by engaging with students in new media.
- Convenience—Students are now untethered from traditional places of learning and can read or listen to the audio of a chapter while walking to class, working out, or commuting to campus.

Challenges

While there are numerous benefits to students when new media is incorporated into educational endeavors, students may also experience challenges related to personal factors, distraction, and expectations of life balance.

- Personal Factors—Socioeconomic factors may exacerbate the access to cutting-edge technology, and students who do not have the resources available to access new media may be excluded from classes embracing the new media learning paradigm. Further, nontraditional students attending college later in life may not be as adept at new media and technology as traditional, millennial students known as digital natives. If this is the case, the instructor should be aware of other sections that do not use new media or be prepared to make a case for the importance of new media in your classroom.

  Workable solutions include requiring low stakes assignments to be turned in online to allow all students to work out kinks and build confidence. It may also be useful to strategically pair students to practice elements of new media to allow students who are inexperienced to learn through observation.
- Distraction—Students may report difficulties staying on task or otherwise using the technology in an appropriate, effective, and ethical manner. Expectations for use of technology should be stated in the syllabus, and the instructor should enforce these policies consistently (Ledbetter and Finn, 2013).
- Expectations of Life Balance—Students may not expect to use new media technology as art of their academic experience and may prefer to separate their academic and personal media presence. In a 2013 study, 52.9 percent of students did not connect with faculty on Facebook while enrolled in a course. However, 40 percent of students will "friend" past instructors (Wang, 2013). In order to circumvent this resistance, consider utilizing online discussion boards that are designated for the course. These discussion boards can also be opened for less formal discussions that might occur on social media. Forums for homework help or planning groups to attend a lecture can be created in this designated space.

Faculty Experiences

Benefits

Students are not the only ones who benefit from adopting a new media learning paradigm. Faculty members may also save administrative time, connect to students, decrease paper and increase effectiveness of receiving assignments and providing feedback, and develop a new skill set.

- Saves Administrative Time—From a faculty standpoint, using new media can expedite grading because physical papers do not have to be collected and redistributed. It also allows the instructor to grade papers and offer feedback from anywhere with an Internet connection.
- Connection to Students—The response time to students can be timelier than trying to arrange face-to-face meetings. Virtual meetings can occur through video conferencing. This is an added benefit for distance learning students that allows for virtual office hours. New media use allows instructors to digitally meet students on platforms they are already using. This demonstrates effort on the part of the instructor and can build rapport. Using new media can result in more engaged students and creates opportunities for active learning.
- Submission and Receipt Simplification—By navigating to a more digital and new media presence, instructors can be unencumbered by stacks of paper. Assignments and assessments can occur online through student management services. Going online with these assignments also creates a time-and-date stamp for submissions and places responsibility on the student for submission in a timely fashion.
- Constructive Challenge—Implementing use of new media can invigorate teaching as it prompts the instructor to consider how to adapt activities for new media.

Challenges

These benefits, however, are not met without some challenges—particularly when instructors first decide to adopt a new media learning paradigm. For example, it can be time consuming and there will be a learning curve associated with the platforms the instructor plans to integrate. Additionally, acknowledging student expertise, multitasking across media, cost of the media, and student adeptness with the tools integrated are all challenges faculty may face. Importantly, these challenges should not constitute barriers to adopting a new media learning paradigm; rather, these challenges should be considerations for how, when, and why faculty decide to integrate new media as content or process into higher education instruction.

- Time Consuming—Using new media can take a considerable amount of time to plan. Activities and assignments must be loaded ahead of time for students to access.
- Learning Curve—Instructors can experience a steep learning curve with implementing new media in the classroom. For some instructors, using apps may be too many steps away from their comfort level with technology.

- Student Expertise—When using new media, it is important to recognize that the instructor may not always be the expert in the classroom. It is possible that students have a greater comfort level with the technology and even with the platform through experience in other courses. Owning up to inexperience demonstrates transparency and the desire to be innovative in the classroom. It is a humbling, but worthwhile endeavor to ask students for assistance with troubleshooting.
- Media Multitasking—One of the biggest drawbacks to incorporating new media in the classroom is that it opens the door for media multitasking. It is difficult to monitor when students deviate from the assigned task to tend to personal matters like email or social media. The best practice is to have a statement about on-task media use in the class syllabus and hold students accountable.
- Cost—There may be budgetary concerns to implementing new media in the classroom. Not all departments can afford subscription services or to add new hardware such as clickers to the classroom. However, there are often supplemental materials that can be provided with a textbook, or with proper planning the subscription can be a required purchase for students. Additionally, there are many subscription trials or educational discounts available for instructors and students.
- Student Adeptness—A user-centered approach should be used in implementing new technology in the classroom. Students may default to the modern day "the dog ate my homework" excuse and try to claim that the "technology wouldn't work." To eliminate such excuses, the instructor should take a user-centered approach and should not assume that students arrive in the course with the aptitude for technology. This can be accomplished either live in the classroom or through the use of learning videos. Topics should include how to log on, submit an assignment, or manipulate a program. For hybrid, distance learning, or even as a reference tool for traditional classrooms, a short video can be filmed and posted in the class management system. Supplying students with a screen cast is a supportive tool for visual learners to follow a sequence of steps.

INFLUENCE

Theory Development

Perhaps the biggest growth area for instructional scholars spanning disciplines such as communication, education, instructional technology, and media interested in the new media paradigm is theory development. Developing modern descriptive and predictive theories that posit how student learning and new media intersect in today's learning environment is critical to furthering scholarship and keeping pace with technological advances. Though theories and constructs such as Davis' (1989) technology acceptance model, Kolb's (1984) experiential learning theory, Mottet, Frymier, and Beebe's (2006) rhetorical and relational goals theory, and media richness theory (Daft and Lengel, 1986) provide some vantage point for exploring new media and learning, both scholars and educators share a great need for advanced explanations that consider additional challenges and unique characteristics of evolving media and instruction. For example, new media may present further task (e.g., usability), cognitive (e.g., communication overload), and financial (e.g., purchasing multiple media platforms or devices per class) burdens that negatively affect learning or restrict access to learning. Thus, how does theory address student burdens distinct to new media and instruction experiences that may disrupt learning? Further, many current theories focus on cognitive processing, pedagogy, or media. Though some theories retain heuristic value across modality and context, such as connectivism (Siemens, 2004), theories that speak directly to the adaptability of the new media instructional paradigm and integrate multiple facets of new media and instruction are needed. Developing theories that address new media instruction is an area ripe for study and investigation.

Media Advancement

The new media learning paradigm offers a rich opportunity for media advancement. Creating diverse tools for educators and students to integrate media as teacher, example, or process is desired. Though some educators have the skill and knowledge to develop individualized platforms (e.g., video games) for their classes, a need exists for entrepreneurs and computer programmers to develop experiential learning media. Generating platforms that offer students virtual experiences to practice skills ranging from communication to chemistry provides additional learning opportunities for traditional, hybrid, and online classroom students. Further, developing options for personalization such that instruction can be tailored to individual student needs may offer an enhanced educational experience for students.

Also, students frequently request examples or portrayals of the learning concept or assignment they are expected to understand or produce. This desire for observation necessitates creating or locating a breadth of examples for contemporary classes. Though there are instructional practices to combat this (e.g., instruct students to bring in a media clip that addresses a particular course concept), media advancement such as curating media for instructional purposes may help in this endeavor. Further, with recent legal changes mandating closed captioning or transcripts for audio and video media, technology that can produce closed captions or quickly transcribe media artifacts for education is needed. Though some of this technology does exist, more media advancements in this area would make the inclusion of media in instruction more widespread and accessible.

Lastly, media advancements that address media as process provide an exciting area for innovation. Media as process, or media that facilitates learning, requires knowledge and skill to develop the media or technology in addition to the foresight for instructional use. Inventions such as the Acclaim platform that provide a space for students in a class to post video presentations to which course peers and the instructor can post comments directly to the video that are time stamped for the moment in the video at which the comment poster initiated the post foster learning in ways consistent with current communication, instructional, pedagogy, and education scholarship. In the instance of Acclaim, we know that feedback should be specific and contextualized. By time stamping the comment and visually seeing the comment at the same moment as the video, the student is able to recognize the action and receive praise or constructive criticism together. Media advancements such as Acclaim extend instructional opportunities for educators and provide access to practices that are theory based and supported by empirical research. More media advancements like this would expand and enhance educators' and students' learning experiences.

The teaching and learning paradigm shift due to new media embraces the ways in which media, both as message and medium, shape our understanding of the world around us. Classrooms are not independent of this reality, and education benefits from adopting a new paradigm that embodies new paradigm as a central component of how we interact with others, access information, and make sense of the world around us. This chapter has reviewed previous paradigms of learning and articulated a new media learning paradigm. Additionally, this chapter has explored how this paradigm may be adopted into college and university classrooms as a framework for teaching and learning in higher education. The chapter concluded with a description of ways in which the new media learning paradigm may influence theoretical and practical innovations, as well as affect higher education classrooms and institutions.

REFERENCES

Alt, D. (2015). College students' academic motivation, media engagement and fear of missing out. *Computers in Human Behavior, 49*, 111–119.

Bigge, M. L., and Shermis, S. S. (1999). *Learning theories for teachers* (6th ed.). New York, NY: Addison Wesley Longman.

Carrington, A. (2015). The pedagogy wheel. Retrieved from http://designingoutcomes.com/assets/PadWheelV4/PadWheel_Poster_V4.pdf.

Chehayl, L. K. (2010). A 21st-century conversation: Preparing today's students for tomorrow's success. *Journal of Curriculum and Pedagogy*, 7, 97–102. doi:10.1080/15505170.2010.10471347.

Daft, R. L., and Lengel, R. H. (1986). Organizational information requirements, media richness, and structural design. *Management Science, 32,* 554–571. doi:10.1287/mnsc.32.5.554.

Davis, F. D. (1989). Perceived usefulness, perceived ease of use, and user acceptance of information technology. *MIS Quarterly, 13,* 319–340. doi:10.2307/249008.

Edgar, D. W. (2012). Learning theories and historical events affecting instructional design in education: Recitation literacy toward extraction literacy practices. *SAGE Open, 2,* 1–9. doi:10.1177/2158244012462707.

Emanuel, R. (2013). The American college student cell phone survey. *College Student Journal, 47*(1), 75–81.

Framework for 21st century learning. (n.d.) Retrieved from http://www.p21.org/about-us/p21-framework.

Frisby, B. N., Kaufmann, R., and Beck, A. C. (2016). Mediated group development and dynamics: An examination of video chatting, Twitter, and Facebook in group assignments. *Communication Teacher, 30,* 215–227. doi:10.1080/17404622.2016. 1219038.

Garner, J. T., and Buckner, M. M. (2012). Skyping class: Using videoconferencing in organizational communication classes. *Communication Teacher, 27*(1).

Gredler, M. E. (2005). *Learning and instruction: Theory into practice* (5th ed.). Upper Saddle River, NJ: Pearson.

Heaslip, G., Donovan, P., and Cullen, J. G. (2014). Student response systems and learner engagement in large classes. *Active Learning in Higher Education, 15*(1), 11–24.

Hosek, A. M. (2016). Teaching engaged research literacy: A description and assessment of the Research Ripped from the Headlines project. *Communication Teacher, 30,* 45–56. doi:10.1080/17404622.2015.1102302.

Kaufmann, R., and Frisby, B. N. (2013). Let's connect: Using Adobe Connect to foster group collaboration in the online classroom. *Communication Teacher, 27,* 230–234. doi:10.1080/17404622.2013.798014.

Kivunja, C. (2014). Do you want your students to be job-ready with 21st century skill? Change pedagogies: A pedagogical paradigm shift from Vygotskyian social constructivism to critical thinking, problem solving, and Siemens' digital connectivism. *International Journal of Higher Education, 3,* 81–91.

Kolb, D. A. (1984). *Experiential learning: Experience as the source of learning and development.* Englewood Cliffs, NJ: Prentice-Hall.

Ledbetter, A. M., and Finn, A. N. (2013). Teacher technology policies and online communication apprehension as predictors of learner empowerment. *Communication Education, 62,* 301–317. doi:10.1080/03634523.2013.794386.

Madden, S., Winkler, R. B., Fraustino, J. D., and Janoske, M. (2016). Teaching, tweeting, and teleworking: Experiential and cross-institutional learning through social media. *Communication Teacher, 30,* 195–205. doi: 10.1080/17404622.2016.1219 040.

Monroe, P. (1925). *A textbook in the history of education.* New York, NY: MacMillan.

Mottet, T. P., Frymier, A. B., and Beebe, S. A. (2006). Theorizing about instructional communication. In T. P. Mottet, V. P. Richmond, and J. C. McCroskey (Eds.), *Instructional communication: Rhetorical and relational perspective* (pp. 253–282). Boston, MA: Allyn & Bacon.

Murray, J. P., and Murray, J. I. (1992). How do I lecture thee? *College Teaching, 40,* 109–114.

Our History. (n.d.) Retrieved from http://www.p21.org/about-us/our-history.

Perry, W. G., Jr. (1970). *Forms of intellectual and ethical development in the college years: A scheme.* New York, NY: Holt, Rinehart, and Winston.

Perry, W. G., Jr. (1981). Cognitive and ethical growth: The making of meaning. In A. Chickering and Associates, *The modern American college: Responding to the new realities of diverse students and changing society* (pp. 76–116). San Francisco, CA: Jossey-Bass.

Schunk, D. H. (2004). *Learning theories: An educational perspective.* Upper Saddle River, NJ: Pearson.

Shannon, C. E. (1948). A mathematical theory of communication. *The Bell System Technical Journal, 27,* 379–423. Retrieved from http://ieeexplore.ieee.org/.

Siemens, G. (2004). Connectivism: A learning theory for the digital age. *Journal of Instructional Technology and Distance Learning, 2,* 3–10.

Spivey, M. F., and McMillan, J. J. (2013). Using the Blackboard course management system to analyze student effort and performance. *Journal of Financial Education, 39*, 19–28.

Stowell, J. R., Oldham, T., and Bennett, D. (2010). Using student response systems ("clickers") to combat conformity and shyness. *Teaching of Psychology, 37*, 135–140.

The Design-Based Research Collective. (2003). Design-based research: An emerging paradigm for educational inquiry. *Educational Researcher, 32*, 5–8.

Trilling, B., and Fadel, C. (2009). *21st century skills: Learning for life in our times*. San Francisco, CA: Josey-Bass.

Vygotsky, L. S. (1978). *Mind in society: The development of higher psychological processes*. Cambridge, MA: Harvard University Press.

Wang, R. (2013). Connecting with instructors on Facebook: Why and why not? (Order No. 1540911). Available from ProQuest Dissertations & Theses Global (1418032398). Retrieved from http://search.proquest.com/docview/1418032398?accountid=7098.

Chapter Three

Media and Digital Literacy

A Framework for Instructional Strategy

Jason M. Martin and Jason Zahrndt

DEVELOPING A FRAMEWORK

A basic, if not advanced, level of media and digital literacy is a vital characteristic necessary to actively engage in contemporary society. This knowledge allows individuals to communicate with one another, to seek entertainment, to become further educated, and to be critical consumers of various forms of media and digital content. Not only does an understanding of media and digital literacy provide an array of positive, beneficial opportunities, it also empowers people to recognize and thwart propaganda and fake news, thus protecting them from inaccurate or misrepresented information, fraudulent activities, and other potentially negative content and situations. From an educational standpoint, teachers, instructors, and professors must be up to date with their level of media and digital literacy as a way to maximize student engagement while enhancing both the quality of education and accomplishment of learning outcomes. Students must continue expanding and strengthening their levels of media and digital literacy throughout their educational pursuit as they ultimately become members of the workforce and a democratic society.

This chapter provides an overview of media and digital literacy from perspectives related to its multifaceted importance, historical evolution, core components, educational relevance, and future possibilities. It is organized into seven sections: (a) Importance of Media and Digital Literacy; (b) Groundwork of Terminology; (c) Background and Historical Context; (d) Theoretical Understanding; (e) Core Constructs of Media Literacy; (f) Media and Digital Literacy in Contemporary Higher Education; and (g) The Future of Media and Digital Literacy. First, the importance and significance of media and digital literacy is discussed. Second, media literacy and digital literacy, along with other key terms, are defined. Third, an overview of the emergence of media and digital literacy is broken down chronologically. Fourth, theoretical perspectives, including information theory and the theory of media literacy, are outlined. Fifth, media literacy is examined as it relates to ethical awareness, media access, media awareness, media evaluation, and media production. Sixth, media and digital literacy's impact on college students and college education is discussed. Finally, the future of media and digital literacy is discussed.

IMPORTANCE OF MEDIA AND DIGITAL LITERACY

Nearly 90 percent of individuals in the United States are online today, roughly three-quarters (77 percent) currently own a smartphone, approximately 70 percent use social media, and half the public now own a tablet (Smith, 2017). This abundance of digital technology and seemingly infinite access to various forms of media in everyday life increases the importance for individuals to be sufficiently media and digitally literate. These modern forms of literacy are not only important for individual but also national success. The twenty-first-century skills of media and digital literacy are imperative if the United States is to compete in the global environment economically, educationally, and intellectually (American Library Association Digital Literacy Task Force, 2013).

Media and digital literacy are a combination of fundamental skills that allow individuals to navigate and participate in contemporary society, which is inundated with media and information (Hobbs, 2010). They allow us to: (a) make responsible choices and access information; (b) analyze messages; (c) create content; (d) reflect on conduct and communication behavior; and (e) take social action (Hobbs, 2010). These essential competencies for citizenship in the digital age also possess practical value by allowing individuals to seek opportunities, locate and critically analyze information, reap the benefits of educational opportunities, and improve the communities in which they live (Hobbs, 2010). Individuals who do not acquire these fundamental abilities "cannot have full dignity as a human person or exercise citizenship in a democratic society where to me a citizen is to both *understand* and *contribute* to the debates of the time" (Center for Media Literacy, n.d., para. 6). Over time, these skills have become increasingly necessary, and as technology and media have evolved, an assortment of positives and negatives have emerged.

For centuries, local social networks existed but were limited by time and space with regard to their numbers and ability to share information and spread ideas. These constraints have been redefined, if not eliminated, with the advancement of technology and, more so, social media, which "have become important tools for managing relationships with a large and often heterogeneous network of people who provide social support and serve as conduits for useful information and other resources" (Steinfield, Ellison, Lampe, and Vitak, 2012, p. 115). Social media is especially useful for creating and maintaining interpersonal relationships (Ellison, Vitak, Gray, and Lampe, 2014), but the impact of technology and social media has not necessarily resulted in more genuine friendships.

Recently, the amount of time individuals spend in the public realm has declined, and despite having more leisure time, more of it is spent alone or isolated by technology (Cortright, 2015). These trends have resulted in people being less likely to regularly socialize with neighbors and maintaining lower levels of trust due to less frequent interaction. Even more concerning, we know that "declining levels of trust and the measurable decrease in social capital are indicators that as a society, we're growing apart" (p. 6). Despite the era of Facebook, Twitter, and seemingly endless electronic connectivity, the number of Americans who claim to have no close friends has roughly tripled in recent decades while their discussion networks have become smaller (McPherson, Smith-Lovin, and Brashears, 2006). While social media technology has been shown to increase people's sociability (Watkins and Lee, 2010), the incorporation and advancement of technology in individuals' lives is more generally thought to restrict and reduce social and communication skills.

One population in particular has experienced a significant technological impact. Children spend approximately four and a half hours each school day texting, watching television, and playing video games, and as they have less time for face-to-face interaction due to increases in digital media use, children's social skills and the ability to empathize may be declining (Uhls et al., 2014). The impact of networked society, and a barrage of quick-fix information pieces, is resulting in young people becoming less likely to undertake deep, critical analysis of issues and challenging information and more likely to make shallow choices, expect instant gratification, and lack patience (Anderson and Rainie, 2012). Mobile communication devices interfere with human relationships when present in social settings, which has negative effects on closeness, connection, and conversation quality, especially when personally meaningful topics are discussed (Przybyski and Weinstein, 2012). Despite the negative influence of technology on social and communication skills, there are certainly upsides to its use and advancement and an increasing need for higher levels of media and digital literacy.

There is, now, a consistent shortage of books and other physical texts, and as the global population expands and literacy rates increase, more people are asking for access to "texts" than ever before (United Nations Educational,

Scientific and Cultural Organization, 2014). To increase access, reading on mobile devices has become more popular. "Mobile reading represents a promising, if still underutilized, pathway to texts," and "digital libraries and mobile reading initiatives may have more impact than traditional, paper-based initiatives" (pp. v–vi). Databases and other electronic technology provide results from tens of thousands of journals, books, magazines, newspapers, broadcasts, websites, and other sources of information, research, and entertainment. Access to information is only one aspect of digital and media literacy, and these skills are a necessity in contemporary digital, network-based society.

Shifts in how information is shared and consumed have been ongoing for generations, and presently, the capacity to analyze, evaluate, and create messages is vital to an individual's ability to be effective consumers and communicators. This necessity of being digitally and media literate impacts individuals in an array of ways, including educationally, economically, socially, and politically. Not having media and digital literacy skills, especially in the field of education, is the equivalent of being handicapped for both students and educators (Jones and Flannigan, 2006). The possession of media and digital literacy is an essential competency that provides individuals knowledge necessary to find and access appropriate information, create and share messages, and take action (e.g., contribute ideas, make informed health decisions, volunteer to educate others, find jobs and socialize online, vote). For instance, media and digital literacy education is increasingly embraced by health practitioners as a tool to promote health strategies (Austin, 2014) and is associated with higher levels of online political engagement and increased exposure to diverse viewpoints (Kahne, Lee, and Feezell, 2012). The necessity of media and digital literacy makes it an important aspect of one's educational attainment, which has caused higher education practitioners and institutions to adjust accordingly.

Post-secondary institutions must educate today's students, often described as "immature, needy, and tethered to the adults in their lives," to think critically, be creative, and commit to continual learning (Levine and Dean, 2012, p. 163). Thus, institutions must reconfigure not only themselves but also courses offered to correspond with the existence and capabilities of modern technology. Students should learn about domestic and global diversity, majors need to support interdisciplinary focuses, and general education must concentrate on communication skills, human customs, and the environment, as well as individual life roles and values. While media and digital literacy have forced higher education to adapt, a variety of organizations have emerged to assist educators and learners.

Numerous national and international organizations cite media literacy as a tool for preparing children and adults for life throughout the twenty-first century and are devoted to media literacy as it relates to social, political, and cultural education. They include: Center for Media Literacy, Media Literacy Council, ASCD, National Association for Media Literacy Education, Center on Media and Child Health, Media Education Foundation, Aspen Institute, Media Literacy Project, The News Literacy Project, National Council of Teachers of English, Free Press, and United Nations Educational, Scientific and Cultural Organization (UNESCO). These institutions recognize the position media and digital literacy should have in our society.

GROUNDWORK OF TERMINOLOGY

The concept of literacy is constantly changing based on people's needs, society's demands, and technology's impacts. For more than 50 years, new literacies have been introduced, including information literacy, media literacy, library literacy, computer literacy, visual literacy, news literacy, and digital literacy (Bawden, 2001; Hobbs 2010). Being literate in today's world requires individuals not only to be effective speakers and listeners but also to be able to create and decipher messages using symbols from an array of forms (Hobbs and Moore, 2013). Learners, whether young or adult, are exposed to and need to accumulate both old and new literacies, including not just rhetoric but also print, visual, information, media, critical, computer, news, and digital literacies. Since their inception, definitions and applicability of both media and digital literacy continue to transform, evolve, and advance. Despite being fairly new concepts, they have stimulated a considerable amount of expert and scholarly debate globally about how each is defined. Combined, media and digital literacy are a collection of life skills necessary for individuals to fully participate in today's media-saturated, information-heavy society (Hobbs, 2010). The terms may be examined individually or collectively.

Media Literacy versus Digital Literacy

Media Literacy

Multiple definitions for media literacy exist; for example, Potter (2010) provides 23 different definitions from scholars and citizen action groups. Media literacy was succinctly defined during the Aspen Institute's 1992 National Leadership Conference on Media Literacy as "the ability to access, analyze, evaluate, and create media in a variety of forms" (Aufderheide, 1993, p. v), characteristics that serve as the foundation for others' definitions. The Center for Media Literacy (n.d.) expands this earlier definition:

> Media literacy is a twenty-first-century approach to education. It provides a framework to access, analyze, evaluate and create messages in a variety of

> forms—from print to video to the Internet. Media literacy builds an understanding of the role of media in society as well as essential skills of inquiry and self-expression necessary for citizens of a democracy. (para. 2)

According to the National Communication Association (1998), a media literate person "understands how words, images, and sounds influence the way meanings are created and shared in contemporary society in ways that are both subtle and profound" and is "equipped to assign value, worth, and meaning to media use and media messages" (p. 1).

Media literacy has become a significant component of education across all levels. The National Association for Media Literacy Education (2007) created six core principles of media literacy that "articulate a common ground around which media literacy educators and advocates can coalesce" (p. 2). Media literacy education: (a) necessitates active inquiry and critical thinking about messages individuals receive and create; (b) moves literacy beyond reading and writing to including all forms of media; (c) develops and strengthens skills for learners of all ages that require "integrated, interactive, and repeated practice"; (d) cultivates knowledgeable, introspective, and involved contributors necessary for a democratic society; (e) acknowledges media as part of culture and a functioning agent of socialization; and (f) encourages the use of personal skills, beliefs, and experiences to create individual interpretations of media messages (pp. 2–5). In recent years, new elements of media literacy, including digital literacy and information literacy, transliteracy, and multiliteracies, have been acknowledged as a response to evolving social and technological environments, along with the creation and arrival of new media (Aczel, 2014). The concept of digital literacy is subsequently discussed.

Digital Literacy

The concept of digital literacy was introduced by Gilster (1997), who described it as the ability to comprehend and utilize information from various digital sources. He explained that digital literacy is concerned with "mastering ideas, not keystrokes" (p. 15) and requires a special mindset or type of thinking. Gilster was not the first to use the phrase, which had previously been used in the 1990s to mean the ability to read and comprehend hypertext, and his account was criticized for being confusing and lacking a clear explanation of the concept and its underlying skills and attitudes (Bawden, 2001). Gilstler summarized four core competencies of digital literacy—Internet searching, hypertext navigation, knowledge assembly, and content evaluation—but did not provide a specific list of skills associated with it (Bawden, 2008). These competencies translate to qualities that allow an individual to: (a) retrieve and critically think about information; (b) publish and communicate information after accessing it; (c) recognize the value of traditional tools associated with networked media; (d) see social networks as sources of information and assistance; and (e) assemble knowledge by collecting reliable information from diverse sources (Bawden, 2001).

More recently, the American Library Association Digital Literacy Task Force (2013) defined digital literacy as "the ability to use information and communication technologies to find, understand, evaluate, create, and communicate digital information, an ability that requires both cognitive and technical skills" (p. 2). A digitally literate person is as someone who: (a) has cognitive and technical skills needed to locate, comprehend, interpret, construct and share various forms of digital information; (b) utilizes digital technologies properly and efficiently while searching for and retaining information, interpreting search results, and evaluating the credibility of information; (c) identifies relationships between "technology, lifelong learning, personal privacy, and appropriate stewardship of information"; (d) utilizes these skills coupled with necessary technologies to engage with peers, co-workers, family members, and members of general society; and (e) becomes an active member of civic society by using these skills to "contribute to a vibrant, informed, and engaged community" (p. 2). Given their connotative and denotative overlap, digital literacy and media literacy are sometimes coupled together.

Comparing Media Literacy and Digital Literacy

In summary, digital literacy includes the personal, technological, and intellectual skills necessary to navigate today's digital world, and media literacy represents critical engagement with mass media, which includes digital technology (Media Smarts, n.d.). Media literacy and digital literacy, along with information literacy, are umbrella concepts that focus on a critical approach toward media messages (Koltay, 2011). While the two terms are closely related and include critical thinking as a core skill, there are notable differences with how both have been approached educationally (Media Smarts, n.d.). Media literacy typically focuses on educating critically engaged consumers of media, and digital literacy is generally more related to enabling individuals to participate in digital media wisely, safely, and ethically. "However, it is important to keep in mind that competencies for digital literacy and media literacy are not separate, but rather complementary and mutually supporting and are constantly evolving and intersecting in new and interesting ways" (para. 5).

Media literacy and digital literacy are often used synonymously and are vital twenty-first-century skills necessary for navigating life in today's media- and information-rich society (Hobbs, 2010). The five competencies of media and digital literacy (access, analyze and evaluate, create, reflect, and act) "work together in a spiral of empowerment, supporting people's active participation in lifelong learning through the processes of both consuming and creating messages" (p. 18). These concepts, investigated together and separately, have become increasingly important.

BACKGROUND AND HISTORICAL CONTEXT

As media products advanced through the twentieth century, the importance of media literacy became more pronounced. Just as film became a common feature in daily life, film and media education also rose to prominence. The idea of using the growing popularity of cinema in courses across the curriculum to increase student engagement with the materials occurred to teachers as early as the 1920s (Kamerer, 2013). Over the next 60 years, media studies found a strong foothold in universities. Media literacy functioned as an important feature of an educated citizenry to ensure the public was capable of determining bias, accuracy, and other characteristics of popular media (Kamerer, 2013; Tisdell, 2007). The concept of media literacy went through substantial changes with the rise of personal computers and digital media in the 1980s.

By the early 1990s, digital media had emerged in various consumer markets. Audio compact discs surpassed both vinyl records and cassettes as the dominant distribution method of the music industry (Kamerer, 2013). The rise of video gaming consoles in the home created a new interest in the education of computer programming. As Internet usage increased through the 1990s, the prevalence of consumer computer equipment exploded. In 1984, only 8.2 percent of census responders owned a computer in their home; by the time of the 1997 census, 36 percent reported having a computer in the home, with only 18 percent having Internet access, and by 2007, over 69 percent of people owned a computer and nearly 62 percent had Internet access (Statistical Abstract, 2014).

One example that speaks to the incredible growth of the Internet in the American consumer world was the AOL installation disk and CD. According to Steve Case (2016), former CEO of AOL, the ubiquity of the disk and CD contributed to the increase in subscribers from 200,000 to over 25 million in under seven years. Media literacy during these two decades expanded from an analysis of texts to an ability to understand and use computers and computer systems, as well as the communication of ideas and information in entirely new ways across these systems.

At the turn of the millennium, the Internet had become a driving force for communication and sales. During the 2000s, the Internet embraced Web 2.0, a concept named by Darcy DiNucci (1999) that presented the next evolution of the Internet as based around the ability for individuals to communicate directly. No longer would companies, news organizations, or media producers distribute information to consumers. The growth of blogs and other social media sites, such as MySpace, LiveJournal, and Facebook, revealed that direct communication between Internet users, especially over mobile devices, would lead to a major shift in the idea of media literacy.

With the advent of mobile, Internet-connected devices, the ability for people to communicate exploded. In September of 2016, Facebook recorded an average of 1.18 billion daily users, with over 92 percent of those users coming from the mobile environment (Facebook, 2017). As of October 2016, YouTube users upload over 300 hours of video per minute, and they watch over 3.25 billion hours per month; additionally, mobile devices accounted for over half of those views (Smith, 2016). With over two billion smartphone users worldwide in 2016, communication and media producers have a worldwide audience that was impossible with previous technology. The key change was individual production ability as individuals can produce and communicate without major television networks, movie studios, news outlets, or other centralized groups (eMarketer, 2017). In light of these changes to media production and consumption throughout the past century, media literacy means more than applying a critical eye to media products; it means applying a critical eye to our interactions with others and ourselves.

THEORETICAL UNDERSTANDING

Theoretical approaches to media literacy are varied and this chapter will not attempt a comprehensive analysis or even summary of all of them. Three holistic approaches provide an understanding of the perception and function of media literacy. Thus, this discussion begins with the context of semiotics in understanding media literacy, then progresses to an application of information theory, and finally ends with a discussion of cognitive media literacy theory as proposed by Potter (2004b).

Semiotics, as applied to media literacy, is a common method for exposing hidden or underlying meanings in a media product. Beginning in the late 1940s, Adorno critiqued cultural products as tools of the culture industry to unconsciously influence the public, laying the foundation for much of the semiotic media analysis (Adorno, 2001). Take, for example, Adorno's description of the common trope of Western films using white and black hats and clothing to communicate ideas of good and evil. Later applications of semiotic analysis included the unpacking of advertising images to discover underlying meanings of gender, racial, political, or other commentaries beyond the initial analysis (Gaines, 2010). The *Killing Us Softly* video series by Jean Kilbourne exemplifies this type of critical analysis by highlighting and analyzing the gender and sexual bias in advertisements.

While semiotic media analysis provides a useful understanding of media and its impact on our perceptions of the world, it does not delve into the activity of communication. An analysis of the communication process is important to understand the transmission of information. The basic tenets of information theory as posited by Claude Shannon (1948) describe how information is input into an encoder (i.e., the code is sent across a channel and the code is decoded and output for a receiver). Information encoded into ones and zeroes and the resulting transmission and decoding of this information forms the basis of all digital communication. The presence of noise hinders this process, usually in the channel, that reduces the accuracy of the decoded signal.

In order to achieve a semiotic analysis of media, information theory should be used to see how media of all kinds encode and decode information. Eco (1976) discussed this in detail in *A Theory of Semiotics*, addressing the idea that the sign itself functions as a code. The white and black hats of Westerns may communicate good and evil for some, but they also communicate ideas of life and death, innocence and experience, purity and sin, etc. Each understanding may function as noise in the system, thus creating difficulty in determining different meanings from the colors, and each then leads to different understandings of their context, the Western film. Noise in the semiotic system is therefore not just in the channel, but possibly at the point of the information's beginning, encoding, decoding, and reception.

Potter's (2004a) approach to media literacy takes into account both information theory and a key aspect of most recent new media. He explains:

> We need to recognize that individuals' interactions with the media are almost always in a state of automaticity. The flood of media messages is so great and so constant that most people stay in a relatively unconscious state where their attention is governed by automatic routines. (p. 256)

The incredibly high volume of new media productions—YouTube, Flickr, Facebook, and other web-based media distribution and social media sites—creates an impossibly noisy scenario for media consumption on a large scale. Noise in the system further compounds the need to determine accurate or factual information from false information. The most recent election cycle of 2016 has challenged Americans with this task, and studies are showing that generations raised with the Internet are no more capable of distinguishing fake from real, unreliable from credible (see Wineberg, McCrew, Breakstone, and Ortega, 2016). Media literacy today goes beyond the cultural analysis and even an understanding of the digital systems we use.

To Potter (2004b), media literacy means taking information, the message that resides in the fact or the ideas communicated through the media product, and turning it into knowledge, which resides in the mind of the viewer, reader, or listener (the receiver). The incredibly noisy, media-laden world that exists today puts a new burden on a person to interact more consciously and deliberately with media. Thus, Potter presents the theory of cognitive media literacy, where each individual contextually creates knowledge. Knowledge will differ for each person, and each person validates that knowledge construction in multiple ways. Potter's perspective helps us take into account the vast diversity of individuals producing media today to understand what it means to be media literate.

CORE CONSTRUCTS OF MEDIA LITERACY

The Center for Media Literacy recognizes five core questions and five key concepts as the foundation for inquiry-based media literacy pedagogy (Thoman and Jolls, 2005). This section begins with a review of the major questions followed by an overview of the key concepts.

The five core questions for the Center for Media Literacy are concerned with the message (Thoman and Jolls, 2005). First, authorship is associated with the concept that all media messages are "constructed" and answers the question, who created this message? Format is associated with the notion that media messages are constructed through creative language, which has its own rules, and answers the question, what creative techniques are used to attract one's attention? Third, audience is associated with the fact that different individuals experience identical media messages differently and answers the question, how might different people understand this message differently from me? Content is associated with the understanding that media have embedded values and points of view and answers the question, what lifestyles, values, and points of view are represented in, or omitted from, this message? Finally, purpose is associated with the belief that most media messages are organized to gain profit and/or power and answers the question, why is this message being sent? These questions help frame an understanding of message construction and development.

In addition to the five questions mentioned above, the Center for Media Literacy also created five overarching constructs or concepts (Thoman and Jolls, 2005). These pillars have been identified as "the basic principles found to be common throughout the literature and throughout the strong media literacy education programs across the country" (Hallaq, 2016, p. 65). Thus, these constructs—ethical awareness, media access, media awareness, media evaluation, and media production—are each subsequently discussed in the following sections.

Ethical Awareness

Ethical and social values are components of all communication (Hobbs, 2011), and, as such, individuals should considerer a variety of ethical issues as both producers and consumers of digital media. James et al. (2009) outline identity, privacy, ownership and authorship, credibility, and participation as "distinct ethical fault lines in these rapidly evolving frontiers" (p. 9). Other considerations related to the ethical use and creation of media include copyright, fair use, attribution, and novel forms of sharing (Hobbs, 2011). Parents, as providers of computers, Internet access, and mobile phones, have a responsibility to teach their children how to ethically and safely use these powerful forms of communication (Bhat, Chang, and Linscott, 2010). Members of the media industry have a tremendous responsibility, which makes constructing their ethics and awareness important (Hardy, Dhanissaro, and Thangsurbkul, 2011). Educators also bear a burden as they not only have a responsibility to teach their students about ethical issues related to digital media in various ways, including media production (Gibbons, 2012; Parker, 2013) and online harassment (deWinter and Vie, 2008), but also must be ethical users of digital tools themselves (Harris, 2009).

Media Access

Media access is related to "finding and using media and technology tools skillfully and sharing appropriate and relevant information with others" (Hobbs, 2010, p. 19). Accessing messages and other content allows individuals to accumulate pertinent and helpful information and understand its meaning effectively (Thoman and Jolls, 2005). Twenty-first-century learning engages with "infinite access to knowledge and information ('content') increasingly through the internet" (p. 8). Accessing such knowledge and information allows individuals to: (a) acknowledge and comprehend an affluent vocabulary of terms, symbols, and methods of communication; (b) acquire tactics for uncovering information from an array of sources; and (c) utilize appropriate information appropriate to different tasks and scenarios (p. 28).

Access is the initial step for media and digital literacy because it relates to using, finding, and comprehending symbolic resources, and it is always media specific (Hobbs, 2011). While the ability to access information is highly important, individuals ultimately "need to be able to evaluate and use information critically if they are to transform it into knowledge" (Buckingham, 2007, p. 46). This requires the user to consider sources of information, the intentions of those who produced the content, and how it represents the world while "understanding how technological developments and possibilities are related to broader social and economic forces" (p. 46).

Media Awareness

Media literacy allows individuals to develop an awareness of media structures (e.g., economic structure, ownership and control, commercial structure, ideological implications of various structures), media impact (e.g., influence on beliefs, values, and perceptions, effect on social structures), and media reform concerns (Duran, Yousman, Walsh, and Longshore, 2008). Media awareness also creates opportunities for media activism and participation (e.g., advocacy groups; Duran et al., 2008). From this perspective, media awareness relates to Hobbs' (2010) media literacy competence act, which encourages individuals to work individually and collectively "to share knowledge and solve problems in the family, the workplace and the community, and [participate] as a member of a community at local, regional, national, and international levels" (p. 19). Media awareness also relates to individuals': (a) ability to save money through shopping online; (b) familiarity with various media formats (e.g., mp3, jpeg, avi); (c) interest in acquiring new knowledge about other cultures through online activities; (d) capacity to evaluate the credibility of online information; and (e) level of confidence related to personalizing information received through online news sites (Hallaq, 2016).

Media Evaluation

In order to successfully evaluate media, individuals must comprehend messages and utilize critical thinking "to analyze message purpose, target audience, quality, veracity, credibility, and point of view, and potential effects of consequences of messages" (Hobbs, 2011, p. 12). Evaluation also encourages consumers to relate messages to personal experience (Thoman and Jolls, 2005). Therefore, evaluating media messages allows individuals to: (a) enjoy evaluating messages of various categories and types; (b) gauge a message's quality according to its substance and form; (c) evaluate messages according to ethical, spiritual, or democratic convictions; and (d) generate verbal, written, or electronic responses to complex messages (p. 28).

Media Production

The production, or creation, of media is related to "composing or generating content using creativity and confidence in self-expression, with awareness of purpose, audience, and composition techniques" (Hobbs, 2010, p. 19). The creation of messages allows people to "'write' their ideas, using words, sounds, and/or images effectively for a variety of purposes, and they are able to make use of various technologies of communication to create, edit, and disseminate their message" (Thoman and Jolls, 2005, p. 28). In doing so, individuals will: (a) utilize the processes of brainstorming, planning, composing, and revision; (b) apply written and oral communication effectively while mastering language usage rules; (c) construct and choose images effectively to accomplish various outcomes; and (d) utilize communication technologies to construct messages (p. 28). The core constructs of media literacy—ethical awareness, media access, media awareness, media evaluation, and media production—have become part of the higher education landscape and curriculum.

MEDIA AND DIGITAL LITERACY IN CONTEMPORARY HIGHER EDUCATION

Media and digital literacy education provide the skills needed to maximize what individuals value most about media and technology's empowering characteristics while, at the same time, minimizing its negative features (Hobbs, 2010). Founded in 1997, the National Association for Media Literacy Education (NAMLE) has been a significant contributor to media literacy education. NAMLE explains that "the purpose of media literacy education is to help individuals of all ages develop the habits of inquiry and skills of expression that they need to be critical thinkers, effective communicators, and active citizens in today's world" (2007, p. 1). Ventimiglia and Pullman (2016) further argue that integrating digital literacy throughout the curriculum is greatly needed in today's higher education in order to ensure that students may: (a) find and vet information online; (b) see problems from digital perspectives; (c) become self-directed learners; (d) obtain digital solutions; (e) learn software quickly; and (f) design and create digital solutions. Today's college students represent the "first generation of digital natives to attend college," and "no change is larger or will have a greater impact on higher education than this generation's use of digital technology (Levine and Dean, 2012, p. 20). In order to meet the needs of the twenty-first-century student, media and digital literacy must have a healthy representation in higher education curricula.

Today's College Students

The addition of media and digital literacy to higher education is significant not only because of the unique focus but also because the modern college student needs a renewed media-based literacy. For context, according to the National Center for Education Statistics (NCES, 2016), approximately 20.5 million students attended American colleges and universities in the fall 2016, the majority of whom were female (57 percent) and enrolled full-time (62 percent). While overall U.S. college enrollment is falling (Long, 2016), an increasing number of black and Hispanic students are attending college (NCES, 2016). Nearly three-quarters (74 percent) of today's undergraduate students have at least one nontraditional characteristic (e.g., transfer student, work full- or part-time, first-generation student, part-time student, have dependent[s]; NCES, 2016). Traditional students (under 25) represent approximately 60 percent of undergraduates in the United States (NCES, 2016) and are an amalgamation of the oldest members of Generation Y (i.e., Millennials) and youngest individuals from Generation Z, depending on which generation continuum is applied. Today's college students are the first generation of digital natives, represent the most diverse generation historically in higher education, and are more immature, dependent, coddled, and entitled than their predecessors (Levine and Dean, 2012).

Students, therefore, are likely to be intimately familiar with the Internet, highly reliant on digital devices (e.g., computers, cell/smart phones, tablets), and extremely media savvy. Millennials, the first always-connected generation, are typically confident, self-expressive, liberal, optimistic, and open to change; they expect technology to serve them and be readily available (Taylor and Keeter, 2010). Members of Gen Z, who have been inundated with digital technology since birth, are defined by "intimate and pervasive use of digital technologies" and "have placed social media at the center of [their] social world rather than as a supplement to face-to-face relationships" (Marron, 2015, p. 123). Combined, today's college students are heavily defined by technology; they are extremely connected yet isolated, a contradiction that results in feeble interpersonal, face-to-face communication, and problem-solving skills (Levine and Dean, 2012). This ever-present technology influences how students learn, approach their college experience, and interact with other students.

Regardless of the generational label, the majority of today's college students have grown up in the digital age and have, therefore, been influenced by digital technology. To put it another way, "if Millennials are the first digital natives, Gen Z represents the first generation to have lived entirely in a digital era" (Marron, 2015, p. 123). Contemporary students communicate and access information via a model that differs from previous generations, was created by the Internet, and is powered by mobile technology (Rishi, 2007). While the majority of traditional college students may be characterized as tech savvy and digitally driven, not all postsecondary students have equal access to technology and are equally competent with regard to their levels of media and digital literacy. This results in what has been affectionately referred to as the digital divide. To put it mildly, the digital divide creates even more chaos when trying to encourage a media and digital literacy in students.

Student Preferences and Expectations

Overall, today's college students generally have positive feelings about technology, feel prepared to utilize technology when entering college, and are eager to multiply and strengthen academic uses of technology (Dahlstrom, Brooks, Grajek, and Reeves, 2015). These students increasingly rely on mobile devices (e.g., smartphones, tablets, and laptops) for academic purposes such as reading course material (Schramm, 2015) and studying (Armitage, 2015). Despite the increasing use of smartphones and tablets on college campuses, laptops remain the most frequently used devices for learning among college students (Pearson, 2015). Most students believe technology enhances their engagement with other students, professors, and course materials and that digital learning technology helps them feel more prepared for class, boosts their efficiency and effectiveness (i.e., saves time), and impacts their grades positively (McGraw-Hill Education, 2016). The majority of today's college students indicate that optimal learning occurs in blended classrooms where work is a combination of face to face and online (Dahlstrom et al., 2015).

Considering the positive effects of technology on students, it behooves instructors to reinforce appropriate and effective use while collaborating and receiving institutional support. College educators must continue evolving as they teach students digital and media literacy skills; this requires education and support and a collaborative effort between faculty, institutions, organizations, and researchers. Colleges and universities need to make updated technology, technical support, and training available for instructors and staff, which will maximize technological efficiency while minimizing its distractions and improving the overall student experience (McCoy, 2016).

Measuring Media Literacy Levels

Consensus has not been reached among researchers and educators with regard to defining, using, and assessing media literacy education (Christ, 2004; Hobbs and Jensen, 2009; Potter, 2010). Additionally, a primary concern within the field is the need to generally measure the effectiveness of media literacy curricula (Martens, 2010; Potter, 2004b; Schilder, Lockee, and Saxon, 2016). Despite various approaches of assessment, media literacy education is typically assessed in one of three ways: (a) by evaluating separate constructs or outcomes not directly related to media literacy knowledge, skills, and attitudes; (b) by measuring selective components; and (c) holistically, mostly through quantitative instruments (Schilder et al., 2016). Efforts have been made to measure media literacy and media literacy skills in general (e.g., Arke and Primack, 2009; Hobbs and Frost, 2003), as well as how these skills relate to specific contexts such as eating disorders (McLean,

Paxton, and Wertheim, 2016) and smoking (Primack, Gold, Land, and Fine, 2006). Attempts have also recently been made to develop instruments to measure new media literacy (Koc and Barut, 2016; Literat, 2014), news media literacy (Ashley, Maksl, and Craft, 2013; Maksl, Ashley, and Craft, 2015; Vraga, Tully, Kotcher, Smithson, and Broeckelman-Post, 2016), and digital online media literacy (Hallaq, 2016). Challenges related to media literacy assessment include the lack of systematic implementation of media literacy assessments and unclear definitions of media literacy criteria and outcomes (Schilder et al., 2016). In light of these challenges, what does the future hold for media and digital literacy?

THE FUTURE OF MEDIA AND DIGITAL LITERACY

The future of higher education is clouded by various uncertainties. Discovering new ways to teach the digital generation, reducing costs, and increasing the number of graduates are among the primary concerns identified by educational leaders (Tugend, 2016). Cultural and demographic shifts will continue to alter society's complexion and the use of technology and evaluation of media messages. As new technology emerges, post-secondary educators will be challenged to not only keep up but also to integrate it into their classrooms. The development of "a common set of technology competency expectations for university professors" has been recommended because students, regardless of their age, should never encounter educators who are not entirely capable of utilizing technology to transform learning (United States Department of Education, 2017, p. 88).

Media and digital literacy are increasingly important skills needed to identity fake news and misinformation. Youth, including college students, struggle to distinguish advertisements from news and identify where information came from or biases that may be present (Wineberg et al., 2016). Instructors, therefore, need to help students become responsible digital media consumers and, as Wineberg and colleagues suggest, more skilled in civic online reasoning (i.e., the ability to judge the credibility of online information). This, in turn, will allow students to more accurately identify misinformation and better understand that alternative facts are falsehoods. The future of media and digital literacy, and more specifically media and digital literacy education, will be shaped by changes and education reform. Despite these looming transformations, media and digital literacy must remain vital cornerstones of our democratic society.

REFERENCES

Aczel, P. (2014) Reconceptualizing (new) media literacy. *Perspectives of Innovations, Economics & Business, 14,* 47–53.

Adorno, T.W. (2001). *The culture industry: Selected essays on mass culture* (2nd ed.). New York, NY: Taylor & Francis.

American Library Association Digital Literacy Task Force. (2013). *Digital literacy, libraries, and public policy: Report of the Office for Information Technology Policy's Digital Literacy Task Force.* Washington, DC: American Library Association Office for Information Technology Policy. Retrieved from http://www.districtdispatch.org/wp-content/uploads/2013/01/2012_OITP_digilitreport_1_22_13.pdf.

Anderson, J. Q., and Rainie, L. (2012). Millennials will benefit and suffer due to their hyperconnected lives. Pew Research Center. Retrieved from http://www.pewinternet.org/files/old-media//Files/Reports/2012/PIP_Future_of_Internet_2012_Young_brains_PDF.pdf.

Arke, E. T., and Primack, B. A. (2009). Quantifying media literacy: Development, reliability, and validity of a new measure. *Educational Media International, 46,* 53–65. DOI: 10.1080/09523980902780958.

Armitage, A. (2015). Use of mobile devices for studying skyrockets among college students. *Education Week.* Retrieved from http://blogs.edweek.org/edweek/DigitalEducation/2015/03/use_of_mobile_devices_for_studying_skyrockets.html.

Ashley, S., Maksl, A., and Craft, S. (2013). Developing a news media literacy scale. *Journalism & Mass Communication Educator, 68,* 7–21. DOI: 10.1177/1077695812469802.

Aufderheide, P. (Ed.). (1993). *Media literacy: A report of the National Leadership Conference on Media Literacy.* Washington, DC: The Aspen Institute.

Austin, E. W. (2014). Media literacy. In T. Thompson (Ed.), *Encyclopedia of health communication,* pp. 831–833. Thousand Oaks, CA: Sage.

Bawden, D. (2001). Information and digital literacies: A review of concepts. *Journal of Documentation, 57,* 218–259.

Bawden, D. (2008). Origins and concepts of digital literacy. In C. Lankshear, and M. Knobel (Eds.), *Digital literacies: Concepts, politics, and practices,* pp. 17–32. New York, NY: Peter Lang.

Bhat, C. S., Chang, S., and Linscott, J. A. (2010). Addressing cyberbullying as a media literacy issue. *New Horizons in Education, 58*(3), 34–43.

Buckingham, D. (2007). Digital media literacies: Rethinking media education in the age of the Internet. *Research in Comparative and International Education, 2,* 43–55.

Case, S. (2016). *The third wave: An entrepreneur's vision of the future.* New York, NY: Simon and Schuster.

Center for Media Literacy. (n.d.). *What is media literacy? A definition . . . and more.* Retrieved from http://www.medialit.org/reading-room/what-media-literacy-definitionand-more.

Christ, W. G. (2004). Assessment, media literacy standards, and higher education. *American Behavioral Scientist, 48*(1), 92–96.

Cortright, J. (2015). City report: Less in common. *City Observatory.* Retrieved from http://cityobservatory.org/wp-content/files/CityObservatory_Less_In_Common.pdf.

Dahlstrom, E., Brooks, D. C., Grajek, S., and Reeves, J. (2015). *ECAR study of undergraduate students and information technology, 2015.* Louisville, KY: Enducause Center for Analysis and Research.

deWinter, J., and Vie, S. (2008). Press enter to "say": Using Second Life to teach critical media literacy. *Computers and Composition, 25,* 313–322. DOI: 10.1016/j.compcom.2008.04.003.

DiNucci, D. (1999). Fragmented future. *Print, 53*(4), 32.

Duran, R. L., Yousman, B., Walsh, K. M., and Longshore, M. A. (2008). Holistic media education: An assessment of the effectiveness of a college course in media literacy. *Communication Quarterly, 56,* 49–68. DOI: 10.1080/01463370701839198.

Eco, U. (1976). *A theory of semiotics.* Bloomington, IN: Indiana UP.

Ellison, N. B., Vitak, J., Gray, R., and Lampe, C. (2014). Cultivating social resources on social network sites: Facebook relationship maintenance behaviors and their role in social capital processes. *Journal of Computer-Mediated Communication, 19*, 855–870. DOI: 10.1111/jcc4.12078.

eMarketer. (2017). *Number of smartphone users worldwide from 2014 to 2020 (in billions)*. Retrieved from https://www.statista.com/statistics/330695/number-of-smartphone-users-worldwide/.

Facebook. (2017). *Stats*. Retrieved from http://newsroom.fb.com/company-info/.

Gaines, E. (2010). *Media literacy and semiotics*. New York, NY: Palgrave.

Gibbons, D. (2012). Developing an ethics of youth media production using media literacy, identity & modality. *Journal of Media Literacy Education, 4,* 256–265.

Gilster, P. (1997). *Digital literacy*. New York, NY: Wiley.

Hallaq, T. (2016). Evaluating online media literacy in higher education: Validity and reliability of the digital online media literacy assessment (DOMLA). *Journal of Media Literacy Education, 8,* 62–84.

Hardy, S., Dhanissaro, P. J. P., and Thangsurbkul, W. (2011). Peace revolution's online social platform: From inner revolution to global evolution of ethical media production. *Journal of Media Literacy Education, 3,* 84–89.

Harris, F. J. (2009). Ethics from web 1.0 to web 2.0: Standing outside the box. *Knowledge Quest, 37*(3), 56–61.

Hobbs, R. (2010). *Digital and media literacy: A plan of action.* Washington, DC: The Aspen Institute.

Hobbs, R. (2011). *Digital and media literacy: Connecting culture and the classroom.* Thousand Oaks, CA: Sage.

Hobbs, R., and Frost, R. (2003). Measuring the acquisition of media-literacy skills. *Reading Research Quarterly, 38,* 330–355.

Hobbs, R., and Jensen, A. (2009). The past, present, and future of media literacy education. *Journal of Media Literacy Education, 1*(1), 1–11.

Hobbs, R., and Moore, D. C. (2013). *Discovering media literacy: Teaching digital media and popular culture in elementary school.* Thousand Oaks, CA: Sage.

James, C., Davis, K., Flores, A., Francis, J. M., Pettingill, L., Rundle, M., and Gardner, H. (2009). *Young people, ethics, and the new digital media: A synthesis from the GoodPlay Project.* Cambridge, MA: The MIT Press.

Jones, B. R., and Flannigan, S. L. (2006). *Connecting the digital dots: Literacy in the 21st century.* The New Media Consortium. Retrieved from http://www.nmc.org/pdf/Connecting%20the%20Digital%20Dots.pdf.

Kahne, J., Lee, N., and Feezell, J. T. (2012). Digital media literacy education and online civic and political participation. *International Journal of Communication, 6,* 1–24.

Kamerer, D. (2013). Media literacy. *Communication Research Trends, 32*(1), 1–25.

Koc, M., and Barut, E. (2016). Development and validation of New Media Literacy Scale (NMLS) for university students. *Computers in Human Behavior, 63,* 834–843. DOI: 10.1016/j.chb.2016.06.035.

Koltay, T. (2011). The media and the literacies: Media literacy, information literacy, digital literacy. *Media, Culture & Society, 33,* 211–221. DOI: 10.1177/0163443710393382.

Levine, A., and Dean, D. R. (2012). *Generation on a tightrope: A portrait of today's college student.* San Francisco, CA: Jossey-Bass.

Literat, I. (2014). Measuring new media literacies: Towards the development of a comprehensive assessment tool. *Journal of Media Literacy Education, 6,* 15–27.

Long, H. (2016). College enrollment is dropping. Bad sign? CNN. Retrieved from http://money.cnn.com/2016/05/20/news/economy/college-enrollment-down/.

Maksl, A., Ashley, S., and Craft, S. (2015). Measuring news media literacy. *Journal of Media Literacy Education, 6*(3), 29–45.

Marron, M. B. (2015). New generations require changes beyond the digital. *Journalism & Mass Communication, 70,* 123–124. DOI: 10.1 1177/1077695815588912.

Martens, H. (2010). Evaluating media literacy education: Concepts, theories and future directions. *Journal of Media Literacy Education, 2*(1), 1–22.

McCoy, B. R. (2016). Digital distractions in the classroom phase II: Student classroom use of digital devices for non-class related purposes. *Journal of Media Education, 7,* 5–32.

Mc-Graw-Hill Education. (2016). 2016 digital study trends survey. Retrieved from http://www.mheducation.com/highered/explore/studytrends.html.

McLean, S. A., Paxton, S. J., and Wertheim, E. H. (2016). The measurement of media literacy in eating disorder risk factor research. *Journal of Eating Disorders, 4(*30). DOI: 10.1186/s40337-016-0116-0.

McPherson, Smith-Lovin, and Brashears. (2006). Social isolation in America: Changes in core discussion networks over two decades. *American Sociological Review, 71,* 353–375.

Media Smarts. (n.d.). *The intersection of digital and media literacy.* Retrieved from http://mediasmarts.ca/digital-media-literacy/general-information/digital-media-literacy-fundamentals/intersection-digital-media-literacy.

National Association for Media Literacy Education. (2007). *Core principles of media literacy education in the United States.* Retrieved from https://drive.google.com/file/d/0B8j2T8jHrlgCYXVHSVJidWtmbmc/view.

National Center for Education Statistics. (2016). *Back to school statistics.* Retrieved from https://nces.ed.gov/fastfacts/display.asp?id=372.

National Communication Association. (1998). *K-12 speaking, listening, and media literacy standards and competency statements.* Retrieved from http://www.natcom.org/uploadedFiles/About_NCA/Leadership_and_Governance/Public_Policy_Platform/K-12Standards.pdf.

Parker, J. K. (2013). Critical literacy and the ethical responsibilities of student media production. *Journal of Adolescent & Adult Literacy, 56,* 668–676. DOI: 10.1002/JAAL.194.

Pearson. (2015). *Student mobile device survey 2015: National report: College students.* Retrieved from http://www.pearsoned.com/wp-content/uploads/2015-Pearson-Student-Mobile-Device-Survey-College.pdf.

Potter, W. J. (2004a). Argument for the need for a cognitive theory of media literacy. *American Behavioral Scientist, 48*(2), 266–272.

Potter, W. J. (2004b). *Theory of media literacy: A cognitive approach.* Thousand Oaks, CA: Sage.

Potter, W. J. (2010). The state of media literacy. *Journal of Broadcasting & Electronic Media, 54,* 675–696. DOI: 10.1080/08838151.2011.521462.

Primack, B. A., Gold, M. A., Land, S.R., and Fine, M. J. (2006). Association of cigarette smoking and media literacy about smoking among adolescents. *Journal of Adolescent Health, 39,* 465–472.

Przybylski, A.K., and Weinstein, N. (2012). Can you connect with me now? How the presence of mobile communication technology influences face-to-face conversation quality. *Journal of Social and Personal Relationships, 30,* 237–246. DOI: 10.1080/02681102.2013.804396.

Rishi, R. (2007). Always connected, but hard to reach. *Educause Quarterly, 20*(2), 7–9.

Schilder, E. Lockee, B., and Saxon, D. (2016). The challenges of assessing media literacy education. *Journal of Media Literacy Education, 8,* 32–48.

Schramm, M. (2015, July 30). Survey: 78% of students prefer digital course material. *USA Today.* Retrieved from http://college.usatoday.com/2015/07/30/students-prefer-digital-text/.

Shannon, C. E. (1948). A mathematical theory of communication. *The Bell System Technical Journal, 27,* 379–423. Retrieved from http://ieeexplore.ieee.org/.

Smith, A. (2017). Record shares of Americans now own smartphones, have home broadband. Pew Research Center. Retrieved from http://www.pewresearch.org/fact-tank/2017/01/12/evolution-of-technology/.

Smith, K. (2016). *36 fascinating YouTube statistics for 2016.* Retrieved from https://www.brandwatch.com/blog/36-youtube-stats-2016/.

Statistical Abstract. (2014). *Households with a computer and internet use: 1984 to 2012.* Retrieved from http://census.gov/topics/population/computer-internet.html.

Steinfield, C., Ellison, N. B., Lampe, C., and Vitak, J. (2012). Online social network sites and the concept of social capital. In F. L. Lee, L. Leung, J. S. Qiu, and D. Chu (Eds.), *Frontiers in new media research* (pp. 115–131). New York, NY: Routledge.

Taylor, P., and Keeter, S. (2010). *Millennials: Confident. Connected. Open to change.* Pew Research Center. Retrieved from http://www.pewsocialtrends.org/files/2010/10/millennials-confident-connected-open-to-change.pdf.

Thoman, E., and Jolls, T. (2005). *Literacy for the 21st century: An overview & orientation guide to media literacy education.* Malibu, CA: Center for Media Literacy. Retrieved from http://www.medialit.org/sites/default/files/01_MLKorientation.pdf.

Tisdell, E. J. (2007). Popular culture and critical media literacy in adult education: Theory and practice. *New Directions for Adult and Continuing Education, 115*, 5–13.

Tugend, A. (2016, June 22). Educators discuss the future of higher education. *New York Times.* Retrieved from https://www.nytimes.com/2016/06/23/education/educators-discuss-the-future-of-higher-education.html.

Uhls, Y. T., Michikyan, M., Morris, J., Garcia, D., Small, G. W., Zgourou, E., Greenfield, P. M. (2014). Five days at outdoor education camp without screens improves preeten skills with nonverbal emotion cues. *Computers in Human Behavior, 39,* 387–392.

United Nations Educational, Scientific and Cultural Organization. (2014). *Reading in the mobile era: A study of mobile reading in developing countries.* Paris: UNESCO. Retrieved from http://unesdoc.unesco.org/images/0022/002274/227436e.pdf.

United States Department of Education. (2017). *Reimagining the role of technology in higher education: A supplement to the national education technology plan.* Office of Educational Technology. Retrieved from https://tech.ed.gov/files/2017/01/Higher-Ed-NETP.pdf.

Ventimiglia, P., and Pullman, G. (2016). From written to digital: The new literacy. *Educause Review, 51,* 36–48.

Vraga, E., Tully, M., Kotcher, J. E., Smithson, A. B., and Broeckelman-Post, M. B. (2016). A multi-dimensional approach to measuring news media literacy. *Journal of Media Literacy Education,* 7(3), 41–53.

Watkins, S. C., and Lee, H. E. (2010). *Got Facebook? Investigating what's social about social media.* The University of Texas at Austin. Department of Radio, Television, Film. Retrieved from http://www.theyoungandthedigital.com/wp-content/uploads/2010/11/watkins_lee_facebookstudy-nov-18.pdf.

Wineberg, S., McCrew, S., Breakstone, J., and Ortega, T. (2016). *Evaluating information: The cornerstone of civic online reasoning.* Stanford History Education Group. Retrieved from https://purl.stanford.edu/fv751yt5934.

Chapter Four

Faculty Development in the Digital Age

Training Instructors in New Media Pedagogy

Russell Carpenter

DIGITAL PEDAGOGY

New media scholars constantly monitor changes and updates to technologies for research, teaching, and learning. Scholars researching new media are not the only ones affected by these changes. With an emphasis on student learning, faculty developers—administrators and scholars in higher education institutions focused on supporting faculty in research, teaching, and service—are charged with not only understanding but also leading efforts to train instructors in digital pedagogy.

Many definitions of digital pedagogy have emerged as higher education institutions, new media scholars, and faculty developers have begun to explore implications and possibilities. For example, the Digital Pedagogy Lab offers "educational outreach" focused on "the implementation of critical digital pedagogy in education at all levels." A definition of digital pedagogy is prominently and helpfully featured on the site: "Digital Pedagogy is precisely not about using digital technologies for teaching and, rather, about approaching those tools from a critical pedagogical perspective. So, it is as much about using digital tools thoughtfully as it is about deciding when not to use digital tools, and about paying attention to the impact of digital tools on learning" (Digital Pedagogy Lab, n.d.). The Digital Pedagogy Lab's definition suggests the importance of focusing on the impact of digital and new media tools on pedagogy. In addition, the University of Kentucky's Center for the Enhancement of Learning & Teaching (CETL) highlights programs that promote critical perspectives on digital pedagogy, defined as:

> Combining critical pedagogy with larger questions around technology use and issues related to privacy, accessibility, privilege, and power, the Digital Pedagogy initiatives seeks to empower faculty to make better decisions around technology, particularly as it relates to the impact on the students and their learning experience. We want to use the tools to suit our and our students' needs, not have the tools use us. (Digital Pedagogy, n.d.)

Princeton University's McGraw Center for Teaching & Learning focuses its digital pedagogy mission on "design[ing], develop[ing], implement[ing], and maintain[ing] an educational technology infrastructure to encourage the thoughtful evaluation of technology for pedagogical advancement" (McGraw Center for Teaching & Learning, 2016, para. 1). Finally, the University of Chicago employs the term "digitally-infused pedagogy," which "fully takes into account how technology affects teaching" (Learn About Digital Pedagogy, 2016, para. 2).

These definitions and approaches provide important context for understanding programming that higher education institutions might foster to develop relevant and applicable faculty development efforts to train instructors how to effectively use new media and design digital-friendly courses. To remain viable, higher education institutions must identify creative and new ways to address challenges related to teaching and learning with new media. Some higher education institutions have developed digital pedagogy and new media faculty development efforts under the umbrella term "innovation."

Innovative pedagogical and programming methods include providing access to new media technologies. To support these efforts, faculty development programs have focused on helping instructors understand the range of possible tools, how to access them, and possible uses and purposes. Table 4.1 provides a sample of tools and purposes common in faculty development programs. Instructors must often make decisions about tools that are new and unfamiliar, increasing the amount of time it takes them to research, test, and integrate new media into their teaching.

While tools are critical to the success of digital pedagogy, instructors are faced with additional challenges. Pedagogical content must be relevant, experiential, and engaging for twenty-first-century learners. New media use and implementation may not come naturally to current faculty. To combat this issue, higher education institutions should facilitate relevant and applicable faculty development programs to train instructors how to effectively evaluate, use, and integrate new media into courses.

Many of the pedagogical and professional initiatives implemented at academic institutions are of critical importance—those that focus on pedagogy, promotion and tenure, student learning, and academic success, for exam-

Table 4.1. Sample new media tools for teaching and learning

Sample New Media Tools	*Teaching and Learning Purpose*
VoiceThread	VoiceThread is a web-based application that allows students to collect media such as images, videos, and presentations. A VoiceThread allows students to have conversations and add comments using text, audio, and video with microphones, phones, web cams, or uploaded files.
Instagram	Instagram is a social media application that allows students to apply creative filters to photographs. Students can use hashtags to post information and create engaging learning experiences.
Pinterest	Pinterest is a content-sharing, web-based service that allows students to "pin" images, videos, and objects to their boards. Students can collect and archive artifacts related to their research.
Wikispaces	Wikispaces is a web-based platform for creating user-generated web pages. Students can create their own wiki pages that are editable by individuals or teams.

ple—and major efforts are in place to address the ubiquitous nature of new media. Several trends necessitate new media faculty development that is innovative, responsive, and learner centered while supporting the need for updated pedagogies. Faculty members will need to:

- learn effective uses of new media;
- analyze the range of possibilities for integrating new media into their teaching; and
- understand approaches for designing digital-friendly courses.

While faculty members often receive disciplinary and research-focused training, they receive limited preparation in pedagogy. Thus, higher education institutions would benefit from updates to programming that advance understandings of new media instructional practices.

This chapter provides an overview of the necessary changes to faculty development as new media technologies continue to emerge. A charge to implement faculty-centered development that focuses on new media and digital pedagogy is discussed and new media training initiatives, topics, and procedures are examined.

BACKGROUND AND HISTORICAL CONTEXT: EMERGING FACULTY DEVELOPMENT PRACTICES

Many scholars have addressed the importance of faculty development in higher education institutions (Condon et al., 2016; Gillespie and Robertson, 2010; Sorcinelli and Austin, 2005). King and Felten's (2012) special issue of the *Journal of Faculty Development* focused on "threshold concepts" in faculty development—ideas for faculty developers that have the potential to transform. As a framework for this special issue, authors focus on student learning, scholarly teaching, transfer, digital thresholds, teaching with service learning, and co-inquiry processes involving students. In this special issue, McGowan (2012) identified faculty members' uses of educational technologies as particularly troublesome, as many faculty "are still reticent to incorporate technology effectively in their teaching. Why not? Interest, motivation, time, incentives and the abundance of available tools are surely partial explanations" (p. 25).

Context for Faculty Development in the Digital Age

A number of scholars have examined technology and media in faculty development (Baepler, 2010; Gibbs, Major, and Wright, 2003; Kaminski and Bolliger, 2012; Kitano, Dodge, Harrison, and Lewis, 1998; McGowan, 2012; Schnackenberg, Maughan, and Zadoo, 2004; Shih and Sorcinelli, 2007; Sorcinelli, 2007). Kitano et al. (1998), for example, noted that progress in integrating new technologies into higher education classrooms has been slow despite emerging evidence of benefits for students when technologies are applied in ways that support teaching and learning (p. 263). Since then, Gibbs et al.'s (2003) research revealed that the top use of technology for instruction is corresponding with students (92.9 percent), classroom instruction (85.7 percent), course preparation (85.7 percent), out-of-class course content delivery (82.1 percent), and classroom instruction for student research or labs (32.1 percent) (p. 80).

Research by Sorcinelli (2007) suggested that "Participants in our study from liberal arts, research, and comprehensive institutions named the integration of technology into traditional teaching and learning settings as one of the top three challenges facing their faculty colleagues" (p. 7). Faculty development scholars Schnackenberg et al. (2004) have implemented programming that explores new media pedagogy. Results of their study supported that "it is clear that many students believe in and enjoy engaging in lessons that utilize technology" (p. 29). Their research also leads them to believe that faculty "would like to learn more about the integration of technology into teaching" (p. 29). In Shih and Sorcinelli's (2007) TEACHnology, the overarching goal is to introduce pedagogical change to faculty through deliberate and continuous engagement with technology applications compatible with their existing values and practices (p. 24). As McGowan (2012) noted, despite layers of support and evidence, many faculty are still reticent to incorporate technology effectively in their teaching (p. 27). McGowan explained that the practice of trying, revising, failing, trying again, and rejoicing when it works has become the professional narrative of teaching with technology for many faculty (p. 27). Finally, Eddy and Bracken (2008) examined ways in which the use of video clips in teaching can provide a means to better connect students to class content, especially when the film is incorporated with active learning (p. 132).

Some scholars have begun researching the potential future implications of new media in faculty development. A recent special issue of the *Journal of Faculty Development*, for example, examined the future of faculty development and featured two important perspectives that help define and contextualize digital technology's potential to enhance instruction. Irvin, Marshall, and Carr (2016) developed a digital classroom observation tool that stands to change the ways we view and conduct fundamental faculty development programming. In the same issue, Weber and Barth (2016) examined technologies that they deemed innovative to enhance the teaching of faculty in increasingly popular online or blended environments.

New media instruction presents unique challenges for faculty developers. Pedagogical approaches and programs that support highly effective instruction must adapt on a regular basis. Content extends beyond that which is focused on effective teaching or classroom trends. Moreover, content employed in faculty development efforts must not only be relevant but also involve teaching and learning experiences, observations, and enhancements. Programs must also consider ways in which students learn in the twenty-first century. Active learning (Baepler, Walker, Brooks, Saichaie, and Petersen, 2016), deep learning (Sweet, Blythe, Phillips, and Carpenter, 2016; Sweet, Blythe, and Carpenter, 2015b), and flipping the classroom (Carpenter, Sweet, Blythe, Winter, and Bunnell, 2015; Sweet, Blythe, and Carpenter, 2015a; Waldrop and Bowdon, 2015), for example, are current trends discussed among faculty developers. These topics also presume capacity with new media. Moreover, they are pedagogical approaches commonly employed through and with the use of new media. As faculty developers and instructors pursue digital pedagogies, these approaches will continue to open new opportunities for enhancing teaching and responding to the changing landscape of higher education.

Training Instructors in Effective New Media Use

Instructors must be trained in current new media technologies, as a start, and also understand the theoretical basis for related software, media platforms, and mediated forms. While instructors often bring a wealth of knowledge from their teaching experience, they make important decisions about ways new media can enhance pedagogy. Widely, higher education institutions lack a focus on comprehensive or even thorough digital pedagogy faculty development to support instructors in best practices, theoretical understandings, or foundational concepts. This issue becomes increasingly problematic for two reasons:

1. Students often expect to engage with digital technologies and new media to learn and access course content.
2. Institutions often focus on triaging technology problems over teaching possible productive educational uses of digital media.

Combined, these two issues can lead to a distrust among faculty when faced with the opportunity or possibility to incorporate new media into the classroom.

Given these challenges and needs, new media faculty development should consider several priorities:

- Experience with new media for teaching and learning;
- Access to freely available digital technology platforms;
- Knowledge of student population, demographics, and access to digital technologies on campus and away from campus; and
- Classroom space and configuration.

These priorities impact new media use but are often overlooked as considerations. Institutional politics can factor in these discussions as well, especially in classroom design and access to in-class technologies to facilitate teaching and learning with new media. To this end, higher education institutions should consider several priorities for new media faculty development:

- Ensure that faculty development initiatives are human centered;
- Enlist the expertise of faculty who have experience with and passion for integrating new media into the classroom;
- Provide faculty with options for new media platforms supported by pedagogical rationales; and
- Pair new media-focused faculty development initiatives with discussions about learning theory, student success, and accessibility.

Priorities for Implementing Digital Pedagogical Faculty Development Programming

Higher education faculty development efforts are often led by experts in technology with varying levels of experience or training in pedagogy. The issue with these designs, of course, is that new media interests can lead pedagogical priorities. A new media–deterministic perspective can overlook areas of teaching and learning that will, of course, determine the extent to which new media enhances deep, transferable learning for students. In the Noel Studio for Academic Creativity, for example, the Teaching & Learning Media Services team offers faculty design, feedback, and assessment support for new media projects. Projects, however, must enhance teaching for deep learning in the class. Media consultants in this program collaborate with faculty interested in enhancing their teaching to promote deep learning for students by designing and integrating new media resources into their pedagogical approaches. Tools and personal projects with minimal student-learning impact, though, are not the priority, as interesting as these projects can be. This program considers the potential learning impact on students and pedagogical development by faculty, posing three questions before formally entering into a partnership:

- What is the potential pedagogical value of the new media project?
- Does the project stand to enhance deep learning among students?
- How many students are impacted by this new media teaching and learning project?

These questions help media consultants prioritize projects that enhance instruction and, more specifically, help faculty provide meaningful learning experiences through new media. Thus, the program focuses on the faculty first, pedagogical approach second, and new media third. New media, thus, is designed to enhance pedagogy based on the faculty member's instructional goals and the learning outcomes as envisioned and articulated by the faculty member. If faculty are focused on new media projects for research or other related academic uses, while perfectly ambitious and compelling, the program provides resources and feedback but does not commit ongoing support for these efforts. The program emphasizes faculty development for new media that enhances ways in which students engage with a class resource or approaches for faculty to design more meaningful assignments and learning objects that facilitate transfer of knowledge over memorization or simple use of new media as containers of information.

This program, as a model for new media faculty development, encourages reflective instruction. During the beginning of the process, faculty might question why they need new media, how it will enhance student learning, and ways in which the use of new media will specifically enhance teaching.

OVERVIEW OF EXISTING FACULTY DEVELOPMENT CONFIGURATIONS

Faculty development initiatives focus on a variety of relevant and important topics. Many programming efforts are organized to provide meaningful experiences for faculty during their first year (acclimating to teaching, students, publication, and service expectations at the institution), second to third years (often considered junior faculty), third to sixth years (pre-tenure, tenure-track faculty), sixth to tenth years (tenured faculty), and over ten years (tenured, senior-level, full professor). Priorities at each of these stages differ. For example, service expectations and leadership opportunities often increase once a faculty member has earned tenure.

Examining the Theoretical Basis and Rationale for Programming

Faculty developers must prioritize the most critical programming efforts for faculty at their institution. This process often entails assessing and evaluating faculty teaching needs and understanding student learning outcomes. At times, faculty will provide suggestions, and in other cases, faculty developers will need to assess opportunities for program development. This process entails an understanding of the basis for program-focused decisions and rationale for these initiatives. Faculty developers might use their institution's strategic plan as one way of evaluating and developing a rationale for programming efforts.

New media–focused initiatives can serve several mission-critical purposes. All academic institutions involve teaching, although it is widely understood that some incentivize success in research and scholarship as well. While teaching priorities vary from institution to institution, common values exist that support a foundation and rationale for faculty development focused on new media:

- New media integration in teaching can enhance student learning;
- New classroom assignments and projects can provide valuable data-collection, research, and publication opportunities for faculty, graduate students, and undergraduate students in the form of Scholarship of Teaching and Learning (SoTL) initiatives; and
- New media teaching resources can provide students with access to concepts, demonstrations, and information that are otherwise inaccessible or convoluted.

Advancing a theoretical understanding for new media faculty development, several factors could determine the extent to which higher education institutions are successful. The primary issue is access to course content. Millennial (Carlson, 2005) and Generation Z learners (Morin and Stanley, 2017), will approach learning with expectations for immediate access to highly engaging, technologically rich, and mobile resources. Faculty advancing their education five, ten, or twenty years ago did not engage information in the same way, although perhaps have had access to new media resources, platforms, and tools in recent years. Thus, new media design and learning can seem distanced or, in some cases, simply not a priority for teaching. Moreover, integrating new media into the classroom can seem burdensome if the expectation is that lessons, modules, and instructional techniques will need significant and time-consuming attention. Faculty development programs cannot guarantee that they will save faculty members time when deciding whether to integrate new media into their teaching; however, these efforts can ensure faculty that they are intentional in their efforts and designing learning experiences using best practices based on evidence of research in scholarly teaching or based on SoTL evidence.

To this end, new media initiatives can become instrumental to faculty development programs across institutions of a variety of contexts, missions, and sizes. With an emphasis on scholarly teaching—instructional practices based on research and evidence—new media initiatives can serve as compelling and valuable opportunities for faculty spanning career trajectories, priorities, or rank.

Innovations in Pedagogy

Faculty developers might consider justifications for additional focus on new media pedagogy. To this end, higher education institutions will need to focus on innovation in pedagogy. While innovation is a major topic of higher education instruction and administration (Sweet, Blythe, and Carpenter, 2016), institutions might adopt concepts that allow for new ways to educate students. In an age of constant change, competition for high-quality students, and changes in funding models, institutions will be forced to embrace a proactive role and set new standards for quality teaching, which is where new media and digital technologies factor.

Innovations in pedagogy will necessarily involve new media and digital technology. Faculty will be expected to incorporate new media in on-ground and online courses and to demonstrate its uses in meaningful, substantive, and engaging ways. That is, new media uses will move beyond surface-level integration—commonly used for experimental or promotional purposes—to enhance student learning. Initiatives like the University Innovation Alliance (UIA)—a network of research-intensive academic institutions spanning the

United States focused on enhancing undergraduate education—are leading the way for new research and development in pedagogy.

Institutions participating in the UIA excel at research, as all are considered "Highest Research Activity" status in the Carnegie Classifications, but they also focus on innovative student learning. Arizona State University (ASU), the University of Central Florida (UCF), and the University of Texas (UT), for example, all employ new media to enhance online course and program offerings for students. These institutions have embraced—in productive and challenging ways—the affordances awarded to them by understanding how students learn within mediated on-ground and online environments. Investments in innovative learning, undergraduate education, and faculty development are substantial at these institutions, and all have complex support networks to build new media teaching and learning infrastructures. To achieve this goal of innovation requires cultures of student learning, of course, paired with faculty learning. New media necessitates committed and ongoing efforts toward the enhancement, proliferation, and sustainability of faculty development. Moreover, Pope-Ruark (2016) suggested that the American Association of Colleges & Universities' (AAC&U) definition of high-impact educational practice might be ready for expansion to include a focus on innovation and technology.

Faculty development initiatives within higher education institutions should take the lead in designing, implementing, and sustaining new media pedagogical programming to enhance faculty teaching and student learning. This decision places pedagogy at the center and allows new media development to build around and enhance high-quality scholarly teaching. New media integration in the classroom stands to enhance pedagogy in several ways:

- Providing immediate educational and instructional content to students;
- Allowing for flexibility in academic experiences for student learners; and
- Increasing learning engagement for students.

THEORETICAL UNDERSTANDINGS

Faculty development theory is changing as quickly as new media itself. Research in journals like the *Journal of Faculty Development*, *To Improve the Academy*, and *Innovative Higher Education*, among others, encourage new thinking about issues related to faculty development. Important within the context of new media pedagogy, faculty development programs are often linked to academic affairs units. These programs will often include investments in faculty as part of their value added to the institution. Moreover, though, programming is becoming less focused on top-down instruction for faculty and more focused on interactive opportunities for faculty to take part in learning experiences with other faculty.

New media and digital pedagogy provide ideal opportunities to offer faculty incentives for taking part in teaching-enhancement processes. At Eastern Kentucky University (EKU) a provost-appointed team—the Faculty Innovation Workgroup—designed and implemented a full-scale plan for moving faculty development programming online specifically through the use of new media. The process is considered to be "for faculty, by faculty," meaning that the output of the workgroup is driven by what faculty from across campus want and need.

The product of the Faculty Innovation Workgroup's efforts is a system called "DEEP," which stands for "Developing Excellence in Eastern's Professors" (DEEP, 2016). Through a highly collaborative process, faculty provided input into the pedagogical topics contained within the system, beginning with a course on metacognition, and the design of the system itself. Each course—built within the institution's Learning Management System (LMS)—includes digital videos, interactive digital tools, and multimodal (combining alphabetic text, oral communication, and visual elements) learning objects that help faculty achieve a set of pre-established faculty learning

System Organization		
Each course, based on pedagogical topic, proceeds in levels to ensure that the structure and materials are consistent across the system.		
Level	**Bloom's Taxonomy**	**Definition by Level**
1. Learner	Remembering and understanding knowledge	Review key concepts on pedagogical topic to identify and transfer knowledge gained.
2. Practitioner	Applying knowledge	Recall knowledge gained with emphasis on practicing pedagogical skills and building strengths.
3. Advocate	Analyzing, evaluating, and promoting knowledge	Share best practices of teaching and learning with colleagues and students.
4. Scholar	Creating new knowledge based on the pedagogical topic	Develop and refine innovative skills that contribute to original research, scholarship, or teaching.

Figure 4.1. Structure of DEEP system available at studio.eku.edu/ DEEP. *Source*: Figure created by Russell Carpenter.

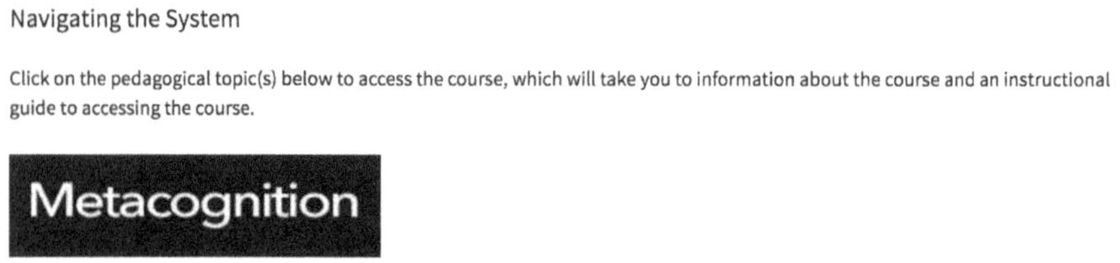

Navigating the System

Click on the pedagogical topic(s) below to access the course, which will take you to information about the course and an instructional guide to accessing the course.

Metacognition

Figure 4.2. DEEP online course button available at studio.eku.edu/ DEEP. *Source*: Figure created by Russell Carpenter.

outcomes (Hurney, Brantmeier, Good, Harrison, and Meixner, 2016). Kalantzis and Cope (2010) find that the "new learner" is comfortable in multimodal, digital spaces, while the "new teacher" is comfortable working with learners in new, multimodal, and social media spaces (p. 204). DEEP employs new media to enhance the delivery of faculty development (Figures 4.1 and 4.2). Digital content allows for modularity and customization.

Based on the results of a pilot test of DEEP, faculty expect mediated content in their own faculty development experiences. Comments on the design of DEEP obtained through a pre-launch testing survey (Table 4.2) focused on the delivery of mediated content and potential for it to enhance pedagogy:

- "Navigation is fairly easy and clear. An updated version may include a video with instructions for each section explained by a narrative/host."
- "The visuals are pretty simple clip-art type illustrations, which do not significantly affect learning."
- "In addition to recommendations above, consistency of graphic design would be a plus."

EKU is not unique in its effort to employ new media and digital content to design faculty development experiences. Higher education institutions are enlisting the collective intelligence of their faculty to design major, sophisticated faculty development systems that employ new media to distribute pedagogical-focused content to faculty on demand. In these cases, institutions have decided to commit to new media pedagogy and harness the most up-to-date strategies as an asset for their faculty. Institutions will continue to employ new media in compelling ways as major financial, intellectual investments in faculty. These efforts will likely focus on enriching teaching and learning—or, more specifically, creating innovative learning experiences—as competition for quality students and highly committed and productive faculty increase. At the same time, faculty will continue to proactively identify ways in which these developments in teaching through and with new media will enhance research, scholarship, and service productivity.

Faculty development and instruction are not independent of these considerations and to separate these pillars of major higher education institutions would be fatalistic for all sides. Systems designed to enhance innovative teaching and learning, like DEEP, will continue to factor prominently. Driven by pedagogy and goals of scholarly teaching, these systems are constructed by, facilitated, and sustained by new media–driven contexts. Institutions can only offer their students and faculty the limits of what humans can envision and create. Through innovative uses of new media, digital pedagogical opportunities will become more accessible to large numbers of faculty members across college and departmental boundaries. Similar systems, of course, become the ideal hub for instructional resources focused on the enhancement of new media instructional resources.

Faculty Development

Faculty development and digital pedagogy will become more tightly interwoven as higher education institutions find new ways to employ tools to advance institutional missions, which often feature faculty—understandably—at the center. Faculty development scholars and leaders will continue to have opportunities to shape ways in which new media is rolled out on their campuses and, perhaps most importantly, to shape ways pedagogical content is transformed and enhanced through these efforts.

Pedagogy

Much like the proliferation of new media, "remediation" of print (Bolter and Grusin, 1998) did not do away with print-based texts, new media will not do away with on-ground instruction. At least not for the foreseeable future. Embrace of—and thus understanding of and harnessing of—new media tools and resources will enhance pedagogy for several reasons, including:

- enabling access;
- encouraging participation; and
- entertaining students during the learning process.

Importantly, new media may also enhance student learning in high-impact practices such as service-learning, writing-intensive courses, undergraduate research, and collaborative projects (Kuh, 2008).

Table 4.2. DEEP usability testing form

DEEP Usability Testing Form

[To be developed as Google Form and sent to faculty testers in each college electronically. Areas included in form: Area, Question/Prompt, Goal, Response]

We will develop questions based on content areas. Goals are internal based on what we would like to learn or know about that area of the system.

0 - Instructions: Please share your thoughts about each area of the system: Samples and Readings, Ease of Navigation, Content, Overall Learning Experience

1 - Samples and Readings			
Area	**Question/Prompt**	**Goal**	**Response**
Clarity of instructions and questions in the system	Explain how well you understand the purpose of each component. If necessary, list any resources you used to complete the section.	Determine if instructions are clear and evaluate faculty members' preparation for the section without having to consult a source.	
Ease of viewing	Describe your ability to use the system and list any complications you may have had.	Identify any challenges to accessing the reading and viewing materials or samples.	
Length of time	Evaluate the length of time required to review the readings and samples in terms of reasonable length.	Determine ideal and reasonable length of time required for readings and samples.	
Suggestions for samples and readings	Evaluate and list areas of improvement for the section.	Understand system needs in Samples and Readings area.	
2 - Ease of Navigation			
Area	**Question/Prompt**	**Goal**	**Response**
Organization	Identify any of the system features (by level) that were difficult or confusing to navigate. List any organizational features that enhanced your experience in navigating the system. Suggest features that would enhance your experience for consideration in an updated version. Evaluate the system design and your ease in locating previously completed material.	**Level:** Faculty will understand where they need to go for information, prompts or instructions, content, readings, and resources. **Between Levels:** How faculty move from one level to the next and locate previously viewed tasks and resources.	
Visual elements	Evaluate the visual elements in terms of your understanding of the content. Explain how they assisted or deterred your navigation of the system.	**Level:** Faculty will benefit from consistent visual elements that support navigation of pedagogical content. **Between Level:** Visual elements will build upon and/or relate to visual elements from the previous level.	

Suggestions for Ease of Navigation	Recommend suggestions for improving the section's navigability.	Understand system needs in Ease of Navigation area.	
3 - Content			
Area	**Question/Prompt**	**Goal**	**Response**
Pedagogical topic	Analyze the relevance of this topic. Propose ways that you might incorporate what you learned into your teaching. List topics would you like to see in future courses. Evaluate the balance of appropriate coverage in breadth and depth.	Determine which topics to develop in future and whether content of the current course is useful. Determine if this topic should be a single course or a series.	
Relevance	Evaluate and explain the relevance of the readings and samples to your teaching at EKU. Suggest any additional or alternative readings and samples.	Determine the usefulness of readings included in the system as they related to current teaching practices at EKU.	
Development and progression	Evaluate the order, pacing, and length of sections. Explain any knowledge you used in previous sections to further understand the current section. Provide your level of clarity with saving your progress.	Ensure that faculty members can complete sections and pick up where they left off. Make sure that there are tasks that can be completed in a spare half hour between other tasks and ensure that content is reinforced in subsequent sections.	
Potential or missing content	Propose any additional content.	Ensure that the most relevant and important content is included in the system.	
Ideas for courses	Suggest additional courses you would like to see developed in the future.	Ensure timely content.	
4 - Overall Learning Experience			
Area	**Question/Prompt**	**Goal**	**Response**
Challenge	Describe how this learning experience encourages you to think differently about the subject matter.	Determine whether the faculty member recognized the need to engage in new learning about teaching.	
Thoroughness	Describe how this experience prompts a deeper understanding of the content. Identify information that you can use from this section to enhance your teaching skills.	Understand how faculty are able to apply information to make meaningful change in the classroom.	

Willingness to begin other courses	Describe how your experience entices you to explore more courses to enhance your teaching.	Determine whether the faculty member would choose this format for engaging in reflection and learning about teaching in the future.	
Willingness to encourage others	Describe how your experience will make you want to share your experience with other faculty. List ways that the content of the course will help build teaching confidence.	Understand the extent to which the course gives faculty more confidence to apply, discuss, and share pedagogical content. Determine whether faculty member would recommend this format to colleagues.	
Suggestions for overall learning experience	Provide suggestions for improvement.	Understand system needs for Overall Learning Experience.	

THEORETICAL UNDERSTANDINGS OF FACULTY DEVELOPMENT IN THE DIGITAL AGE

To understand new media and digital pedagogies, it might be beneficial to define digital media. Digital media refers to audio and video content that has been digitized and is often available through web access or via computer transmission. It is often considered in association with new media.

New media pedagogies provide the opportunity to show and model rather than merely tell. Teaching scenarios become engaging, interactive, and even entertaining through the effective use of well-design digital video, for example. Lister, Dovey, Giddings, Grant, and Kelly (2009) take new media to refer to: new textual experiences, including entertainment, pleasure, and patterns of media consumption (games and simulations); new ways of representing the world, including immersive environments; and new relationships between users and consumers and media technologies, including the ways we use media in everyday life (p. 12). Gitelman and Pingree (2003) offer a deeper exploration of the term "new media" in their argument that "all media were once 'new media'" (p. xi). More specifically, though, new media often includes content available online or via cloud-based platforms and integrates digital images and sounds available on demand.

ADOPTION

Future faculty development programming adopted for implementation should include a balance of on-ground and online initiatives. Programs that enhance new media and digital pedagogy might include digital video creation and editing, LMS integration, instructional technology training, instructional media development, and mobile learning applications.

Faculty institutional priorities usually include scholarship, teaching, and service. A focus on instruction, however, in new media faculty development can increase faculty engagement. Strategies for adoption could also include: 1) enlisting insight into the most widely used new media from faculty, 2) focusing on pedagogical uses of specific new media, and 3) inviting ongoing faculty input into decisions regarding new media.

Faculty development initiatives focused on new media and digital pedagogy stand to enhance instructional techniques and encourage faculty learning on their own to ensure that they can incorporate concepts in future classes. A focus on digital pedagogy should incorporate approaches, strategies, and tools that are transferable across disciplines. Digital pedagogy examples should be designed in ways that faculty will see benefits in their own instruction. Concepts should transfer readily to a variety of classroom contexts. Digital pedagogy should cut across instructional settings. Integrating digital pedagogy in higher education institutions can present challenges, but it is critical that potential benefits—along with hurdles—are addressed.

A THEORETICAL MODEL FOR PROGRAM DESIGN

Faculty developers will benefit from a theoretical model for program design that could lead to the adoption of efforts across the curriculum. One such model that is readily adaptable for such use is the Revised Bloom's Taxonomy. For such a model, faculty developers might turn to Anderson and Krathwohl (2001). The Revised Bloom's Taxonomy provides a framework to help instructors consider how their approaches to teaching with new media, and the promotion of a digital pedagogy, might help them move toward "creating" course tools and content while allowing students to do the same.

Table 4.3. Tracking chart for integrating new media into the classroom

Cognitive Process Dimension	New Media Selection	Learning Objective

Integrating with Students

Moreover, an attention to the Revised Bloom's Taxonomy will help instructors consider how their new media options and selections contribute to student learning. Table 4.3 offers one way to organize such a process for instructors integrating new media into the classroom to enhance student learning.

Linking Teaching and Learning with New Media Pedagogy

Faculty developers can help instructors link teaching and learning with new media pedagogy. While faculty developers might not provide answers regarding new media solutions, which often serves as a simple troubleshooting answer, it is more likely that possibilities should be based on a set of questions regarding the course goals or learning outcomes. Such questions might include:

- What is the intended learning outcome expected from the use of new media?
- How might new media enhance the learning experience of students?
- In what ways might students retain information learned in the class through new media?

In addition, instructors might also consider teaching and learning issues related to access. As Carpenter et al. (2015) explained, pedagogical decisions involving technology can depend on the level of reliable access to wireless Internet (Wi-Fi) or computers. This issue can become an important consideration at higher education institutions in rural areas. Instructors might pose several questions:

- How many of my students are impacted by assignments that require new media access or creation away from the classroom?
- Will students have access to new media resources while on campus?
- What is the level of technology access of students in the class?

Answering these questions, as a start, will allow for more robust integration of new media for instructors and students.

STRATEGIES FOR IMPLEMENTATION

It is possible to identify strategies for implementing new media. Foremost, new media implementation should be driven by pedagogical need and justification. Instructors might discuss the use of new media, rationale, and learning goals in advance with students. Once those parameters are established between the instructor and students, plan time during two to three class meetings for students to create projects. The instructor can facilitate questions and encourage idea generation as students learn to use the media to achieve course learning goals.

Teaching

On the instructor side, it is important to commit time for students to create in class. Allowing for in-class media-creation time suggests to students that this process is important. Students will also learn from your on-the-spot feedback, which will enhance learning for students while reducing anxiety if students are not accustomed to using new media for academic purposes. The instructor's role becomes that of facilitator.

Learning

Students—when approaching the learning process—must see the value of new media. New media projects should be closely aligned with course goals. Rather than assigning superficial new media projects, instructors might consider ways in which learning experiences can build on one another from the beginning of class to the end. In addition, instructors might consider the value of a showcase opportunity, which allows for a celebration of student new media projects as a culminating experience. Students also learn through presenting their new media work during the process. By way of example, the Noel Studio for Academic Creativity collaborates with numerous faculty members each semester culminating in a showcase of teaching and learning innovation. These collaborations enhance faculty development and student learning through the use of new media (Carpenter, Apostel, and Hyndman, 2012; Fairchild and Carpenter, 2015).

Sustainable Resources

In these productive collaborations, the Noel Studio provides space and access to laptops and Wi-Fi. Students create new media projects within the space at milestone dates in the semester after attending multiple workshops about the technology selected for the project. The instructor attends the sessions and works, side by side, with the Noel Studio facilitator. Students have focused time to create with an expert facilitator's support.

This practice adds sustainability to the process. Students have focused time to create while learning to employ new media options. In addition, the instructor learns along with students. Instructors can create these new media learning opportunities in their own classroom, and even if students are using low-tech materials to think through their projects, the learning experience can prove valuable.

SUSTAINABLE PROGRAMMING

New media pedagogy should enhance deep and transferable learning (Condon et al., 2016). Students who learn deeply are able to apply knowledge in one academic area to others. Teaching for deep learning places students at the center of the process. Students then select new media options based on the intended learning outcomes of students and concepts that students can transfer from one experience to the next.

Goals and Transferability of New Media Pedagogical Approaches

Instructors might select personal pedagogical goals for new media approaches. These goals can help instructors track what pedagogical approaches students respond to best and what new media options support and reinforce this learning. Ideally, students are learning course content in addition to new media applications. Faculty will continue to learn ways to best apply new media in their own processes. Moreover, they can build skills in new media that will help them in different academic situations in the future.

Concepts for Understanding Programming Effectiveness

Faculty development programs often base perceptions of program effectiveness and success for faculty on satisfaction surveys. Such methods do not offer an in-depth or ongoing understandings of knowledge gained from the experience. It is also likely that such efforts do not ask faculty what they have learned or applied in their teaching over time—a month, three months, five months, or a year after the event. For the individual faculty member, it is common to consider the media platform first before the pedagogical focus.

Programming effectiveness and success are best understood with a focus on faculty long-term growth and information retained while also focusing on understanding usage and application of new media tools, strategies, and classroom integration. Immediate use, while important, can serve as a starting point, with a focus on long-term learning through new media. Longitudinal assessments can offer faculty development perspectives that lead to long-term decision making and digital pedagogical enhancements.

Transfer of New Media Pedagogy

Faculty development efforts focused on digital pedagogy and teaching and learning with new media can focus on transfer—concepts and approaches learned in one academic scenario that are replicable or adaptable in another. In the Noel Studio, facilitators focus on helping faculty reflect in meaningful and substantial ways on their pedagogical development.

Reinforcing transferability of new media pedagogy enhances the ability to focus on core concepts—fundamental approaches central to any teaching and learning scenario. The four core concepts presented in Table 4.4 serve as guiding principles for faculty development in new media and digital pedagogy programming and initiatives.

Impact on Student Learning in the Classroom and Beyond

New media and digital pedagogy are more than important conversations at higher education institutions. Institutions must take the lead in designing and studying the ways that new media engage students and faculty. It is not only critical to those stakeholders but also the communities in which these higher education institutions are situated. When higher education institutions discover innovative, reliable, and accessible ways to enhance pedagogy through new media, communities benefit as well. Secondary school teachers can use pedagogical courses made available and accessible via new media to enhance their own classrooms. Higher education institutions will employ new media to connect in new ways with student learners while also supporting faculty development through access to tools and teaching-enhancement resources. Most importantly, higher education institutions must use new media to meet and anticipate student expectations. To ensure that programming efforts do not fall short, faculty developers should scale efforts to meet future needs of students and the faculty teaching them.

Institutions can generate the most innovative practices for new media and digital pedagogical development. High-quality faculty development efforts enhance teaching and learning and provide opportunities for research and development. The focus will remain on pedagogy, with new media and digital pedagogy developments encouraging faculty to think about the possibilities for their own instruction. Much like scholars have examined when supporting faculty in implementing new pedagogical approaches into the classroom, new media and digital pedagogy instruction can be incremental or

Table 4.4. Core concepts for faculty development in new media and digital pedagogy

Core Concept	*Description*
1	Teaching with new media should enhance deep learning in students.
2	Digital pedagogy development is a process of discovery.
3	New media purposes inform delivery.
4	New media teaching and learning should be student centered.

modular, and the resulting faculty development initiatives to support these efforts can provide best practices.

REFERENCES

Anderson, L. W., and Krathwohl, D., eds. (2001). *A taxonomy for learning, teaching and assessing: A revision of Bloom's Taxonomy of educational objectives*. New York, NY: Pearson.

Baepler, P. (2010). A teaching, technology, and faculty development timeline. *Journal of Faculty Development, 24*(2), 40–48.

Baepler, P., Walker, J. D., Brooks, D. C., Saichaie, K., and Petersen, B. A. (2016). *A guide to teaching in the active learning classroom: History, research, and practice*. Sterling, VA: Stylus.

Bolter, J. D., and Grusin, R. (1998). *Remediation: Understanding new media*. Cambridge, MA: MIT Press.

Carlson, S. (2005, October 7). The net generation goes to college. *Chronicle of Higher Education*. Retrieved from http://www.chronicle.com/article/The-Net-Generation-Goes-to/12307.

Carpenter, R., Apostel, S., and Hyndman, J. (2012). Developing a model for ePortfolio design: A studio approach. *International Journal of ePortfolio, 2*(2), 163–172.

Carpenter, R., Sweet, C., Blythe, H., Winter, R., and Bunnell, A. (2015). A challenge for the flipped classroom: Addressing spatial divides. In *Implementation and critical assessment of the flipped classroom experience*. Ed. Abigail Scheg. Hershey, PA: IGI Global. 139–156.

Condon, W., Iverson, E. R., Manduca, C. A., Rutz, C., and Willett, G. (2016). *Faculty development and student learning: Assessing the connections*. Bloomington, IN: Indiana University Press.

DEEP. (2016). Noel Studio for Academic Creativity. Retrieved from http://www.studio.eku.edu/DEEP.

Digital Pedagogy. (n.d.). Retrieved from http://www.uky.edu/celt/content/digital-pedagogy.

Digital Pedagogy Lab. (n.d.). Retrieved from http://www.digitalpedagogylab.com/hybridped/digitalpedagogy/.

Eddy, P. L., and Bracken, D. (2008). Lights, camera, action! The role of movies and video in classroom learning. *Journal of Faculty Development, 22*(2), 125–134.

Fairchild, J., and Carpenter, R. (2015). Embracing collaborative opportunities: Examining an ePortfolio bootcamp. *Communication Center Journal, 1*(1), 61–71.

Gibbs, J. E., Major, C. H., and Wright, V. H. (2003). Faculty perceptions of the costs and benefits of instructional technology: Implications for faculty work. *Journal of Faculty Development, 19*(2), 77–88.

Gillespie, K. J., and Robertson, D. R., eds. (2010). *A guide to faculty development*. San Francisco, CA: Jossey-Bass.

Gitelman, L., and Pingree, G. B., eds. (2003). *New media 1740–1915*. Cambridge, MA: MIT Press.

Hurney, C., Brantmeier, E. J., Good, M. R., Harrison, D., and Meixner, C. (2016). The faculty learning outcome assessment framework. *Journal of Faculty Development, 30*(2), 69–77.

Irvin, A., Marshall, K., and Carr, S. (2016). Feedback for the future: Building a classroom observation tool for the TCU community. *Journal of Faculty Development, 30*(2), 37–46.

Kalantzis, M., and Cope, B. (2010). The teacher as designer: Pedagogy in the new media age. *E-Learning and Digital Media, 7*(3).

Kaminski, K., and Bolliger, D. (2012). Technology, learning, and the classroom: Longitudinal evaluation of a faculty development model. *Journal of Faculty Development, 26*(1), 13–17.

King, C., and Felten, P., eds. (2012). Spec. Issue Threshold Concepts in Educational Development. *Journal of Faculty Development, 26*(3).

Kitano, M. K., Dodge, B. J., Harrison, P. J., and Lewis, R. B. (1998). Faculty development in technology applications to university instruction: An evaluation. *To Improve the Academy, 17*, 263–290.

Kuh, G. D. (2008). High-impact educational practices: What they are, who has access to them, and why they matter. Washington, DC: Association of American Colleges & Universities. Retrieved from https://keycenter.unca.edu/sites/default/files/aacu_high_impact_2008_final.pdf.

Learn About Digital Pedagogy. (2016). Digital Pedagogy and Teaching. University of Chicago. Retrieved from https://online.uchicago.edu/page/learn-about-digital-pedagogy.

Lister, M., Dovey, J., Giddings, S., Grant, I., and Kelly, K. (2009). *New media: A critical Introduction* (2nd ed.). New York, NY: Routledge.

McGowan, S. (2012). Obstacle or opportunity? Digital thresholds in professional development. *Journal of Faculty Development, 26*(3), 25–28.

McGraw Center for Teaching & Learning. (2016). Retrieved from https://mcgraw.princeton.edu/digital-pedagogy.

Morin, C., and Stanley, C. (2017). Connecting high-impact practices, scholarly and creative teaching, and faculty development: An interview with Dr. Aaron Thompson. *Journal of Faculty Development, 31*(2), 1–6.

Pope-Ruark, R. (2016). 3 easy ways to embrace high-impact learning. *Chronicle of Higher Education*. Retrieved from http://www.chronicle.com/article/3-Easy-Ways-to-Embrace/238111?cid=cp57.

Schnackenberg, H., Maughan, M. D., and Zadoo, E. (2004). From Socrates to cyberspace: Enhancing teaching and learning through technology. *Journal of Faculty Development, 20*(1), 21–30.

Shih, M., and Sorcinelli, M. D. (2007). Technology as a catalyst for senior faculty development. *Journal of Faculty Development, 21*(2), 23–31.

Sorcinelli, M. D. (2007). Faculty development: The challenge going forward. *Peer Review: Emerging Trends and Key Debates in Undergraduate Education, 9*(4), 4–8.

Sorcinelli, M. D., and Austin, A. E. (2005). *Creating the future of faculty development: Learning from the past, understanding the present*. San Francisco, CA: Jossey-Bass.

Sweet, C., Blythe, H., and Carpenter, R. (2016). *Innovating faculty development: Entering the age of innovation*. Stillwater, OK: New Forums Press.

Sweet, C., Blythe, H., and Carpenter, R., eds. (2015a). *It works for me, flipping the classroom*. Stillwater, OK: New Forums Press.

Sweet, C., Blythe, H., and Carpenter, R. (2015b). Teaching for deep learning. *Thriving in Academe*. National Education Advocate, *33*(4), 12–15.

Sweet, C., Blythe, H., Phillips, B., and Carpenter, R. (2016). *Transforming your students into deep learners*. Stillwater, OK: New Forums Press.

Waldrop, J., and Bowdon, M., eds. (2015). *Best practices for flipping the college classroom*. New York, NY: Routledge.

Weber, N. L., and Barth, D. J. (2016). Motivating instructors through innovative technology and pedagogy. *Journal of Faculty Development, 30*(2), 97–105.

Chapter Five

Learning Interfaces

Collaboration and Learning Space in the Digital Age

Nigel Haarstad

A SHIFTING LANDSCAPE

During the last decade (2005–2015), higher education experienced an explosion of new online courses and degree programs. While many academic leaders reported that online learning was critical to their long-term strategies, they believed that lower retention rates were a significant barrier to the growth of online instruction (Allen and Seaman, 2013). One reason for this dissatisfaction, and the resulting lower retention numbers, is that online learners sometimes feel disconnected from others (van Tyron and Bishop, 2009). This disconnect can hinder students from interacting and building knowledge together. Moreover, instructors have reported difficulties in facilitating student interactions online (Rovai, 2007). Thus, there is a critical need to create online learning environments that have the capability to sustain a strong sense of community that supports students both socially and cognitively. This chapter will outline research pertaining to community and collaboration facilitated through these new learning interfaces.

EMERGENCE

Recently, there has been a dramatic increase in the number and type of online courses offered worldwide, and there is a growing consensus that e-learning will be critical to the future of education (Allen and Seaman, 2014). While the impact of the Internet on higher education certainly marks a new era in education, many of the questions we are facing today are not new.

Debates about the impact of learning interfaces on pedagogy have been around for generations. For example, many argue that Plato thought that learning ought to take place solely through conversation. Likewise, Socrates argues that writing only teaches or reminds those who already have knowledge. Both were concerned that writing did not engage pupils' questions or challenge their interpretations (Mintz, 2016). More recently, technologies have also transformed *where* learning takes place. For example, the printing press made books accessible outside of monasteries and universities so that learning could take place in one's home (Male and Burden, 2014). This was a dramatic shift in the accessibility of knowledge, yet the contents of these books were still largely determined by a relatively small group of authors and publishers (Dede, 2008). In 1870, the chalkboard became prevalent in the classroom when the Education Acts made school free and mandatory for all children. The creation and implementation of the chalkboard resulted in a huge population of schoolchildren who inspired the development of teaching techniques appropriate for large-group learning. Many of these techniques relied on the blackboard as a reusable demonstration space visible to the entire class at once, unlike a book or slate (Wylie, 2012). The printing press and chalkboard, once considered innovative classroom new media, changed both where and how learning happened, paving the way to the student-centered and active learning we see today.

We face similar challenges today as the Internet drives significant changes to our society and to higher education. For example, the Internet has drastically increased the availability of knowledge, in terms of both sheer volume and the fact that mobile devices put that knowledge at our fingertips at all times. Technologies for synchronous collaboration across vast distances are changing both possibilities and expectations for distance education, and increases in broadband infrastructure raise our expectation for media-rich experiences. Indeed, the landscape of higher education is already influenced by these technological affordances: 49 percent of students have taken a course in the past year which was offered *completely* online, and 81 percent of undergraduates said that at least some of their courses were blended, or offered partially online (Grajek, 2016). Additionally, 99 percent of universities use a learning management system (Dahlstrom, Brooks, and Bichsel, 2014). These systems provide comprehensive software that often integrates with other university systems to support the administration, delivery, and assessment of courses in traditional face-to-face, blended, or online learning environments (Wright et al., 2014, April 21). Despite these trends toward online learning, many faculty still have legitimate questions and concerns. A recent survey by Educause found that faculty claim that they would adopt technology more if they had evidence of its impact on student learning. Faculty from a wide variety of institutions said that they would integrate more or "better" technology into the classroom if they had a clear indication or evidence that students would benefit (Brooks, 2016). Fortunately, there is a wide body of research available to help faculty evaluate the potential affordances and limitations of different types of technology and new media in the online classroom.

THEORETICAL UNDERSTANDING

When teaching online, one should not necessarily attempt to re-create the face-to-face classroom experience. Replication should not be the end goal. We know that the online environment mediates communication in ways we don't encounter in face-to-face settings. This does not mean that we should disregard the abundance of existing instructional research, rather we must examine what we know contributes to a collaborative classroom environment, then ask how new media interact with the strategies that have worked in face-to-face environments. To build a theoretical foundation, instructors would be wise to visit research pertaining to e-learning, learning interfaces, and instructional technology that spans numerous academic disciplines from educational psychology to computer science.

A large body of literature has examined learning interfaces from a user experience or user interface design perspective. For example, education researchers (e.g., Aragon, Johnson, and Shaik, 2002; Bassoppo-Moyo, 2006; Keegan, 1996; Ko and Rossen, 2010) study variables such as planning, time management, learning styles, and assessment with regard to online courses. In the field of communication, however, fewer studies have examined how new media change the student experience (Limperos et al., 2015). Those studies that do explore e-learning settings indicate that many of the same variables important to successful face-to-face courses (e.g., interaction, immediacy, motivation) are just as important in e-learning settings (Carrell and Menzel, 2001; Conaway, Easton, and Schmidt, 2005). Learning interface research that focuses on the user and user experience can be helpful as instructors attempt to connect the seemingly disconnected students in their online courses.

Theoretical developments related to new media and distance education is an area of consistent growth and exploration. With that said, various theoretical lenses have been developed that highlight distance education and new media implementation. Transactional distance theory is one theory that focuses on the intersection between the learning interface and communication, and offers a logical starting point for this discussion.

Transactional Distance

Transactional distance theory holds that the physical separation of the learner and instructor can lead to psychological and communication gaps that, in turn, create misunderstandings and feelings of isolation (Moore, 2007). The structure of the course, dialogue between the instructor and learners, and the extent to which learners are autonomous are dimensions of transactional distance (Stein, Wanstreet, and Calvin, 2009). The three constructs of transactional distance—dialogue, structure, and autonomy—have been studied as the building blocks for interaction among learners, instructors, content, and technology (Chen, 2001). Researchers investigate these elements in order to understand how to reduce the chance for miscommunication and misunderstanding concerning the nature of the course, the intent of the instructor and learner, and the content itself. Considering the prevalence of collaborative and interactive tools, Stein and colleagues (2009) contend that transactional distance could be defined as "the space where the work of preparing to learn online occurs, the place where a learner works through the issues of how to learn by engaging with others in a new teaching-learning space" (p. 307). If so, what does it feel like to experience that space, to negotiate through and in that space in order to be connected and engaged in the meaning-making activities of the learning environment?

Research related to transactional distance theory indicates that *dialogue* is a primary tool for reducing transactional distance and misunderstanding in an online course (Stein, Wanstreet, and Calvin, 2009). For example, Spector (2007) describes *voice* as the skill involved in knowing when and how to communicate in an online space. Members of a course need to learn how to express themselves in online educational environments and how to create a sense of their presence and identity as learners. Thus, learners need to fill in the spaces created by the lack of visual and verbal cues.

While dialogue reduces transactional distance, increased structure, by itself, may increase transactional distance (Dron, Seidel, and Litten, 2004). For example, Tait (2003) describes transactional distance as a space where learning tasks are negotiated. Viewed in this light, it is possible that increased structure offers less opportunity for learners to engage in dialogue and construct their presence in the course. Rather than planning out the details of every individual interaction that could take place, Conrad (2002) suggests that a "good beginning" to a course constitutes having worked out the concerns about instructional roles, course organization, and social acceptance and support from other learners (p. 215). Being aware of transactional distance from the student's point of view can help instructors understand how the learner moves from dependency on the instructor to interdependency and from the feeling of distance to a feeling of interconnectedness with peers in the course. All in all, a clear understanding of transactional distance may result in a comfortable learning environment and the retention of learners in online courses.

Social Presence

Like transactional distance, social presence is an issue related to classroom climate that plays a central role in facilitating situated learning. The term "social presence," coined by Short, Williams, and Christie (1976), refers to the degree to which individuals perceive immediacy, intimacy, and understand their particular role in a social setting. Other studies indicate that social presence is a quality of the medium and communications media vary in the degree of social presence basing on their transmission ability of nonverbal and vocal information (Gunawardena and Zittle, 2009; Swan and Shih, 2005). Further, Ubon and Kimble (2004) indicate that social presence is a prerequisite to establishing an online community capable of fostering collaboration. Moreover, Ubon and Kimble (2004) assert that the degree of social presence can mold the quality and quantity of interaction in the course.

According to Lave and Wenger (1991), situated learning theory supports the notion that learning takes place in social situations where individuals develop skills by interacting with others who can provide them with insights about existing knowledge and previous personal experiences within a community of practice. Their study argues that knowledge is acquired in a context that normally involves the practical use of that knowledge. Thus, social interactions play a fundamental role in order to involve learners in a community of practice. Social technologies in particular have great potential and educational value due to their inherent capacity to increase learners' motivation and engagement through participation and knowledge creation (Greenhow, 2011).

Immediacy

Instructor immediacy is another characteristic that has been found to affect student learning outcomes and student experiences in the classroom (Witt, Wheeless, and Allen, 2004). Instructor immediacy comprises any verbal (e.g., complimenting students and sharing personal stories related to content) and nonverbal (e.g., making eye contact or smiling) behaviors that seek to enhance relational closeness or similarly reduce psychological distance (Mehrabian, 1967). Instructors may engage in various combinations of verbal and/or nonverbal immediacy behaviors at one time.

In an online instructional context, where the students may or may not hear or see the instructor, immediacy often results from interface cues or channels that students use to form perceptions of verbal and nonverbal behaviors (O'Sullivan, Hunt, and Lippert, 2004). As a result, it is not uncommon for research that focuses on instructor immediacy in online contexts to include two technologically driven concepts known as social presence and electronic propinquity. Both social presence and electronic propinquity are theoretical frameworks that emphasis the "man-machine" relationship and ultimately seek to explain if people can achieve a sense of connectedness or community through communication technology when they are not physically present or close (Korzenny, 1978; Short, Williams, and Christie, 1976).

In other contexts, social presence has been described as a sense of being close or co-present with others in a mediated communication situation (Heeter, 1992; Short et al., 1976). Lee (2004) defined social presence as "a psychological state in which virtual (para-authentic or artificial) social actors are experienced as actual social actors in either sensory or nonsensory ways" (p. 45). Additionally, Allmendinger (2010) defined social presence as "the cognitive synthesis of several factors that occur naturally in face-to-face communication" (p. 45).

No matter one's definition of social presence, in research centering on the effects of social presence in online classes, the closeness felt by students via mediated instruction has been linked to increased satisfaction with the course (Richardson and Swan, 2003; Swan and Shih, 2005), learning satisfaction (Arbaugh and Benbunan-Fich, 2006), and greater perceptions that students can learn in classes in which closeness is fostered (Richardson and Swan, 2003). This begs the question: What factors are responsible for fostering closeness in online courses? Current research indicates that instructional technologies that have more technological affordances (e.g., multimedia and interactive) are better at fostering closeness than those that do not have similar features (Cui, Lockee, and Meng, 2012; Stoerger, 2011). This body of literature indicates that social presence is best achieved through a multimodal approach to instruction.

Modality

A number of recent studies in communication pay attention to the modality of communication via new media. While much of this scholarship investigates perceived learning or knowledge retention, a modality's ability to adequately convey a user's presence seems fundamental to the goal of fostering collaboration and community. Studies will often approach new media with a narrow focus on how a particular communication phenomenon (e.g., instructor authority) is mediated by a particular mode of communication (e.g., video vs. text).

When looking at the broader literature and research on education, the impact of modality on learning can be traced to early research which investigated the effects of using audio-visual technology in the classroom (Lumsdaine and May, 1965). These early research efforts to understand the impact of video on learning primarily involved theorizing and investigating differences between face-to-face instruction versus instruction using video. As technology and scholarship evolved, the understanding of modality has become more nuanced. Video, audio, pictures, and text are modes, and modality refers to the channel through which a "mode" is processed (Downs, Boyson, Alley, and Bloom, 2011; Sundar, 2007). Deconstructing modality to its constituent modes allows for a clearer understanding of exactly how different presentations of information might impact student experiences and learning in an online course.

The way that we process information from multiple modalities does have an impact on cognition and recall (Mayer and Anderson, 1991). Downs and colleagues (2011), for example, conducted a study using iPods as a tool for the delivery of instructional material and found that students scored highest on a knowledge test (cognitive learning) when they were able to access lecture material that was multimodal (audio with text narration; audiovisual) in comparison to students who has access to information that was presented via a single modality (audio only). Similarly, Frisby, Limperos, Record, Downs, and Kercsmar (2013) found that multimedia information presented in a simulated online course was far superior in promoting perceived and actual learning than information presented via a single mode. Thus, as Sundar (2007) notes, the presentation of information via different modalities does indeed impact how we perceive and respond to messages.

The significant impact on message response is likely due to cognitive differences in the way information is processed via multiple modalities versus a single modality. The dual-coding theory (Clark and Paivio, 1991) and the multimedia learning theory (Mayer, 2001; Mayer and Moreno, 2002) assert that people who receive information through a single format or channel (e.g., text only, audio only, or pictures only) process information in an associative manner, whereas information that is presented in a multimedia format (all formats combined) tends to process information in a referential manner. According to Mayer and Anderson (1991) and subsequent research guided by these perspectives (see Mayer, 2001), referential processing is preferable to associative processing because information that is received, processed, and stored in a referential manner is far superior in terms of producing learning outcomes than information that is processed in an associative manner. Similarly, Limperos and colleagues (2015) found that the presentation of multimodal information in an online class increases both perceived and measured learning. In our technology-driven age, the importance of multimodal delivery cannot be understated.

There are instances, however, where new technologies fundamentally alter our expectations about communication process. Sundar and Limperos (2013) discuss this when they note that, within the literature on uses and gratifications theory, the use of the term "audience" has now been largely replaced by the term "users" because media have become much more interactive over the past two decades. Moreover, they contend that the proliferation of interactive features in new media has "expanded our expectations as well as bandwidth for the degree of interaction and activity that we prefer to have with modern media interfaces" (Sundar and Limperos, 2013, p. 516). The presence of interactive features on a digital platform can signify a participatory and open quality, leading to positive perceptions of the content in that space (Sundar, 2008). We can conclude, then, that modality can influence not only the process of learning, but also student expectations for the classroom experience and student ability to interact with one another. A modality's capacity to adequately convey a user's presence seems fundamental to the goal of fostering collaboration and community.

Community of Inquiry Framework

Social presence is one component of another approach to understanding community in online courses: the Community of Inquiry framework. This framework was originally designed with asynchronous text-based discussions in mind (deNoyles, Syndey, and Chen, 2014), and has been used to conceptualize community in many online discussion studies. Garrison, Anderson, and Archer (2000) propose that there are three essential elements that contribute to a successful educational experience: social presence, cognitive presence, and teaching presence—which make up the CoI framework. In keeping with the literature outlined above, social presence is conceptualized as the ability of learners to project themselves socially and emotionally while being perceived as "real" people in mediated communication (Garrison and Arbaugh, 2007).

Indicators of social presence include open communication (e.g., self-disclosure), group cohesion (e.g., encouraging collaboration), and emotional expression (e.g., humor) (Garrison and Arbaugh, 2007). A high level of social presence supports the discourse necessary to build cognitive presence, the extent to which learners are able to construct and confirm meaning through sustained reflection and discourse (Garrison and Arbaugh, 2007). This construction of meaning is described in four progressive phases: triggering event, when an issue is identified for further inquiry; exploration, which is an exchange of ideas or information; integration, when ideas are connected and expanded on; and finally, resolution, when new ideas are applied to other contexts, such as work or education (deNoyles, Syndey, and Chen, 2014).

In addition to social presence and cognitive presence, a critical element of the Community of Inquiry framework is teaching presence, defined as the "design, facilitation, and direction of cognitive and social processes for the purpose of realizing personally meaningful and educationally worthwhile learning outcomes" (Anderson, Rourke, Garrison, and Archer, 2001, p. 5). There are three categories of teaching presence: instructional design and organization, facilitation, and direct instruction. Instructional design and organization is the structure, process, interaction, and evaluation of the discussion. Facilitating discourse includes connecting ideas, asking for clarification, and diagnosing misconceptions. The final component is direct instruction, in which a participant in the course, usually the instructor, injects knowledge and explains content (Garrison, Anderson, and Archer, 2010). This framework is useful for guiding educators in the design and development of effective online discussions that support a community in which students openly communicate with one another and think critically in an effort to build knowledge together under expert guidance (Garrison and Arbaugh, 2007).

Certainly, the scholarship covered above is but a small selection from a vast collection of research on new media in online learning spaces. However, a thorough understanding of the role of transactional distance, immediacy, social presence, multi-modal approaches, and the Community of Inquiry framework can help scholars and practitioners build a useful foundation for considering the adoption and influence various new media have on community and collaboration.

ADOPTION

The body of scholarship presented in the previous section outlines foundational components of community in online settings and how new media change users' expectations. This section will apply the aforementioned theoretical understanding by exploring the adoption of various types of new media interfaces in the classroom. In doing so, this section hopes to answer the questions: How do certain new media platforms promote collaboration and community and how might new media platforms limit those same goals?

Learning Management Systems

One of the most ubiquitous new media technologies in today's education landscape is the learning management systems (LMS). A survey by Educause found that 99 percent of institutions of higher education employ an LMS (Dahlstrom, Brooks, and Bichsel, 2014). In the early days of development, the LMS served as a series of private web pages on which an instructor could display course content or share files. As they do today, the early LMS also helped manage enrollment, course administration, and provided a space for the instructor to track and communicate grades to students (Szabo and Flesher, 2002). Today they often serve an important role as the locus for community and collaboration by providing the means to communicate within a course through features such as discussion boards, collaborative writing tools, and instant messaging.

Discussion Boards

Contemporary learning management systems, such as Blackboard, Moodle, Canvas, or Desire to Learn, offer a number of features which can increase social presence and foster community. The discussion board, a staple of the LMS, is a popular method of creating such a community in online classes by engaging students in asynchronous discussions (Andresen, 2009). As one example, a survey conducted at the University of Central Florida reports that 95 percent of 358 teaching faculty respondents used online discussions, and 87 percent required class discussion participation (Lynch, Kearsley, and Thompson, 2011). Despite their prominence, online discussions pose a number of challenges. Care must be taken to optimally structure discussions so that students co-construct knowledge, rather than simply answering a prompt as they would on a quiz. Also, instructors must effectively facilitate them, promote equity in participation, and do so within the confines of limited time constraints typically faced by instructors (Mazzolini and Maddison, 2007).

While discussion boards have long been a core component of the LMS, new features have made learning management systems much more multimodal and conducive to building social presence and interactivity. Core features such as content pages and discussion posts can now handle embedded video, images, and audio files much more easily. Also, most learning management systems integrate with a variety of other platforms designed to foster collaboration and social presence, such as interactive polling (e.g., "clickers") and collaborative writing software such as Google Docs or Office 365, and have features to facilitate communication among individual students and groups of students via built-in messaging features.

Collaborative Writing Technologies

The LMS platform presents exciting opportunities for student collaboration and community learning space. However, applications beyond a learning management system have direct implications for learning as well. Google Docs, for instance, has been an area of study as researchers investigated writing processes and perceptions of Google Docs and suggests that learners support each other in terms of knowledge and strategy, leading to a positive perception of collaboration in the web-based environment (Kessler, Bikowski, and Boggs, 2012). Those positive student-collaboration results have been corroborated by other studies. For example, Kennedy and Miceli (2013) reported that those working with others tended to have more positive perceptions and greater appreciation of wikis, as they were more likely to feel connected to others or to feel a sense of community. A wiki page can have a positive effect on feelings of group membership because, as Ebersbach and Glaser (2004) note, "working on a common project does have a highly integrative function. Participants will identify with the piece of work they produce and also with the group it emerged from" (p. 5). Further, Sellnow-Richmond, Spence, and Bevins (2015) assert that wikis promote "a more process-centered, collaborative, and democratized space" (p. 6). Google Docs, wiki pages, and other tools allow for dynamic student-centered collaboration.

Annotation software, wikis, and other collaborative technologies facilitate what Collis and Moonen (2005) described as contribution-oriented pedagogy. Instructors can now use learning tools not only to provide content and grade student work, but also to partner with the learner by allowing students to participate in the creation of course content. Collaboration might even take place between cohorts of a course, or asynchronously across many years. Public annotation tools, one type of new learning interface which enable this type of activity, like Hypothes.is, allow students in a course to add their own annotations to a public document. Students can also read and respond to the annotations made by others, like peers at another university or students who commented on the document during a previous offering of a course.

While wikis and collaborative authoring platforms like Google Docs are built for real-time collaboration, some users do find them limiting. Mehlenbacher, Autry, and Kelly (2015) studied student use of Google Docs in an online class comprised of mostly residential students. They found that their students often had a desire to meet in person to plan group projects, even though the class met online and promoted the use of Google Docs for collaboration. The study revealed that student desire to meet in person was driven by a desire to communicate more effectively. The authors surmise that the text-centric platform used for collaboration in this study meant that students could not take advantage of subtle nonverbal interpersonal communication used to negotiate team roles and agreements.

Instant Messaging

Messaging apps are another interface making their way into the online classroom. The potential for these programs to help foster community and collaboration is promising. One such messaging service, Slack, brands itself as "team communication for the 21st century" (Slack, 2016, n.p.). This particular service, when used in a classroom setting, provides students with the ability to participate in synchronous discussion with others in their course, including their classmates and the instructor. Students can attach files, link to web pages, embed content, and organize their conversation by topic, offering a rich, interactive, multi-modal experience. One feature which seems particularly salient to the idea of community building is that these conversations can be private, providing a sort of "back channel" for students in an online course to have discussions about the course privately or in small groups. While this could also be accomplished via email, text, or social media, situating these conversations in the same virtual space as other class communication may help to build a sense of community more closely tied to the course (Whalen, 2016, February 24).

Slack provides one rather unique contribution to the online classroom setting worth considering: humor is built into the interface. Slack provides an integration for a service known as Giphy, which is a repository of animated images, or GIFs. When a user types "/giphy" and then a keyword or phrase, Slack will embed a random animated GIF related to that topic into the conversation. GIFs are often meant to be funny and, when coupled with some randomization, can add levity to a conversation. Whalen (2016, November 3) reports that Giphys, along with emoji and other features, allowed students to express themselves in a way that led to increased interaction in his course and, in his assessment, an increased sense of community. Slack, and similar interfaces, seem poised to provide many factors which lead to a sense of community: a multi-modal experience, rich social presence through expressive tools, interactivity, and the ability to foster sustained discourse.

Blogging Platforms

Many learning interfaces are meant to be closed spaces, mirroring a face-to-face classroom in that they promote learning, collaboration, and community within the confines of a particular course. An alternative approach is to teach "on the open web" through blogging. Blogs have been shown to facilitate a strong Community of Inquiry (Angelaina and Jimoyiannis, 2012; Pifarre, Guijosa, and Argelagos, 2014). One movement which embraces this approach is known as Domain of One's Own. Started at the University of Mary Washington in 2012, this program aims to provide each student with their own web domain which they can utilize throughout their studies at the university (Udell, 2012). While the project is multi-faceted, the initiative takes a critical approach to the idea of a learning interface, granting the student control over his or her learning space, and providing them with the support (through tutoring and curriculum) to make informed choices about how they manage the intellectual property they produce in a course (Watters, 2015, July 15). Currently there are over 40 schools piloting Domain of One's Own–like projects (Haarstad and Shaffer, 2016, September 22).

Simulations

One experiment in online community building is a platform known as Second Life. This virtual world allows users to interact with one another using personalized avatars in a custom-built virtual world. In theory, the platform's multi-modal affordances should be ideal for facilitating community building.

Users are able to express themselves and interact with one another through verbal and nonverbal communication expressed through their avatars. The space provides a platform to create and interact with user-generated content (Coleman, 2011). However, Second Life has seen a marked decline in use, now mostly populated by niche interest communities (Przegalińska, 2015). Second Life's founder, Phillip Rosedale, surmises that one of the barriers to Second Life's success is its complexity, saying, "You had to have an immense amount of time and skill to get into it" (Roush, 2007, June 18). This is a lesson which may extend to any number of learning interfaces. If platforms become too complex, users may simply decline to take advantage of the communication opportunities afforded by them.

The ongoing adoption of the learning interfaces outlined here indicate that online tools are becoming more capable of fostering collaboration and community in online settings. Text-based interface such as discussion boards, wikis, and collaborative documents have proven capable of supporting communities of inquiry. The LMS and messaging apps are beginning to support rich, multi-modal interaction, while movements like Domain of One's Own and programs such as Hypothes.is are expanding the boundaries of community and collaboration beyond the confines of particular courses.

INFLUENCE

Understanding how these tools are being applied allows faculty to ask questions about the impact of new media on their own pedagogies. What do these affordances and trends mean for educators evaluating which tools to use and how to best use them? What choices might an instructor want to make? Depending on your institution or organization, some of the fundamental new media choices have likely been made for you when the school purchased a learning management system, or through the ecosystem of other digital tools in which your school has invested. Even if these choices are not immediately in the educator or instructor's control, there are still a number of personal choices to make regarding how education technology tools are used to foster collaboration and community. For instance, as learning management systems become much more multi-faceted, they are able to deliver multi-modal content, integrate with other digital platforms designed for collaboration, and foster interactivity. However, these features only benefit learning if they are used thoughtfully and without injecting unneeded complexity or frustration into the course.

It is important to consider students when planning new media use in the classroom. Designing a multi-modal, interactive community of inquiry into a course benefits only those students with access. A recent survey of undergraduate students in the United States found that 96 percent of students owned a smartphone, while laptop ownership has risen to 93 percent (Brooks, 2016). While a vast majority of students own these devices, not all own personal computers. Pedagogy has the potential to further marginalize or exclude those students who cannot afford these devices, just as these same students face the pressure of rising textbook prices and tuition rates.

The onus, then, is on the instructor to determine how all students have a voice in courses that rely on digital tools. Assigning group work may mitigate compounding issues of inequality when assigning activities that leverage student-owned devices. By working in groups, students who do not own a device are able to participate and complete the activity.

Another strategy is to offer a course in an asynchronous format. Students without devices may access the course by visiting a computer lab on campus or at a public library, or via a friend or family member's device. This means that the student may have less flexibility about the time and place in which they can contribute to the course. An asynchronous course format with a clear schedule allows students to plan ahead, and gives them time to utilize shared resources.

Learning interfaces increasingly invite students to create their own intellectual property and upload it, either to an LMS or the open web. Students are now able to not just upload their essays but, increasingly, they are able to share videos, audio, photos, and other digital artifacts. Through projects like Domain of One's Own, students have more control over their intellectual property. However, as learning interfaces make it easier for students to share their work, educators should take care to ensure students' right to privacy. While learning and collaborating on the open web certainly has advantages, there are a variety of reasons a student may not wish to share their intellectual property publicly.

Some of these challenges place a new burden on educators to consider the ethics of the tools we use in our teaching. Likewise, the tools we choose are often not ideologically neutral. A course that asks students to upload their papers to a plagiarism detection service communicates something quite different than a course that gives students agency over how they share their intellectual property. The choices instructors give students have the potential to shape the communities that form in our courses and, by extension, our institutions.

Institutions recognize that student autonomy and voice is crucial and, at the same time, universities rely on analytics to more closely navigate student presence in online learning spaces. User analytics have become more robust in learning interfaces as data analysis promises to reveal which students have clicked on a link, how many minutes of a video they've watched, or how many comments they've left on a discussion board. We should think critically about how this information informs our pedagogy. There is no doubt that this information can be extremely useful as an early-warning system for retention or student engagement. If these analytics reveal that a student isn't engaging with the course, the instructor can intervene to get the student back on track. However, analytics can also drive a theoretical, data-driven approach to education. For educators focused on creating an active, engaged online community, it may be tempting to use these analytics in a punitive way to promote engagement by setting a minimum number of page views, discussion contributions, or other activities. Rather, the research outlined in this chapter suggests that we would be better served by looking beyond the quantity of interactions and rather at the quality of those interactions. For example, is the student's contribution helping them close the transactional distance in the course? Would students benefit from advice on establishing their social presence in the course? When thinking about course design, course-level analytics can indicate whether an instructor has created a space conducive to collaboration and community building, or whether students are just participating to meet the minimum requirements.

Clearly, there are a number of theoretical approaches to understanding the formation of community in the online spaces we create. The variety of learning interfaces available to us have features we can use to lay the groundwork for community and facilitate collaboration, and the richness of communication provided by these platforms is steadily increasing. Depending on one's goals, this may mean deploying more than one tool. As we use these interfaces, though, we should be careful to consider how those tools confine or enable our pedagogies and empower or burden our students. Does a required piece of hardware or software serve as an equalizing force or does it further marginalize already disadvantaged students? Are we using the analytics available to make pedagogically informed choices? The landscape of learning interfaces continues to evolve rapidly. As that evolution continues, we should continue to reflect on our own teaching and how our use of these tools influences community and collaboration in our courses. The landscape of educational technology may seem broad and somewhat fragmented, but these theoretical underpinnings help us evaluate those tools' ability to foster collaboration and build community.

REFERENCES

Allen, I. E., and Seaman, J. (2014). *Grade change: Tracking online education in the United States.* Newburyport, MA: Sloan Consortium.

Allen, I. E., and Seaman, J. (2013). Changing course: Ten years of tracking online education in the United States. Babson Park, MA: Babson Survey Research Group and Quahog Research Group. Retrieved from http://www.onlinelearningsurvey.com/reports/changingcourse.pdf.

Allmendinger, K. (2010). Social presence in synchronous virtual learning situations: The role of nonverbal signals displayed by avatars. *Educational Psychology Review, 22,* 41–56. http://dx.doi.org/10.1007/s10648-010-9117-8.

Anderson, T., Rourke, L., Garrison, D. R., and Archer, W. (2001). Assessing teaching presence in a computer conference environment. *Journal of Asynchronous Learning Networks, 5*(2),

1–17. Retrieved from http://www.sloanconsortium.org/sites/default/files/v5n2_anderson_1.pdf.

Andresen, M. A. (2009). Asynchronous online discussions: Success factors, outcomes, assessments, and limitations. *Educational Technology & Society, 12*(1), 249–257. Retrieved from http://www.ifets.info/journals/12_1/19.pdf.

Angelaina, S., and Jimoyiannis, A. (2012). Analysing students' engagement and learning presence in an educational blog community. *Educational Media International, 49*(3), 183–200.

Aragon, S. R., Johnson, S. D., and Shaik, N. (2002). The influence of learning style preferences on student success in online versus face-to-face environments. *American Journal of Distance Education, 16*(4), 227.

Arbaugh, J. B., and Benbunan-Fich, R. (2006). An investigation of epistemological and social dimensions of teaching in online learning environments. *The Academy of Management Learning and Education, 5,* 435–447. http://dx.doi.org/10.5465/AMLE.2006.23473204.

Bassoppo-Moyo, T. C. (2006). Evaluating e-learning: A front-end process and posthoc approach. *International Journal of Instructional Media, 33*(1), 7–22.

Brooks, D. C. (2016). *ECAR study of undergraduate students and information technology, 2015.* Retrieved from the Educause website: http://www.educause.edu/ecar.

Carrell, L. J., and Menzel, K. E. (2001). Variations in learning, motivation, and perceived immediacy between live and distance education. *Communication Education, 50*(3), 230.

Chen, Y. (2001). Transactional distance in world wide web learning environments. *Innovations in Education and Teaching International, 38*(4), 327–337.

Clark, J. M., and Paivio, A. (1991). Dual coding theory and education. *Educational Psychology Review, 3,* 149–170. http://dx.doi.org/10.1007/BF01320076.

Coleman, B. (2011) *Hello avatar: Rise of the networked generation.* Cambridge, MA: The MIT Press.

Collis, B., and Moonen, J. (2005). Collaborative learning in a contribution-oriented pedagogy. *Procedia Social and Behavioral Sciences, 83,* 367–370.

Conaway, R. N., Easton, S. S., and Schmidt, W. V. (2005). Strategies for enhancing student interaction and immediacy in online courses. *Business Communication Quarterly, 68*(1), 23–35. http://dx.doi.org/10.1177/1080569904273300.

Conrad, D. (2002). Engagement, excitement, anxiety, and fear: Learners' experiences of starting an online course. *The American Journal of Distance Education, 16*(4), 205–226.

Cui, G., Lockee, B., and Meng, C. (2012). Building modern online social presence: A review of social presence theory and its instructional design implications for future trends. *Education and Information Technologies, 18*(4). 661–685. http://dx.doi.org/10.1007/s10639-012-9192-1.

Dahlstrom, E., Brooks, C. D., and Bichsel, J. (2014). *The current ecosystem of learning management systems in higher education: Student, faculty, and IT perspectives.* Retrieved from the Educause website: http://www.educause.edu/ecar.

Dede, C. (2008). A seismic shift in epistemology. *Educause Review, 43,* 80–81.

deNoyelles, A., Sydney, J. M., and Chen, B. (2014). Strategies for creating a community of inquiry through online asynchronous discussions. *Journal of Online Learning and Teaching, 10*(1), 153–165.

Downs, E., Boyson, A. R., Alley, H., and Bloom, N. R. (2011). iPedagogy: Using multimedia learning theory to identify best practices for MP3 player use in higher education. *Journal of Applied Communication Research, 39*(2), 184–200. http://dx.doi.org/10.1080/00909882.2011.556137.

Dron, J., Seidel, C., and Litten, G. (2004). Transactional distance in a blended learning environment. ALT-J, *Research in Learning Technology, 12*(2), 163–174.

Ebersbach, A., and Glaser, M. (2004). Towards emancipatory use of a medium: The wiki. *International Journal of Information Ethics, 2,* 1–8.

Frisby, B., Limperos, A. M., Record, R. A., Downs, E., and Kercsmar, S. C. (2013). Students' perceptions of social presence: Rhetorical and relational goals across three mediated instructional designs. *Journal of Online Teaching and Learning, 9*(4), 468–480.

Garrison, D. R., Anderson, T., and Archer, W. (2000). Critical inquiry in a text-based environment: Computer conferencing in higher education. *The Internet and Higher Education, 2*(2), 87-105. doi:10.1016/S1096-7516(00)00016-6.

Garrison, D. R., Anderson, T., and Archer, W. (2010). The first decade of the community of inquiry: A retrospective. *The Internet and Higher Education, 13*(1), 5–9. doi:10.1016/j.iheduc.2009.10.003.

Garrison, D. R., and Arbaugh, J. B. (2007). Researching the community of inquiry framework: Review, issues, and future directions. *The Internet and Higher Education, 10*(3), 157–172. doi:10.1016/j.iheduc.2007.04.001.

Grajek, S. (2016). Digital capabilities in higher education, 2015: E-learning. Retrieved from http://library.educause.edu.

Greenhow, C. (2011). Online social networks and learning. *On the Horizon, 19*(1), 4–12.

Gunawardena, C. N., and Zittle, F. J. (2009). Social presence as a predictor of satisfaction within a computer-mediated conferencing environment. *American Journal of Distance Education, 11*(3), 8–26. http://dx.doi.org/10.1080/08923649709526970.

Haarstad, N., and Shaffer, K. (2016, September 22). An infographic of one's own. [Web log post]. Retrieved from http://umwdtlt.com/an-infographic-of-ones-own/.

Heeter, C. (1992). Being there: The subjective experience of presence. *Teleoperators and Virtual Environments, 1*, 262–271.

Keegan, D. (1996). *Foundations of distance education* (3rd ed.). New York: Routledge.

Kennedy, C., and Miceli, T. (2013). In piazza online: Exploring the use of wikis with beginner foreign language learners. *Computer Assisted Language Learning, 26*, 389–411.

Kessler, G., Bikowski, D., and Boggs, J. (2012). Collaborative writing among second language learners in academic web-based projects. *Language Learning & Technology, 16*(1), 91–109.

Ko, S., and Rossen, S. (2010). *Teaching online: A practical guide.* Chicago, IL: Routledge.

Korzenny, F. (1978). A theory of electronic propinquity: Mediated communication in organizations. *Communication Research, 5*, 3–24.

Lave, J., and Wenger, E. (1991). *Situated learning: Legitimate peripheral participation.* Cambridge: Cambridge University Press.

Lee, K. (2004). Presence, explicated. *Communication Theory, 14*, 27–50. http://dx.doi.org/10.1093/ct/14.1.27.

Limperos, A. M., Buckner, M. M., Kaufmann, R., and Frisby, B. N. (2015). Online teaching and technological affordances: An experimental investigation into the impact of modality and clarity on perceived and actual learning. *Computers & Education, 83*. 1–9. http://dx.doi.org/10.1016/j.compedu.2014.12.015.

Lumsdaine, A. A., and May, M. A. (1965). Mass communication and educational media. *Annual Review of Psychology, 16*, 475–534.

Lynch, D. J., Kearsley, G., and Thompson, K. (2011). Faculty use of asynchronous discussions in online learning. *International Journal of Instructional Technology and Distsance Learning, 8*(2), 17–24.

Male, T., and Burden, K. (2014). Access denied? Twenty-first-century technology in schools. *Technology, Pedagogy & Education, 23*(4), 423–437. doi:10.1080/1475939X.2013.864697.

Mayer, R. E. (2001). *Multimedia learning.* Cambridge: Cambridge University Press.

Mayer, R. E., and Anderson, R. B. (1991). Animations need narrations: An experimental test of a dual-coding hypothesis. *Journal of Educational Psychology, 83*, 484–490. http://dx.doi.org/10.1037//0022-0663.83.4.484.

Mayer, R. E., and Moreno, R. (2002). Aids to computer-based multimedia learning. *Learning and Instruction, 12*(1), 107–119. http://dx.doi.org/10.1016/S0959-4752(01)00018-4.

Mazzolini, M., and Maddison, M. (2007). When to jump in: The role of the instructor in online discussion forums. *Computers & Education, 49*(2), 193–213. doi:10.1016/ j. compedu.2005.06.011.

Mehlenbacher, B., Autry, M. K., and Kelly, A. R. (2015). Instructional design for stem-based collaborative, colocated classroom composition. *IEEE Transactions on Professional Communication, 58*(4), 396–409. doi:10.1109/TPC.2016.2517538.

Mehrabian, A. (1967). Attitudes inferred from non-immediacy of verbal communications. *Journal of Verbal Learning and Verbal Behavior, 6*, 294–295. http://dx.doi.org/10.1016/S0022-5371(67)80113-0.

Mintz, A. I. (2016). Writing and pedagogy in Plato's *Phaedrus*. *Philosophy of Education Archive,* 159–161. Retrieved from http://ojs.ed.uiuc.edu/index.php/pes/article/viewFile/4481/1385.

Moore, M. (2007). The theory of transactional distance. In M. Moore (Ed.), *Handbook of distance education* (2nd ed., pp. 89–108). Mahwah, NJ: Erlbaum.

O'Sullivan, P. B., Hunt, S. K., and Lippert, L. R. (2004). Mediated immediacy: A language of affiliation in a technological age. *Journal of Language and Social Psychology, 23*(4), 464–490. http://dx.doi.org/10.1177/0261927X04269588.

Pifarre, M., Guijosa, A., and Argelagos, E. (2014). Using a blog to create and support a community of inquiry in secondary education. *E-Learning and Digital Media, 11*(1), 72–87.

Przegalińska, A. (2015). Embodiment, engagement and the strength of virtual communities: Avatars of second life in decay. *Tamara Journal for Critical Organization Inquiry, 13*(4), 48–62.

Richardson, J. C., and Swan, K. (2003). Examining social presence in online courses in relation to students' perceived learning and satisfaction. *Journal of Asynchronous Learning Networks, 7*(1), 68–88.

Roush, W. (2007, June 18). Second earth. *MIT Technology Review*. Retrieved from https://www.technologyreview.com/s/408074/second-earth/.

Rovai, A. P. (2007). Facilitating online discussions effectively. *The Internet and Higher Education, 10*(1), 77–88. doi:10.1016/j.iheduc.2006.10.001.

Sellnow-Richmond, S., Spence, P. R., and Bevins, C. (2015). Social media and collaboration: The wiki's effectiveness as a classroom tool. *Kentucky Journal of Communication, 34*(2), 4–15.

Short, J., Williams, E., and Christie, B. (1976). *The social psychology of telecommunications.* London: John Wiley.

Slack (2016). Team communication for the 21st century. [web page]. Retrieved from https://slack.com/is.

Spector, M. J. (2007). *Finding your online voice: Stories told by experienced online educators.* Mahwah, NJ: Erlbaum.

Stein, D. S., Wanstreet, C. E., and Calvin, J. (2009). How a novice adult online learner experiences transactional distance. *Quarterly Review of Distance Education, 10*(3), 305–311.

Stoerger, S. (2011). Creating instructor presence in an online course. In *Proceedings of the 27th Annual Conference on Distance Teaching & Learning.*

Sundar, S. S. (2007). Social psychology of interactivity in human-website interaction. In A. N. Joinson, K. Y. A. Mckenna, T. Postmes, and U.-D. Reips (Eds.), *The Oxford handbook of internet psychology* (pp. 89–104). Oxford: Oxford University Press.

Sundar, S. S. (2008). The MAIN model: A heuristic approach to understanding technology effects on credibility. In M. J. Metzger, and A. J. Flanigan (Eds.), *Digital media, youth, and credibility* (pp. 72–100). Cambridge, MA: The MIT Press.

Sundar, S. S., and Limperos, A. M. (2013). Uses and grats 2.0: New gratifications for new media. *Journal of Broadcasting & Electronic Media, 57*(4), 504–525. http://dx.doi.org/10.1080/08838151.2013.845827.

Swan, K., and Shih, L. F. (2005). On the nature and development of social presence in online course discussions. *Journal of Asynchronous Learning Networks, 9*(3), 115–136.

Szabo, M., and Flesher, K. (2002). CMI theory and practice: Historical roots of learning management systems. In M. Driscoll and T. Reeves (Eds.), *Proceedings from the World Conference on E-Learning in Corporate, Government, Healthcare, and Higher Education* (pp. 929–936).

Tait, A. (2003). Reflections on student support in open and distance education. *International Review of Research in Open and Distance Learning, 4*(1), 1–9.

Ubon, N. A., and Kimble, C. (2004, July). Exploring social presence in asynchronous text-based online learning communities (OLCS). *Proceedings of the 5th International Conference on Information Communication Technologies in Education*, Greece.

Udell, J. (2012). A domain of one's own. *Wired.* Retrieved from https://www.wired.com/insights/2012/07/a-domain-of-ones-own/.

van Tyron, P. J. S., and Bishop, M. J. (2009). Theoretical foundations for enhancing social connectedness in online learning environments. *Distance Education, 30*(3), 291–315. doi:10.1080/01587910903236312.

Watters, A. (2015, July 15). The web we need to give students. [Web log post]. Retrieved from https://medium.com/bright/the-web-we-need-to-give-students-311d97713713#.1e118s168.

Whalen, Z. (2016, February 24). Notes on teaching with Slack. [Web log post]. Retrieved from http://www.zachwhalen.net/posts/notes-on-teaching-with-slack/.

Whalen, Z. (2016, November 3). Cat facts, animated GIFs, and building community online. [Web log post]. Retrieved from http://umwdtlt.com/cat-facts-animated-gifs-and-building-community-online/.

Witt, P. L., Wheeless, L. R., and Allen, M. (2004). A meta-analytical review of the relationship between teacher immediacy and student learning. *Communication Monographs, 71*(2), 184–207. http://dx.doi.org/10.1080/036452042000228054.

Wright, C. R., Lopes, V., Montgomerie, T. C., Reju, S. A., Schmoller, S. (2014, April 21). Selecting a learning management system: Advice from an academic perspective. *Educause Review.* Retrieved from http://er.educause.edu/articles/2014/4/selecting-a-learning-management-system-advice-from-an-academic-perspective.

Wylie, C. D. (2012). Teaching manuals and the blackboard: Accessing historical classroom practices. *History of Education, 41*(2), 257–272.

Chapter Six

Accessibility and New Media Technologies

Beth Case

ACCESSIBILITY IN THE TWENTY-FIRST-CENTURY CLASSROOM

Classroom accessibility is of the utmost importance for the twenty-first-century student, classroom, and institution. As the population of students with disabilities continues to increase in higher education institutions, instructors should effectively utilize new media technologies. Instructors should recognize challenges faced by students with disabilities and, using the Universal Design model, strategically implement a classroom climate that engages students across the spectrum. This chapter will address the current landscape of accessibility challenges, discuss the potential of new media technologies as the classroom equalizer, and position new media pedagogy and digital tools as sound pedagogy prospective for equality in the higher education classroom.

WHY ACCESSIBILITY MATTERS

In 2011–2012, eleven percent of college undergraduate students reported having a disability. While this number has remained consistent (the same percentage was reported in 2007–2008 [U.S. Department of Education, 2016]), it is likely an underestimation. Many students with "hidden" disabilities such as learning or psychological disabilities may choose not to self-disclose their disability (Trammell, 2009). The probability is high that every instructor will encounter at least one student with a disability at some point during their career. With the proliferation of new media technologies in the classroom, however, this encounter can become less of a challenge and more of an opportunity—not only to engage students with disabilities but to improve and enhance the learning experience for all concerned.

To fully understand the scope of the current learning landscape as it relates to students with disabilities, a brief review of the realm of accessibility, including definitions, legal framework, and historical context, is warranted.

DEFINITIONS

As we will see, accessibility is a complex issue which can be defined differently depending on the perspective of those involved. Therefore, a clear and common taxonomy is vital to ensuring not only an effective discussion but that a mutually beneficial conclusion is attained by all concerned. We will begin with a quick review of the key terms.

Disability

According to the Americans with Disabilities Act, "Disability means, with respect to an individual, a physical or mental impairment that substantially limits one or more of the major life activities of such individual; a record of such an impairment; or being regarded as having such an impairment" (Americans with Disabilities Act of 1990, § 12102). The Act goes on to give examples of disabilities, including both contagious and non-contagious diseases; impairments of vision, speech, and hearing; emotional and mental illness; and learning disabilities among others. Major life activities include "functions such as caring for one's self, performing manual tasks, walking, seeing, hearing, speaking, breathing, learning, and working" (Americans with Disabilities Act of 1990, § 12102).

Accessibility versus Usability

An important concept to understand is the distinction between "accessibility" and "usability." The ADA only requires that programs, services, and activities be accessible. The Americans with Disabilities Act Accessibility Guidelines (ADAAG) define accessibility as "a site, building, facility, or portion thereof that complies with these guidelines," referring to the guidelines laid out by ADAAG (United States Access Board, n.d.-a). Iwarsson and Stahl (2003) describe accessibility as "compliance with official norms and standards, thus being mainly objective in nature" (p. 61).

Usability, on the other hand, is more subjective in nature, referring to "use, i.e. to move around, be in and use the environment on equal terms with other citizens" (p. 62). Thus, accessibility means someone with a disability *can access* a building, information, etc., although it may take extra effort.

Usability, on the other hand, means individuals with a disability can obtain access *with the same ease* as someone without a disability. While the law only requires accessibility, usability is the goal.

Reasonable Accommodation

According to the ADA, "The term 'reasonable accommodation' may include . . . acquisition or modification of equipment or devices, appropriate adjustment or modifications of examinations, training materials or policies, the provision of qualified readers or interpreters, and other similar accommodations for individuals with disabilities" (§ 12111). An accommodation is determined on a case-by-case basis, depending on the specific needs of each individual.

LAWS

Beyond the inherent benefits from a learning perspective for those with disabilities, there are also strong legal mandates to make education accessible to students with disabilities. Through a combination of laws, federal mandates, and court decisions which refined and shaped them, there are many significant precedents concerning the role of accessibility within the learning environment. As new media technologies continue to emerge, the requirements to ensure they are accessible and inclusive also continue to evolve. Regulatory compliance, originally focused primarily on equal access, now encompasses many of the systems used by students with disabilities—both in the classroom and those necessary to be a student. This section will review the key components of the current legal framework concerning accessibility and learning for students with disabilities.

The Americans with Disabilities Act of 1990 (ADA) was signed into law on July 26, 1990, by President George H. W. Bush and amended effective January 1, 2009. Based on the Civil Rights Act of 1964, the ADA prohibits discrimination based on disability (U.S. Department of Justice, Civil Rights Division, n.d.). As it relates to public institutions, the ADA states that "No qualified individual with a disability shall, on the basis of disability, be excluded from participation in or be denied the benefits of the services, programs, or activities of a public entity, or be subjected to discrimination by any public entity" (Americans with Disabilities Act of 1990, § 35.130). The Act also states that individuals with disabilities must be given access that is as effective as that provided to individuals without disabilities.

Section 504 of the Rehabilitation Act of 1973, generally referred to just as the "Rehab Act," was the precursor to the Americans with Disabilities Act. The Rehab Act defines disability in similar terms to the ADA legislation, though the new definition limited the application primarily to programs and activities which receive federal funding. Specifically, the Rehab Act states:

> No otherwise qualified individual with a disability in the United States, as defined in section 705 (20) of this title, shall, solely by reason of his or her disability, be excluded from the participation in, be denied the benefits of, or be subjected to discrimination under any program or activity receiving Federal financial assistance or under any program or activity conducted by any Executive agency or by the United States Postal Service. (U.S. Department of Justice. Section 504, Rehabilitation Act of 1973, § 794 [a])

Before 1998, neither the Americans with Disabilities Act nor the Rehabilitation Act of 1973 specifically addressed what would be considered modern technology. In 1998, President Clinton signed the Rehabilitation Act Amendments of 1998, which specifically strengthened Section 508 and was groundbreaking by providing specific guidelines concerning the use and access to electronic and information technology (EIT) by individuals with disabilities. The revised Section 508 established clear standards by defining accessibility in terms of technology. In addition, it set requirements upon the development, procurement, maintenance, and/or use of accessible EIT to include not only the Internet but also equipment, software, and peripherals. On January 18, 2017, a refresh of Section 508 was published which established the Web Content Accessibility Guidelines (WCAG) 2.0 AA as the standard for web accessibility (United States Access Board, 2017).

However, like the other sections of the Rehabilitation Act, these amendments apply only to federally funded programs (United States Access Board, n.d.-b). Whether Section 508 applies to public colleges and universities has been an issue of debate. Nonetheless, the specific guidelines mentioned in Section 508 are frequently used as a road map for electronic and information technology accessibility since the ADA refers to all services, programs, and activities.

BACKGROUND AND HISTORICAL CONTEXT

Using the foundation of definitions and regulatory framework outlined above, this section reviews many real-world scenarios and examples encountered by students with disabilities. Technology, often deployed with the best of intentions, can inadvertently exclude or complicate the ability to include students with disabilities within a common learning experience. However, as we will see, with thoughtful planning and appropriate use of technology, many of these barriers can be addressed or eliminated entirely.

On-Demand Accommodations

To better appreciate the complexity of real-world accommodations, it is helpful to consider the experience from the student's perspective. A student with a disability at a college or university often goes through a standard registration process in order to receive accommodations. Typically, the student begins by contacting the disability services office and provides documentation concerning their disability. A disability counselor reviews the documentation and meets with the student to determine appropriate accommodations. Next, the instructors are informed about the student and necessary accommodations. While some accommodations require little effort on the part of the instructor, such as recruiting a volunteer note-taker, other accommodations are more labor intensive, such as making sure all documents can be read by screen readers or that all videos shown in class have captions. Some planned classroom activities may need revision or replacement if they are not and cannot be made accessible. Too often, instructors are informed of accommodation requirements with little or no time to properly prepare or alter the course materials. This presents a challenge if the course was not originally designed to be accessible. As a result, last-minute revisions of course materials and activities may cause increased expense, sub-par accessibility, and high levels of stress for all involved. Ultimately, it benefits instructors to design an accessible course from the outset to avoid common pitfalls and create a more inclusive learning environment, not only for students with disabilities but for all students.

Many techniques used to make information accessible benefit students as a whole. For example, providing close captioning allows students to watch a video in noisy environments and perhaps benefits students whose first language is not English. In addition, several Office of Civil Rights (OCR) complaints and lawsuits support the proactive accessibility of courses, especially those which are provided online. Encouraging this "forward-leaning" posture for improving the accessibility of learning materials would seem to go hand in hand with the adoption of new technologies and learning tools within the classroom. Often, the latest technologies are the first to emerge on campuses and in classrooms whenever they can improve or enhance the learning experience. However, new does not always mean better, especially in terms of accessibility for students with disabilities. Consider the landmark events surrounding the early use of e-book readers as learning tools.

The "Kindle Letter"

In 2009, Amazon initiated a pilot program with the University of Washington, Princeton University, Case Western Reserve University, Reed College, Arizona State University, Pace University, and the Darden School of Business at the University of Virginia. Kindle DX tablets containing the required textbooks were provided for free to students in the pilot program. (University of Washington, 2009). The National Federation of the Blind and the American Council of the Blind filed suit against Arizona State University claiming that the program was discriminatory against blind students. Although text-to-speech was available for some books available on the Kindle, the menus on the device itself were not accessible, and therefore blind students would not be able to navigate the device to access their books. A settlement was reached with some of the universities in the pilot program preventing the use of the Kindle tablets (and other e-book readers) until the tools could be made fully accessible (U.S. Department of Justice, 2010).

The Kindle DX accessibility challenge led the U.S. Department of Justice, Civil Rights Division, and the U.S. Department of Education, Office for Civil Rights (OCR), to release a joint "Dear Colleague" letter regarding electronic book readers, which has come to be known as the "Kindle Letter" (U.S. Department of Education, 2010). This letter did not implement or change laws, but clarified how the Americans with Disabilities Act should be applied to new technologies. "It is unacceptable for universities to use emerging technology without insisting that this technology be accessible to all students" (U.S. Department of Education, 2010, para. 5). The Frequently Asked Questions page (U.S. Department of Education, 2011) clarifies that the position taken in the letter applies to all forms of emerging technology, to online content, and applies even if no students with disabilities are enrolled in a course. Therefore, either accessibility should be included from the beginning, or a plan must be in place to provide accessibility on short notice.

Relevant OCR Decisions and Legal Settlements

The availability of accessible resources and materials must also be timely. Several other OCR decisions and legal settlements emphasize the importance of considering accessibility well before there is a request for accommodation. Louisiana Tech University settled with the Department of Justice (DoJ) over the use of an online learning tool which was core to the course but was not accessible. At the heart of the decision was the fact that the contents were not made accessible in a timely manner (U.S. Department of Justice, 2013). Eve L. Hill, Deputy Assistant Attorney General for the Civil Rights Division of the DoJ, said, "Emerging technologies, including Internet-based learning platforms, are changing the way we learn, and we need to ensure that people with disabilities are not excluded or left behind" (U.S. Department of Justice, 2013, para. 3). In this case, the timeliness of the accessible solution was highlighted as a critical part of the accommodation.

However, in addition to the content needing to be accessible, the systems which provide access to the content, such as learning management systems and web sites, must also be made accessible. South Carolina Technical College System (SCTCS) reached a resolution with the OCR regarding inaccessible web sites, which included both course and non-course related sites (Office of Civil Rights, 2013). Pennsylvania State University reached an agreement with the National Federation of the Blind to ensure a variety of technologies would be accessible to blind students (Pennsylvania State University, 2012). Specific problems included inaccessible library catalogs, web sites, and a learning management system, among others (National Federation for the Blind, 2010). The University of Montana reached a resolution with the U.S. Department of Civil Rights for the inaccessibility of class assignments, their learning management system, and the library system in addition to inaccessible scanned documents and videos without captions, among other issues (U.S. Department of Education, 2014).

This is by no means a comprehensive list, nor do agreements and settlements have the force of law. However, they serve as examples of the criteria used by the Department of Justice and the Department of Education when evaluating a discrimination complaint. In these cases, the complaints could have been avoided had the universities proactively factored in accessibility when designing web sites or developing courses.

UNIVERSAL DESIGN

Most classes are designed for the fictional "average" student. However, the majority of students do not fit this "average" image. Students have different skills, motivations, demands on their time, and life experiences. Instead of designing a course for the "average" student, what if a course could be developed with enough flexibility that most students could find a way for the course to fit their needs? To answer this question, instructional professionals routinely utilize Universal Design (UD) principles.

The term "Universal Design" was first coined in the 1970s by Ron Mace, founder of the Center for Universal Design, and was defined as "the design of products and environments to be useable by all people, to the greatest extent possible without the need for adaptation or specialized design" (Center for Universal Design, 2008, para. 1). The concept originated with architecture and product design but has been applied to education under various names such as Universal Design of Instruction (UDI), Universally Designed Teaching (UDT), Universal Instructional Design (UID), Universal Design for Learning (UDL), Universal Design for Instruction (UDforI), and Universal Design of Instruction (UDI) (Burgstahler, 2015a). Each model has a slightly different approach, but all variations support the creation of an educational environment designed to allow most students to fully participate without requiring individual accommodations. Of course, there is always the potential for an additional accommodation, such as providing a sign language interpreter only when a deaf student is taking a course. However, following the principles of Universal Design proactively provides an accessible classroom where the need for individual accommodations is reduced. To summarize, a Universally Designed course is both accessible and usable (Burgstahler, 2015b).

Burgstahler (2015b) provides an example that demonstrates the difference between providing an accommodation and creating a Universally Designed environment. Imagine a building with a door. Most people will be able to open the door and go into the building. Someone in a wheelchair may have difficulty, so a large button is added that will open the door when pressed. The button is an accommodation, something special added to the building for a person with a disability. It still may not provide access to everyone, however, as some individuals may have difficulty pressing the button. Now imagine that the door opened automatically when someone approaches, like those frequently found at grocery stores. Nothing special is needed for the wheelchair user and the accommodation also benefits other users, such as those with their arms full. This is Universal Design.

ADOPTION OF NEW MEDIA TECHNOLOGIES

Increased Accessibility

The continuously evolving realm of technology can be both an enabler and a barrier for students with disabilities, depending on how the learning tools are used throughout the life cycle of a course. This section will review assistive technologies, mainstream technologies, and how they often overlap as new media technologies emerge.

Assistive Technology

The Technology-Related Assistance for Individuals with Disabilities Act of 1988 (Tech Act) describes an assistive technology device as "any item, piece of equipment, or product system, whether acquired commercially off the shelf, modified, or customized, that is used to increase, maintain, or improve functional capabilities of individuals with disabilities" (Technology-Related Assistance for Individuals with Disabilities Act of 1988, § 3). Assistive technology can be as simple as a magnifying glass or as complex as screen-reading software. Historically, assistive technology was often cost-prohibitive, however new media technologies provide affordable alternatives. In some cases, you get what you pay for, but the less expensive options help many individuals who cannot afford higher-end technology. As a result, assistive technology is now more readily available to students with disabilities. This is particularly true for mobile devices.

Some companies have been more proactive in adopting assistive technologies than others. Apple, for example, provides a wide range of assistive technology on their phones and tablets. Currently, Apple's iOS devices come with a built-in screen reader, the ability to play captions and audio descriptions within videos, and options to customize the screen display for greater accessibility and to restrict certain functions to assist individuals with autism stay on task. Voice commands through the Siri interface also provide hands-free access.

Similarly, devices based on Google's Android operating system are moving towards a more accessible design. For example, the Android OS (7.0 and above) has features similar to Apple products, including a screen reader, the ability to control the device with a keyboard or joystick, and the ability to attach a refreshable Braille display, use voice commands, customize the screen, and display captions. Moreover, Google offers a developer toolkit to help developers make their applications (apps) more accessible across all Android OS platforms, which can be downloaded at https://support.google.com/accessibility/android/faq/6376582.

Apps exist for almost any assistive technology imaginable. Dictation apps will type what the user says or let them control the device with their voice. Some magnification apps enlarge the screen; others serve as a sort of electronic magnifying glass, enlarging the image from the camera's view. Additionally, scanning apps allow users to take a picture of a document, which is then converted to text and can be read aloud. Similarly, screen-reading apps can read aloud what is on the screen or in a document.

Mainstream Technology

Some new technologies which were not intended as assistive technology nevertheless are providing people with disabilities renewed freedom and independence.

FaceTime is a video chat system which has become widely popular on iPhones. Despite being limited only to Apple devices, sign language users nonetheless quickly adopted the software as an effective means of communication. FaceTime's video quality was high enough to allow sign language to be read clearly, allowing deaf individuals to communicate directly and easily with friends near and far.

Texting is another mainstream technology which has improved communication for the deaf. In fact, long before texting became mainstream, deaf individuals were using teletype machines, teletypewriters (TTY), and text pagers such as the T-Mobile Sidekick. This allowed them to communicate easily with other deaf individuals, but once everyone started texting, deaf and hearing individuals had an even easier way to communicate with one other.

There are unexpected benefits of technology for persons with disabilities, beyond improved communication, however. GPS helps most everyone find their way around by car, but many GPS apps now have a feature which also provides a walking route. This feature, along with audio directions, allows blind users to more independently navigate their environment.

Although not a recent technology, voice recognition software which was originally intended for professionals to dictate notes, reports, and other documents has found an unexpected support role in accessibility. Those with limited use of their arms or who have limited fine motor control often use voice recognition software to interact and control the computer. There are many such examples of technology which was designed for use by the general public but has provided an additional benefit for people with disabilities.

Digital text-based information can be extremely beneficial to students with disabilities, if it is in an accessible format. Consider an instructor wishing to provide a handout to students. In the past, if a blind student was in the course, the instructor would need to submit the document in advance to disability services for conversion (a process that might take several days) and potentially delay the blind student's access to the material. With digital text posted online, a blind student can access the document using screen reader software at the same time that other students can access the document. It is important to note, however, that not all digital formats are equally accessible. For example, many PDF documents are only images of the text, which computers cannot interpret as text. A better solution is a word processing document that was designed to be accessible using basic formatting techniques, such as the Styles feature in Word. Posting course content online can increase accessibility but only so long as the materials are in an accessible format.

Online libraries can also increase access if online access to the database of materials is accessible. Many journal articles are now available online and in an accessible format, making it easier for blind students to conduct research independently. Online search engines such as Google Scholar (http://scholar.google.com) can further help blind students in their research efforts since both the web interface and many of the search results are accessible. As highlighted in the SCTCS case above, both the content and the methods to access the content are required to be accessible.

Decreased Accessibility

Unfortunately, not all new technology increases accessibility. Some technology can actually reduce the ability of students with disabilities to participate, either by introducing new barriers or by removing support for existing accommodations and solutions. As technological advancements continue to focus on improving the learning experience, they may inadvertently reduce the accessibility for students with disabilities.

Digital text-based information, if not accessible, is the same as giving a blind student a handout on a piece of paper. The most common inaccessible format of digital text is a scanned PDF, which is essentially a photograph of text. As a result, only an image of the document is presented and thus the system lacks the ability to provide text-based searching, navigation, and screen-reading capabilities.

Similarly, online library access can be a barrier if the catalog and the resulting materials are not accessible. This obstacle is evidenced by the previously mentioned settlements with Pennsylvania State University (Pennsylvania State University, 2012) and the University of Montana (U.S. Department of Education, 2014). Even if the materials are in an accessible format, if the searching and navigation systems are not also accessible, the end result is the same.

Phones and tablets are rapidly replacing PCs and laptops in the classroom as primary learning tools. Touchscreens are the default input method for these devices, but without a physical keyboard, the devices are difficult to use for blind and low-vision individuals as well as those with limited fine motor skills. It is easier to type and navigate with the physical keyboard. Videos can be very helpful in conveying information; however, captions are required for videos to be accessible to deaf students and audio descriptions are required for blind students. Without these accessibility features, videos cannot be deemed accessible. These are two common examples of decreased accessibility through technological advancement.

As evidenced by the Louisiana Tech settlement (U.S. Department of Justice, 2013), many third-party applications are not accessible. This often includes the web sites provided by publishers which provide supplemental materials, such as videos, simulations, practice quizzes, and flash cards. These materials can often be beneficial and add variety and depth to the course content. However, until publishers make them accessible, schools that require their use are vulnerable to a legal challenge. Including accessibility as part of the initial design of a course, a system, or any student-facing component of the learning environment is vital to avoiding accessibility pitfalls and to optimizing the role of technology as a classroom equalizer.

INFLUENCE

Given the complex relationship between accessibility, learning, and various mandates, instructors must take a thoughtful approach when introducing new media technologies, either as a course enhancement or to support a universal design goal. As shown, simply introducing new technology without a full consideration of the impacts can actually impair learning. However, employing UD during the development of the course and introducing new technologies as a global enabler for learning greatly reduces the complexity and positions all students to have a more inclusive learning experience. This creates a phenomenal world of accessible learning for all.

Impact on Other Students

It is important to recognize that the benefits of UD extend well beyond accommodating students with disabilities. "Incorporating UD processes when developing [electronic and information technology] is one solution to accommodating people with disabilities that also improves the usability of the products for the rest of the population" (National Council on Disability, 2004, para. 2). When a course is designed to maximize accessibility, it inherently maximizes availability as well, which eases the consumption of information and increases the learning opportunities.

One of the benefits of considering accessibility while designing a course is that it forces the designer to think about and evaluate each component of the course. An improved design results from a thorough review during the initial design while asking key functional questions throughout the development cycle. Designers may ask, why am I including this element? Can I easily make it accessible? If not, is there another element I can use instead? If not, how important is it? By considering the value of each component and only including those facets which truly add value, the overall course is improved.

Steps taken to make content accessible can benefit all students. When documents are accessible to screen readers used by blind students, they also become searchable, making it easier for all students to more easily find the information they need. Captioned videos benefit both deaf students as well as students working in quiet environments such as the library or at home after the kids have gone to sleep. Students for whom English is not their first language also benefit from listening to the audio while reading the captions.

Mainstream Adoption of Assistive Technologies

Many of the fundamental design goals within UD are also used within the consumer space to develop intuitive interfaces to optimize the end user experience (UX). As a result, while not specifically calling out UD goals for inclusion and accessibility, a natural crossover between mainstream and assistive technologies is inevitable. Some assistive technologies originally created to assist people with disabilities have been adopted by the mainstream. As mentioned previously, closed captioning is not just used by individuals with hearing loss. With captions, students can watch videos in the library or on the train, patrons at a sports bar can read the commentary, one partner can watch a movie while the other sleeps.

Another example of assistive technology expanding into the mainstream involves Optical Character Recognition and speech-to-text (STT). Optical Character Recognition is a process by which printed text is digitized, which can then be recognized and read by a computer. In the 1970s, Ray Kurzweil invented the first machine that would take a printed page, convert the image to text, then read the text aloud for the blind (Kurzweil Technologies, 2016). Today, Optical Character Recognition digitizes documents for purposes such as archiving and record keeping and text-to-speech is used in a variety of ways. Significant advances in text-to-speech are opening new areas of technological interfaces such as Siri, Cortana, and Alexa devices. Voice interaction systems rely heavily on text-to-speech as well as voice recognition capabilities. The work of Kurzweil and others in the early years of assistive technology laid the foundation for these modern tools.

ADVICE FOR CREATING A UNIVERSALLY DESIGNED CLASSROOM

By this point, it should be evident that considering accessibility early in the development process and incorporating the tenants of Universal Design is a desired goal, but it can be intimidating to know how to begin.

First, instructors should not be afraid to try new technologies and new approaches to teaching. As seen above, many technological advances make it possible for students with disabilities to participate more fully in the course.

Second, as course materials and activities are planned, the instructor should ask themselves how students with various disabilities would be able to access the materials or participate in the activity. If the instructor has questions about whether students with different disabilities would have problems with course material or what they can do to make it more accessible, the disability office on campus is a great place to start.

Sometimes an instructor may want to include materials or plan an activity that would be difficult or expensive to make accessible to students with certain disabilities. It does not mean the instructor cannot use the material or activity, but a contingency plan must be in place so that the content or activity can be changed if a student with such a disability enrolls in the course.

CONCLUSION

In this chapter, we have reviewed the foundation and legal and real-world framework concerning the need for accessibility in today's classroom with particular focus on new media technologies' ability to remove barriers for students with disabilities, increase learning for all students, and provide a greater potential for equality in higher education. By considering accessibility at the outset of course development, incorporating Universal Design principles throughout the life cycle of the course, and continuously reviewing new technology as opportunities for increased learning, today's instructors are well positioned to provide optimal learning environments for years to come.

Technology is constantly changing. New apps and tools are developed daily while others are discontinued. That is the nature of technology and the beauty of new media—it is ever evolving. But, accessibility is not about a specific technology, it's about how the technology can be used to create an environment that is accessible and welcoming to all students.

REFERENCES

Americans with Disabilities Act of 1990 (ADA), 42 U.S.C.A. § 12101 *et seq.* (amended 2008).

Burgstahler, S. E. (2015a). Universal design of instruction. In S. E. Burgstahler (Ed.), *Universal design in higher education* (pp. 31–64). Cambridge, MA: Harvard Education Press.

Burgstahler, S. E. (2015b). Universal design of technology. In S. E. Burgstahler (Ed.), *Universal design in higher education* (pp. 231–251). Cambridge, MA: Harvard Education Press.

Center for Universal Design. (2008). *About UD*. Retrieved from https://www.ncsu.edu/ncsu/design/cud/about_ud/about_ud.htm.

Iwarsson, S., and Stahl, A. (2003). Accessibility, usability and universal design—positioning and definition of concepts describing person-environment relationships. *Disability & Rehabilitation, 25*(2), 57–67.

Kurzweil Technologies. (2016). *A brief career summary of Ray Kurzweil*. Retrieved from http://www.kurzweiltech.com/aboutray.html.

National Council on Disability. (2004). *Design for inclusion: Creating a new marketplace*. Retrieved from http://www.ncd.gov/publications/2004/Oct282004.

National Federation of the Blind. (2010). *National Federation of the Blind files complaint against Penn State*. Retrieved from https://nfb.org/node/1026.

Office of Civil Rights. (2013). *Resolution agreement South Carolina Technical College System OCR compliance review no. 11-11-6002*. Retrieved from http://www2.ed.gov/about/offices/list/ocr/docs/investigations/11116002-b.pdf.

Pennsylvania State University. (2012). *Settlement between Penn State University and National Federation of the Blind*. Retrieved from http://accessibility.psu.edu/nfbpsusettlement/.

Technology-Related Assistance for Individuals with Disabilities Act of 1988, Pub. L. No. 100–407, 102 Stat. 1044.

Trammell, J. (2009). Postsecondary students and disability stigma: Development of the postsecondary student survey of disability-related stigma (PSSDS). *Journal of Postsecondary Education and Disability, 22*(2), 106–116.

United States Access Board. (n.d.-a). *ADAAG*. Retrieved from https://www.access-board.gov/guidelines-and-standards/buildings-and-sites/113-ada-standards/background/adaag.

United States Access Board. (n.d.-b). *Section 508: The law.* Retrieved from https://www.access-board.gov/guidelines-and-standards/communications-and-it/about-the-section-508-standards/background/section-508-the-law.

United States Access Board. (2017). *About the ICT refresh.* Retrieved from https://www.access-board.gov/guidelines-and-standards/communications-and-it/about-the-ict-refresh.

University of Washington. (2009). Kindle DX pilot project. Retrieved from http://www.cs.washington.edu/news/KindlePilot/.

U.S. Department of Education. (2010). *Joint "dear colleague" letter: Electronic book readers.* Retrieved from http://www2.ed.gov/about/offices/list/ocr/letters/colleague-20100629.html.

U.S. Department of Education. (2011). Frequently asked questions about the June 29, 2010, dear colleague letter. Retrieved from http://www2.ed.gov/about/offices/list/ocr/docs/dcl-ebook-faq-201105.html.

U.S. Department of Education, National Center for Education Statistics. (2016). Digest of Education Statistics, 2014 (2016–006), Chapter 3.

U.S. Department of Education, Office of Civil Rights. (2014). Resolution agreement. Retrieved from http://www.umt.edu/accessibility/docs/FinalResolutionAgreement.pdf.

U.S. Department of Justice. Section 504, Rehabilitation Act of 1973. Retrieved from https://www.dol.gov/oasam/regs/statutes/sec504.htm.

U.S. Department of Justice. (2010). *Justice Department reaches three settlements under the Americans with Disabilities Act regarding the use of electronic book readers.* Retrieved from https://www.justice.gov/opa/pr/justice-department-reaches-three-settlements-under-americans-disabilities-act-regarding-use.

U.S. Department of Justice. (2013). *Justice Department settles with Louisiana Tech University over inaccessible course materials.* Retrieved from https://www.justice.gov/opa/pr/justice-department-settles-louisiana-tech-university-over-inaccessible-course-materials.

U.S. Department of Justice, Civil Rights Division. (n.d.) *Introduction to the ADA.* Retrieved from https://www.ada.gov/ada_intro.htm.

Chapter Seven

Gamification and the New Media Imperative

Clay Ewing

THE RISE OF DIGITAL GAMES

Games are as old as civilization and the act of play has always played a significant role in learning. From games that encourage strategic thinking on the battlefield to role-playing idealized cultural norms, games are an interactive medium with abundant affordances for education. In the past three decades, the rise of digital games has marked a period of exuberance, reflection, and assessment. Perhaps due to the growth of the commercial video game industry, the idea of gamification or using game elements in non-game contexts has become increasingly popular. Separate from this is game-based learning, which uses games as a central point to teach and around which to generate discussion. While these trends have become popular in K–12 environments, their usage in higher education is burgeoning.

BACKGROUND AND HISTORY

Game-Based Learning

Games have a long history as a learning tool. For example, *Chaturanga* emerged in India in 500 BCE with pieces representing warriors and military equipment of the time on the battlefield. Around 500 CE, the game made its way through the Middle East and Europe, being cast as the ultimate test of strategic thinking in a military context. Today, one would recognize *Chaturanga* as chess (Smith, 2009). Thus, games designed with specific learning outcomes have been around for centuries (Abt, 1970).

During the rise of the commercial video game industry in the 1970s and 1980s, many educational titles also flourished. One of the earliest examples is *Oregon Trail*, a simulation game where the player takes the role of a wagon leader guiding their group from Missouri to Oregon. The game began as an interactive history lesson on 19th-century pioneering and has since been adapted for many different platforms and even inspired a zombie apocalypse parody version called *Organ Trail*. *Where in the World Is Carmen San Diego?* is another early hit that taught geography through role-playing as a member of a detective agency. It was so popular that it spun off into a well-received 1990s children's television game show. While these early educational titles were successful, it wasn't until the 2000s that the potential of digital games for learning emerged because of their ability to engage and motivate players (Prensky, 2003).

Educational Games

When games are used in the classroom, they are usually designed by the teacher or already exist as a product that was not specifically designed to be educational. The educational game market is concentrated in early academic grades (Adkins, 2015), and therefore the choices in higher education on specific subjects can be limited. Thus, educators either design their own games and game-like activities or take an existing game and tailor it to suit their needs. Often, instructors will modify a pre-existing game such as *Jeopardy* (Afari et al., 2013) or *Snakes & Ladders* (Telner et al., 2010) to increase interest and motivation in a given subject. This may present an instructional barrier, as a teacher is not necessarily a game designer. As Squire and Jenkins (2003) write, "Educators acting alone are unlikely to fully grasp what makes contemporary commercial games so compelling for their players; game designers acting alone may not fully grasp the challenges of designing problems and activities that will fully achieve pedagogical objectives" (p. 27).

There are some suggestions for narrowing the gap between educators and designers. For instance, game design workshops that allow educators to prototype and play test their ideas before using them in the classroom have shown promise (Crocco et al., 2016). Others have suggested frameworks for designing serious games (Westera et al., 2008). Beyond using games as a medium for learning, some educators take principles found in games and apply them to the design and structure of their classroom.

Gamification

Scholars believe the term "gamification" originated with Nick Pelling in 2002 (Quora, 2012), but it wasn't until the launch of Foursquare in 2009 that the idea of using game design elements in a product to drive user acquisition and retention became more popular. Foursquare enjoyed significant success, as did Nike+, *Chorewars*, Stack Overflow, and Ribbon Hero, by integrating game elements into product design (Deterding et al., 2011). Furthermore, professional talks by Jane McGonigal (2012) and Jesse Schell (2010) helped popularize these ideas with mainstream audiences.

As gamification became a buzzword, educators started to use the term to describe their efforts for integrating games and game-like components into the classroom. For example, Paul Anderson (2011) reflected on principles found in game design whilst describing his efforts to improve a high school biology class. Anderson created a point structure displayed on a leaderboard and broke down different concepts into levels that allowed students the ability to move at a faster or slower pace, independently of their classmates. Additionally, other educators have touched upon gamification when referring to using mini-games (Top Hat, 2011), levels, avatars (Ross, 2011), and badges (Teched Up Teacher, 2014) in their classrooms.

Sebastian Deterding defines gamification as "the use of design elements characteristic for games in non-game contexts" (Deterding et al., 2011, p. 2). Gamification proponents argue that games are inherently engaging and therefore there must be some secret ingredient that can be extracted from their design. Unfortunately, in an effort to commoditize the term, gamification features were simply boiled down to points, badges, and leaderboards. This is the easiest abstraction to make from games when the goal is to sell a game layer as a service or product (Bogost, 2016). However, the key takeaway is that games should be designed as an experience with the recognition that every game is unique. Design elements that work really well in one game may not translate so successfully to another context. Thus, the implementation of game-based components into the classroom can improve a student's learning experience (Crocco et al., 2016), but it's not a guarantee. Therefore, it is important for educators and instructional designers to think through any new implementation with the intended learning objectives in mind.

USE AND THEORETICAL UNDERSTANDING

Off the Shelf, Into the Classroom

Educators looking to use games in the classroom often start with commercial off-the-shelf (COTS) games. These games may have been designed with learning in mind or may exist purely for entertainment. The primary benefit to using these COTS games in the classroom is that these games already exist and are of high production quality. In many video games one will find several learning theories applied not for academic pursuit but because a well-designed game teaches the player how to play. This requires game designers to incorporate instructional design principles and robust feedback mechanisms. As interactive experiences, games allow for personalization and for multiple routes to victory. Perhaps most importantly, games by their very nature are vehicles for active learning.

In order to play a game, the player must interact with the system, which prompts them to analyze their environment and begin solving problems. The popular mobile game *Flappy Bird* is an active example. *Flappy Bird* belongs to a genre known as "endless runners" whereby the level is procedurally generated and thus infinite. The object of the game is to see how far you can get. When the player starts the game, a bird controlled by the player takes a nosedive. To correct this, the player must tap the screen. This results in a momentary upward boost before taking another nosedive. To fly, the player must continue tapping the screen. If they don't learn how to do this, they die. Once they have learned to fly, they must learn how to avoid on-screen obstacles. If they hit an obstacle, they also lose their life. Through this process of trial and error, the player learns how to make their bird fly and avoid on-screen hazards.

Video game strategy and effective instructional design share significant commonalities. For example, Dickey's (2005) engaged learning framework provides educational game designers with a helpful framework. Video games and effective instructional design share unique features like focused goals, feedback, choice, and challenging tasks. For gamers, these connections are obvious. Games have clear objectives: e.g., shoot the bad guys, save the princess, solve the puzzle, etc. A "game" without choice is not truly game. When you make choices in a game, the system provides feedback that lets you know that you chose something and whether it resulted in a positive or negative outcome: e.g., a delightful sound, a change in score, a "game over" or congratulatory win message appearing on the screen, etc. Finally, game designers have mastered the art of crafting challenging tasks. Sometimes it's a scaffolded experience that increases in difficulty as you level up. Other times it's nightmarishly difficult twitch controls that push a player to compulsively try again. These examples show that sound learning principles are prominent in games.

In fact, James Paul Gee, whom Henry Jenkins once described as the Johnny Appleseed of serious games, has documented 36 principles found in video games that can transform one's ability to learn and develop literacy (Gee, 2004). The Situated Meaning Principle and the Semiotic Principle, two of Gee's key components, are particularly present in simulation games. Situated meaning is derived from an embodied experience while the semiotic principle states that learning is about appreciating interrelations within and across multiple sign systems. A sign is a broad term in semiotics to describe anything with meaning. In a video game, a sign could include the characters, environment, dialogues, or even the mechanics. Thus, an example of a sign system in a game might be the relationship between hearing an ominous sound effect when an enemy enters a room. In a simulation game, a player might pull a lever that reduces the amount of water in a garden, thereby causing flowers to die and highlighting the effect an individual component can have on a complex system.

The *SimCity* series is used by many educators in higher education (Adams, 1998; Gaber, 2007; Frye and Frager, 1996) as it allows learners to explore the concept of urban planning at a systemic level and to see the effect of their decisions over time. Minnery and Searle (2014) assessed *SimCity 4*'s effectiveness as a class activity in two higher education classrooms. From their findings, one can see the situated meaning principle in effect as students play the game. For example, one key pedagogic aim "was to help students understand how governance and institutional justification was required for the level and spatial distribution of the different elements making up the outcomes, including justification of trade-offs amongst them, based on sound urban planning principles" (Minnery and Searle, 2014, p. 45). In *SimCity 4*, players are tasked with building a city from the ground up. The game allows players to visualize the terrain of the city and choose where to place residential, commercial, and industrial zones. Additionally, the game incorporates a tax system and imposes restrictions on what the player is allowed to do within its own set of constraints for citizen happiness. Specifically, the complex relationships in real-world city planning are modeled and the player sees in real time the effects of competing demands. The students are then able to connect this embodied learning to the real world. Multiple studies illustrating the Semiotic Principle (Minnery and Searle, 2014; Adams, 1998) have shown that students see the power structure as unrealistic and that the real world requires a lot of compromises. By playing *SimCity 4*, students learn to appreciate how complicated each relationship expressed in the game is in the real world.

Technology, coupled with the interactive affordances of games, has reached the point where scalable personalized learning is now possible. Various games tailor their approach to learning for individuals. For example, Tomlinson's (1999) idea of differentiated instruction can be found in the turn-based strategy game series *Civilization*. When the player starts the game, they can choose one of eight difficulty levels: settler, chieftain, warlord, prince, king, emperor, mortal, and deity. Each difficulty level triggers a different set of values. For example, costs associated with choices in the game change based on the selected level. This allows a player to experience easier or harder paths to victory, which is important when accounting for the motivation and engagement of the player. A good designer balances a game's difficulty level with the player's skill level in order to create cognitive flow, a mental state in which the player is fully immersed and energized on the task at hand (Csikszentmihalyi, 2000). By striking a balance between a learner's skill level and a given task, engagement can be maximized by offering the player a unique personal experience.

A personalized experience must still allow the player to make decisions that are meaningful. Following this principle, a key component to the interactivity in games is that they can offer multiple routes to victory. In the game *Civilization*, a player can win the game through conquest, diplomacy, technology, or culture. For a learner, this self-exploration is empowering. For example, if a person is interested primarily in technology, they must learn the history behind the technology they desire to build. For example, a radio requires electricity, which requires scientific theory. To acquire scientific theory, the civilization must acquire economics and architecture. Therefore, the player must be taken through many generations of preceding, dependent technologies until they hit upon the idea of agriculture. If a student enjoys the game, it is very likely they will try and play it again with a new path to victory. However, if only one path to victory were to exist in the game, it is very likely that a portion of students would become uninterested in that particular path. And instead of wanting to explore and therefore continue to learn more content from the game, the player may become bored and save their progress, yet never come back to play the game.

The idea of saving progress in a game and continuing later doesn't seem revolutionary today. However, it plays a critical role as part of the solution for individualized instruction (Switzer, 2004). Video games provide constant feedback like a teacher would do one on one with each of their students if they had the time. *Civilization* provides a vast amount of content with meaningful feedback for the player to consume on their own time when they are ready. Much like *Civilization*'s technology tree, where the evolution of technology can be seen as a branching network of bodies of knowledge, many subjects cannot be understood until previous content is learned. An educator giving a lecture in a class of a hundred students doesn't have the luxury of presenting the material at each of their individual paces. However, a game has the power to provide this individual feedback and instruction.

Non-Digital Games and Game-Inspired Activities

While making digital games has become more accessible over time, many of the hurdles can be avoided by taking things offline. Board and card games utilize the same concepts as digital games to create engaging experiences. Furthermore, designing a learning system that can be played with paper and facilitated in a classroom is something that many educators are fully equipped to do.

While educators do have enthusiasm for digital technology use, non-digital games for education should not be ignored. Kaufman and Flanagan (2016) have found that non-digital games prepare people better for problem-solving tasks that have higher-level processing of a representation of a past event. These findings reinforce the strengths of non-digital games especially for aiding abstract thinking. In a 2012 study, Antunes and colleagues (2012) created a board game and used it in a general chemistry college course with positive results. In the study, the game acted not only as a vehicle for content delivery but also as an invitation for discussion. Similarly, role-playing simulations in psychology classrooms have been found to be more engaging with a much higher retention rate of knowledge than traditional lectures (DeNeve and Heppner, 1997). Both of these cases highlight the Active, Critical Learning Principle (Gee, 2004), which states that all aspects of the learning environment encourage active and critical learning. As classmates work through and discuss material, each concept can be contemplated, which allows greater contextualization. As discussions progress, students find new questions to raise with their teacher, thereby increasing their depth of learning. Thus, games and simulations have the ability to turn a classroom into a community of learners, a key to constructivist theory (Fosnot, 2013).

Games can be used to supplement classroom learning and educators can also restructure classrooms into a game. What constitutes a class formally becoming a game is up to interpretation but there are two lenses from which we can contextualize the concept: narrative and structure. A narrative lens implies that the class takes on a theme and a story. The class could be set in the future with learners becoming, for example, sentient robots. The robots embark on a series of epic quests to understand the nature of humanity, which culminates in a speech to the Intergalactic League of Species in order to gain sentient status, which recognizes their rights and equality among all other species. In other words, role-playing. On the other hand, a structural lens focuses on applying the systemic elements found in games into a classroom. For example, students might compete against each other and earn recognition for achievements. Structurally, classroom time might be flipped to allow more interaction between students. Therefore, game elements should be pursued based on the learning principles they embody.

The application of role-playing in the classroom is well illustrated by Lee Sheldon in his book *The Multiplayer Classroom* (2011). Instead of a one-off activity, Sheldon reimagined an entire semester as one big game. Students were split into guilds (groups) and assigned territory zones that occasionally changed seating assignments. Assignments were relabeled to solo, pickup, and group quests that allowed students to work alone with a non-guild member or together as a team with their guild. Grades were determined by XP (experience points) received from quests. Occasionally students had the option to do a pickup quest, where two students from different guilds would work together. Sheldon's approach to teaching this undergraduate course on game design focuses primarily on reframing the narrative of class time. However, traditional classroom design was still incorporated (i.e., students still take exams, give presentations, write reports, and read from critical texts). Ultimately, the difference in the role-playing simulation was the student perception of classroom engagement. For example, students compete as part of a guild against other groups of students, just as they would in a game. Students were also free to strategize on how they played the game in order to boost their avatar's XP level. This format has been used in other classrooms as well, most notably in a Latin language class at the Norwich Free Academy where Operation LAPIS imagines students as operatives working to decipher the LAPIS SAECULORUM in order to save civilization. As students work on each quest, they are ultimately learning the language through immersion in an alternate reality (Slota et al., 2013). Both of these classrooms showcase the Committed Learning Principle, where students extend their real world identity to a virtual identity and are continually engaged (Gee, 2004). Forming teams also highlights Gee's Affinity Group Principle where the group is bonded by the shared goal of leveling up, studying, and figuring out how to maximize their team's strength.

Applying Gameful Concepts Through Software

As the affordances of games in education are realized, software developers have started to design products for higher education that apply concepts found in games. Some products have implemented game elements that are commonly found in other non-educational settings, such as badges and leaderboards. Other products have put considerable effort into designing solutions that are specific to learning environments, such as building affinity groups and the amplification of input through system feedback. Taken as a whole, these products are finding new ways to build engagement in the classroom and on college campuses.

By changing the structure of a higher education classroom, gameful learning management systems (LMS) inherently embody learning principles found in game design. Courses that use these systems don't require an instructor to treat class time as a game. Instead, a gameful LMS offers opportunities to reimagine how assignments and content are consumed by students. Two examples of software platforms that explore classroom gamification are Gradecraft and Queso. GradeCraft, developed at the University of Michigan, is an LMS built on gameful principles and was originally used to teach a class on video games and learning. Similarly, Queso is an LMS developed at the University of Miami as a solution for early adopters of gamified classrooms to alleviate the administrative burdens of changing the class structure. Incorporating many game elements into the classroom, such as badge systems, is an added stress for educators that can be simplified through software.

Badges are a popular form of gamification that have made their way into a variety of commercial product offerings. A core idea behind badges is that they serve as a marker of success and achievement. In GradeCraft, badges function primarily as an extrinsic reward. On the surface, a badge represents an external reward in the form of an image recognizing the completion of a task. However, GradeCraft allows instructors to create badges that highlight the skills and actions they feel are important to achieving the goals of the class (Holman et al., 2013). This allows the badges to serve as an indication of student progress when assessed by either the learner or the teacher.

The competitive spirit of game players is a motivator that can be infused into the classroom. Leaderboards are often present in gamified products as a way of instilling a sense of competition. However, in an educational setting, leaderboards must be designed in a way in which a classroom is not seen as a zero-sum game with one student winning big while the rest lose. In Sheldon's multiplayer classroom, the sense of competition is based around teams where being on top does not always correlate to the best grades for each team member. In comparison, GradeCraft students create an alias that appears on the leaderboard so they can see how well they stack up against everyone in the class while remaining anonymous to others. Getting a sense of your overall standing is important for students to see as it can serve as an indicator for poor effort and a reward system for exceptional work.

One difference between video games and classroom expectation is the prospect of failure. In video games, we poke and prod, dying repeatedly in hopes of eventual mastery. In classroom contexts, Gee (2004) calls this the Psychosocial Moratorium Principle, where learners can take risks while avoiding real-life consequences. In Queso, assignments are presented in a way to encourage repeated performances. Instead of a due date, assignments expire. A student clicks a button labeled "attempt" to submit the first version of an assignment. When the instructor assigns points and gives feedback, the student can make revisions and submit the assignment again. This allows a student to keep trying, per the instructor's willingness to grade, until they have shown a mastery of the task assigned. It also changes the experience of homework as multiple assignments could be in progress without a specific due date.

When a player wanders around in an open-world game, they have a vast array of quests. Some quests require completing another quest or reaching a specific level. The choices students/players make creates a personalized experience. Queso and GradeCraft use this idea to create scaffolded assignments. In Queso, instructors are encouraged to create multiple skills to award points on various assignments. A student can then choose assignments based on the skills they need. Assignments can be hidden until a student meets a threshold of points in a given skill level. In GradeCraft, assignments can be hidden until a specific badge has been awarded. This gives learners agency by giving them the opportunity to achieve mastery in the class through multiple routes (Gee, 2004).

Games and courses both have objectives. In games, goals can be viewed at the micro and macro level. A micro goal might be collecting a coin, whereas a macro goal would entail collecting enough coins to purchase a powerful weapon. This happens in courses as well, where completing an individual assignment can be a micro goal while mastery of a subject is a macro goal. The difference is that in a game a player's performance exists within the magic circle of the game and is not tied to real-world consequences. In a classroom, the learner is eventually graded on their performance. As multiple routes through various assignments are introduced, it is easy for a student to be overwhelmed by feeling they must do everything (Holman et al., 2013). To balance this, GradeCraft has implemented a grade predictor whereby a student can play with the various combinations of assignments (or micro goals) available to plan their route for the semester. This gives students more agency in determining their grade (the macro goal) as well as a way to analyze their current performance and pivot to a new strategy if needed. By adding this interactive layer to the software, students also receive an additional level of feedback.

Another principle put forward by Gee (2004) is the Amplification of Input, which states that the output for a learner should be maximized based on minimal input. Queso implements this through various feedback systems. For example, not all assignments require the instructor to act as a gatekeeper. Like Kahn Academy, Queso can track when a video has been watched and can assign points automatically. Unique codes can also be generated for the instructor to hand out to students to redeem for points instantly, removing the time delay usually associated with grading. For example, an instructor might have a series of student debates as a classroom activity. Usually an instructor would keep track of participating students with a spreadsheet and assign points after class. With Queso, each time a debate concluded, the instructor could hand to the student a slip of paper with a code that when entered into Queso, awards them points for participating. This reduces the amount of time spent on grading for the instructor and provides instant feedback to the student.

As shown with Lee Sheldon's multiplayer classroom, affinity groups can establish a community of learners. Queso builds on that idea with peer groups, where students are prompted to give feedback on other group member's assignments. When a student submits an assignment, members of their peer group are notified. Each group member is shown what their peer submitted and asked to write what they liked and suggest ways to improve it. By presenting opportunities for students to critique their peers, the student becomes the teacher. This follows Gee's (2004) Insider Principle, whereby the learner is not just a consumer of content but is also able to customize the learning experience.

Looking at higher education holistically as a community of learners, gameful experiences do not need to be relegated solely to the classroom. The Rochester Institute of Technology, in partnership with Microsoft Research, implemented a game layer called Just Press Play (JPP), for all undergraduates in the School of Interactive Games and Media. JPP presents a series of challenges for participants to undertake as a way of establishing an outlet for students and academic staff to interact outside of the classroom (Clark and Martinez-Garza, 2012). This is different from a gamified classroom or using a game in a class because the focus is solely on building a community in an academic environment. Through a variety of activities, participants are given opportunities to socialize with faculty and students across the school with whom they may or may not share a class. This increased focus on building a community has led to positive outcomes. In particular, a one-time study group achievement gave seniors the intrinsically rewarding feeling that they could have a positive influence on freshmen. What was once a one-time event turned into a recurring event, devoid of the game layer, and the pass rate for the final exam increased by a few percentage points (Clark and Martinez-Garza, 2012).

In summary, games and game design are transforming the way instructors in higher education can teach their students. Various commercial games have been used to introduce topics, which allows learners to gain a greater appreciation for the systems in which they reside and promote active and personalized learning. Seeking higher engagement, educators have designed their own games and classroom activities. These game-based activities have seen measureable increases in abstract thinking and problem-solving skills for learners while providing an opportunity for in-depth discussions. As the enthusiasm for game-based learning grows, so too does the desire to incorporate game design principles into software used in the classroom and on campus. Projects like Queso, GradeCraft, and Just Press Play are applying concepts found in games to their systems in order to increase engagement and build communities of learners. The future of games in education is wide open.

CONCLUSION

Every form of media has the potential to improve learning outcomes and pedagogical practices. As new technologies come to market, the scope and reach of games in education expands. The NMC Horizon Report (2014) estimated that games and gamification would be widely adopted in higher education by 2017. While the examples shown throughout this chapter prove that higher education is experimenting with games, they are by no means commonplace. Games, as an interactive medium, offer a wide variety of affordances for learning. For instance, we know that games increase motivation when they are integrated into the educational process (Joyce et al., 2009). Games can be played outside of class and used as supplementary materials alongside books and films. Games can be used as a class activity thus allowing deep discussion to take place both during and after play. Likewise, the practice of designing games in a classroom can be used to teach systems thinking. Games can also be distilled down into their core elements, focusing on the process of learning and engagement to improve learning management systems. The application of game design principles in higher education may increase student engagement and motivation. Technologies such as virtual reality are being explored by early adopters in the commercial space and offer exciting opportunities. As new ideas take hold and new platforms are released, educators should seek more ways to incorporate innovative learning technologies into the classroom. It is imperative that higher education professionals pursue game-based strategies aggressively in order to reach the twenty-first-century student.

REFERENCES

Abt, C. C. (1970). *Serious games*. New York, NY: Viking Press.

Adams, P. C. (1998). Teaching and learning with SimCity 2000. *Journal of Geography*, *97*, 47–55.

Adkins, S. (2015). The 2014–2019 global edugame market. [White paper]. Retrieved February 10, 2017, from Ambient Insight: http://www.ambientinsight.com/Resources/Documents/AmbientInsight_2014_2019_Global_Edugame_Market_Whitepaper.pdf.

Afari, E., Aldridge, J. M., Fraser, B. J., and Khine, M. S. (2013). Students' perceptions of the learning environment and attitudes in game-based mathematics classrooms. *Learning Environments Research*, *16*(1), 131–150.

Anderson, P (2011). Using game design to improve my classroom. [Video file]. Retrieved from https://www.youtube.com/watch?v=XGE6osTXym8.

Antunes, M., Pacheco, M. A. R., and Giovanela, M. (2012). Design and implementation of an educational game for teaching chemistry in higher education. *Journal of Chemical Education*, *89*(4), 517–521.

Bogost, I. (2016). *Play anything*. New York: Basic Books.

Clark, D. B., and Martinez-Garza, M. (2012). *Prediction and explanation as design mechanics in conceptually integrated digital games to help players articulate the tacit understandings they build through game play*. London: Cambridge University Press.

Crocco, F., Offenholley, K., and Hernandez, C. (2016). A proof-of-concept study of game-based learning in higher education. *Simulation & Gaming*, 1046878116632484.

Csikszentmihalyi, M. (2000). *Beyond boredom and anxiety*. Jossey-Bass.

DeNeve, K. M., and Heppner, M. J. (1997). Role play simulations: The assessment of an active learning technique and comparisons with traditional lectures. *Innovative Higher Education*, *21*(3), 231–246.

Deterding, S., Khaled, R., Nacke, L. E., and Dixon, D. (2011). Gamification: Toward a definition. *CHI 2011*, 1–4.

Dickey, M. D. (2005). Engaging by design: How engagement strategies in popular computer and video games can inform instructional design. *Educational Technology Research and Development*, *53*(2), 67–83.

Dickey, M. D. (2011). Murder on Grimm Isle: The impact of game narrative design in an educational game-based learning environment. *British Journal of Educational Technology, 42*(3), 456–469.

Fosnot, C. T. (2013). *Constructivism: Theory, perspectives, and practice*. Teachers College Press.

Frye, B., and Frager, A. M. (1996). Civilization, colonization, SimCity: Simulations for the social studies classroom. *Learning and Leading with Technology, 24*(2), 21–23, 32.

Gaber, J. (2007). Simulating planning: SimCity as a pedagogical tool. *Journal of Planning Education and Research, 27*, 113–121. doi: 10.1177/0739456X07305791.

Gee, J. P. (2004). *Situated language and learning: A critique of traditional schooling*. London: Routledge.

Holman, C., Aguilar, S., and Fishman, B. (2013, April). GradeCraft: What can we learn from a game-inspired learning management system? In *Proceedings of the Third International Conference on Learning Analytics and Knowledge* (pp. 260–264). ACM.

Joyce, A., Gerhard, P., and Debry, M. (2009). How are digital games used in schools: Complete results of the study. *European Schoolnet*.

Kaufman, G., and Flanagan, M. (2016, May). High-low split: Divergent cognitive construal levels triggered by digital and non-digital platforms. In *Proceedings of the 2016 CHI Conference on Human Factors in Computing Systems* (pp. 2773–2777). ACM.

McClarty, K. L., Orr, A., Frey, P. M., Dolan, R. P., Vassileva, V., and McVay, A. (2012). A literature review of gaming in education. *Gaming in Education*.

McGonigal, J. (2012, June). Jane McGonigal: The game that can give you 10 extra years of life. [Video file]. Retrieved from https://www.ted.com/talks/jane_mcgonigal_the_game_that_can_give_you_10_extra_years_of_life.

Minnery, J., and Searle, G. (2014). Toying with the city? Using the computer game SimCity™ 4 in planning education. *Planning Practice and Research, 29*(1), 41–55.

New Media Consortium. (2014). NMC Horizon Report 2014, Higher Education Edition.

Prensky, M. (2003). Digital game-based learning. *Computers in Entertainment (CIE), 1*(1), 21–21.

Quora. (2012). Who coined the term "gamification?" Retrieved from https://www.quora.com/Who-coined-the-term-gamification.

Ross, P. (2011). Math teacher uses gamification to help at-risk students succeed. Retrieved from http://www.goventureoasis.com/resources/pdf/5111201034254.pdf.

Schell, J. (2010, June). DICE 2010: Design outside the box presentation. [Video file]. Retrieved from https://www.youtube.com/watch?v=nG_PbHVW5cQ.

Sheldon, L. (2011). *The multiplayer classroom: Designing coursework as a game*. Cengage.

Slota, S., Ballestrini, K., and Pearsall, M. (2013). Learning through pperation LAPIS: A game based approach to the language classroom. *The Language Educator*, October, 36–38.

Smith, R. (2009). The long history of gaming in military training. *Simulation & Gaming*.

Squire, K., and Jenkins, H. (2003). Harnessing the power of games in education. *Insight, 3*(1), 5–33.

Switzer, D. (2004). Individualized instruction. In F. P. Schargel and J. Smink (Eds.), *Helping students graduate: A strategic approach to dropout prevention* (pp. 225–233). Larchmont, NY: Eye on Education.

Teched Up Teacher. (2014). Gamify your class level III: Badges. Retrieved from http://www.techedupteacher.com/gamify-your-class-level-iii-badges.

Telner, D., Bujas-Bobanovic, M., Chan, D., Chester, B., Marlow, B., Meuser, J., . . . and Harvey, B. (2010). Game-based versus traditional case-based learning: Comparing effectiveness in stroke continuing medical education.*Canadian Family Physician, 56*(9), e345–e351.

Tomlinson, C. A. (1999). Mapping a route toward differentiated instruction. *Educational Leadership, 57*, 12–16.

Top Hat. (2011). Gamifying English class: Can it be done? Retrieved from https://blog.tophat.com/gamifying-english-class-can-it-be-done.

Westera, W., Nadolski, R. J., Hummel, H. G., and Wopereis, I. G. (2008). Serious games for higher education: A framework for reducing design complexity. *Journal of Computer Assisted Learning, 24*(5), 420–432.

Chapter Eight

The Internet of Things and Wearable Technology as a Classroom Resource

Heather J. Hether, Joe C. Martin, and Andrew W. Cole

A COMMUNICATION REVOLUTION

We are living in the midst of one of the greatest revolutions ever experienced in human communication. The Internet and devices capable of accessing the web pervade our homes, offices, and classrooms, and are increasingly found on our bodies. Like any new advancement, this wave of technology brings in its wake a host of potential challenges and opportunities for the broader world, but also for educational contexts. Already under pressure to modernize the college educational experience, instructors must fully understand these technologies in order to properly assess how (or if) they should be incorporated into the classroom.

In this chapter, we explore the possibilities of two promising electronic classifications for the twenty-first-century classroom: the Internet of Things (IoT) and wearable technologies. Though these categories have some areas of significant overlap, they are, in fact, distinct. An activity tracker, for instance, is both a wearable and a part of the Internet of Things. A smart thermostat is part of the Internet of Things, but is not a wearable. A virtual reality headset (though it may be Internet connected) does not by nature require interconnectivity or Internet access to function and therefore may only be categorized as a wearable, but not necessarily part of the Internet of Things. To better understand these overlapping yet distinct categories and their potential for the educational environment, this chapter will: trace their history, define ways in which they are distinct, develop a theoretical understanding, explore potential for adoption, and finally hypothesize as to the influence such devices are likely to have.

BACKGROUND AND HISTORICAL CONTEXT

Both wearable technology and IoT devices can trace their heritage to the advent of the military-funded ARPANET in the 1960s. This promising new network ushered in the wider, global "Internet" in the final decades of the 20th century (see Abbate, 2000). While the Internet was originally conceptualized as a system that allowed humans to communicate with other humans, it is increasingly a system that allows computers to communicate with other computers. With each new iteration of electronic technology, the Internet makes new inroads into devices that were previously described colloquially as "dumb." This new wave of "smart" devices spans the spectrum from jewelry to refrigerators, and has significantly expanded the breadth and depth of the Internet's invasion into the human experience.

The instructional environment has already been infiltrated by both wearable technology and the IoT. In backpacks, on desks, and on wrists, the modern classroom is likely host to more Internet-enabled devices than students. Even without intentional human interaction, these devices send and receive information, and potentially impact the educational experience. As teachers lecture, Fitbit accelerometers await the next step, Apple Watches exhort to their wearers, "Time to stand," and cell phone push notifications trigger vibrations and screen wakes for Twitter trends and Snapchat stories. These new technologies have already altered the educational environment and will continue to do so. Thus, it is incumbent upon educators to lead the way with technology, rather than be led by it.

Internet of Things

The term "Internet of Things" likely originated in a 1999 presentation by technologist Kevin Ashton to an audience at Procter and Gamble (Ashton, 2009). Ashton theorized ways that radio frequency identification (RFID) technology coupled with Internet connectivity could enable greater supply-chain efficiencies. Ten years after coining the term, Ashton notes the distinction between "the Internet" and "the Internet of Things" with the following words:

> Today computers—and, therefore, the Internet—are almost wholly dependent on human beings for information. Nearly all of the roughly 50 petabytes (a petabyte is 1,024 terabytes) of data available on the Internet were first captured and created by human beings—by typing, pressing a record button, taking a digital picture or scanning a barcode. (Ashton, 2009, para. 2)

In distinction to the above, Ashton shares what could be described as the general vision for the Internet of Things:

> We need to empower computers with their own means of gathering information, so they can see, hear and smell the world for themselves, in all its random glory. RFID [radio-frequency identification] and sensor technology enable computers to observe, identify and understand the world—without the limitations of human-entered data. (Ashton, 2009, para. 5)

Thus, the Internet of Things allows for increased interconnectivity and data generation by devices that are not necessarily controlled by conscious human interaction. So while an Excel spreadsheet typically awaits direct human input before it can save or share data of the steps a person takes in a day, an IoT pedometer can track, save, and share the same data without direct action on the part of the user.

Wearable Technology

While the Internet of Things is a concept with a heritage linked to corporate supply-chain management, wearable technology traces its roots to an MIT graduate watching the film *The Terminator* in 1993 (Miller and Spiegel, 2015). In the film's opening scenes, a cyborg analyzes its surroundings with the aid of a computer that overlays useful information onto people and objects, essentially "augmenting" its vision. Concluding that the potential technology of the aforementioned variety was "cool" (Miller and Spiegel, 2015), Thad Starner (who would later write a dissertation at MIT entitled "Wearable Computing and Contextual Awareness") set out to handcraft a wearable computer based on a design by Doug Platt (Rhodes, n.d.). The device was dubbed "Lizzy" and Starner began wearing it regularly starting in 1993 (Rhodes, n.d.). This initial prototype featured a small screen mounted over one eye, a hip-mounted computer and battery, and a one-handed keyboard (Miller and Spiegel, 2015). With Lizzy, Starner could use the keyboard to save notes of his experiences and interactions in order to later display the previously saved information onto the head-mounted screen. Since the inception of Lizzy in 1993, Starner has, in one form or another, consistently worn some type of wearable technology (Stevens, 2013). Thanks to his groundbreaking experience and expertise, Starner would go on to serve as technical lead/manager for the Google Glass project (Stevens, 2013).

Though Starner may have pioneered the utilization of digital wearable technologies he, and the creators of *The Terminator*, were far from the first to envision wearing a piece of technology. In fact, as early as the 17th century, individuals wore eyeglasses, which later inspired Robert Hooke to remark:

> The next care to be taken, in respect of the Senses, is a supplying of their infirmities with Instruments, and as it were, the adding of artificial Organs to the natural . . . and as Glasses have highly promoted our seeing, so 'tis not improbable, but that there may be found many mechanical inventions to improve our other senses of hearing, smelling, tasting, and touching. (Hooke, 1665)

When one revisits Hooke's predictions in light of technologies such as the Oculus Rift virtual reality headset, it is difficult to see his vision being manifested any more fully. But of course, virtual reality devices are only one category in the modern landscape of Internet-connected and wearable objects.

Wearables and the Internet of Things

Today, fitness trackers, such as Fitbit, have become ubiquitous examples of wearable technology devices (Leslie, 2016). In their most basic forms, fitness trackers utilize a motion sensor (or accelerometer) to measure steps taken by the wearer, or to track a lack of step-movement as periods of sleep. More advanced fitness trackers log stairs ascended by the wearer, and the most advanced iterations boast heart-rate tracking and other complex sensors. Many of these devices depend to some extent upon connections with smartphones or computers in order to store and graph data generated by the user's activities. Fitness tracking devices are compact, relatively inexpensive, and often quite simple—factors that undoubtedly help lead to their relatively wide adoption. The Fitbit Flex, for instance, lacks any physical buttons, though basic functions can be carried out by tapping the device (Make fitness a lifestyle with flex, n.d.). Though fitness trackers like those described above offer impressive capabilities, they represent one of the most basic forms of wearable technology.

Smartwatches are generally more expensive, interactive, and complex than fitness trackers. One of the most popular smartwatches at the time of this writing is the Apple Watch. Introduced in 2015, the Apple Watch offers activity tracking functionality such as steps and heart-rate tracking, but also features numerous other more complex functions such as sending and receiving messages and phone calls (Watch: Series 1, n.d.). Like other wearables, the Apple Watch is, to some extent, dependent upon a wirelessly connected phone in order to offer the full extent of its functionality. The Apple Watch has proven to provide both accurate and precise results in the area of heart-rate monitoring (a potentially useful measure in the educational context). A recent study that assessed the precision and accuracy of various wearable fitness devices against the Onyx Vantage 9590 professional clinical pulse oximeter found that the Apple Watch boasted an impressive 99.9 percent accuracy, rating (El-Amrawy and Nounou, 2015). Such findings speak to the quality of data gathered by at least some wearable devices.

Though some wearable devices have arrived with critical acclaim and high rates of adoption, this is not always the case. One of the most discussed, maligned, and lauded wearables of the early twenty-first century was Google Glass ("Glass"). Replacing lenses with a single translucent screen, Glass displays information to the user and augments the vision of the wearer (for instance, overlaying direction arrows onto the user's view of a road). Though some of the controversy that plagued Glass centered on concerns of a user's ability to be socially "present" amidst a bombardment of text and images on a display millimeters from the eye, most concerns centered on Glass' conspicuous camera and microphone (Bilton, 2015). Simply making eye contact with a Glass wearer meant having a camera lens pointed directly at one's face, an experience that proved to be unnerving for many. Glass is not currently manufactured by Google and its future remains uncertain, a reality echoed on its official web page, where a runner's shoes are shown paused at the edge of murky waters (Glass, n.d.). While Google's Glass may be at a standstill, devices like Microsoft's HoLolens™ are poised to create even more impressive augmented environments that stop just short of an entirely "virtual" experience.

Finally, and arguably the pinnacle of current wearable technology, are virtual reality headsets. Devices such as the aforementioned Oculus Rift create an immersive visual and auditory experience for the user. Utilizing dual 1080×1200 OLED panels, "3D audio," and an infrared position tracking system that boasts "sub-millimeter" accuracy (Step into the rift, 2015), devices like the Rift provide numerous and varied opportunities for both educators and students to create and experience alternate and augmented "realities."

It is important to note that the devices discussed above represent only a fraction of wearable and Internet-connected devices in the modern classroom, and the passage of time will only bring new and more advanced technologies. Yet, even at this nascent stage in the history and application of wearable technology, wearables and Internet-connected objects are already part of the lives of students and educators (see Atkinson and Curtin, 2016; UW Internet of Things Lab, 2016). These devices are not necessarily technologies that must be introduced to the classroom; they are already there. Therefore, how to best utilize the technologies becomes the challenge.

THEORETICAL UNDERSTANDING

The value of new technologies in the classroom inherently depends upon the role these tools can assume in helping students achieve learning outcomes.

Courses are designed around the achievement of a collection of learning outcomes and competencies. Competencies may include cognitive outcomes such as those identified in Bloom's taxonomy (Anderson and Krathwohl, 2001; Bloom, 1956); metacognitive outcomes such as students' understanding of their own learning processes (Kolb 2015; Kolb and Kolb, 2009; Schraw, 1998; Veenman, Van Hout-Wolters, and Afflerbach, 2006); process-oriented outcomes such as working collaboratively (Fidalgo-Blanco et al., 2015); and even emotional outcomes that involve situation-appropriate values, attitudes, and behaviors (Bloom, 1956; Krathwohl, Bloom, and Masia, 1964; Rodriquez, Plax, and Kearney, 1996; Shepherd, 2008). Thus, while educators and students alike may be drawn to new technologies by their promise of innovation, it is critical that educators assess what these tools can contribute to the learning environment and process before they are integrated too quickly into the curriculum.

Pedagogical theory describes how students learn and, thus, how learning outcomes can be achieved. In the current analysis, three pedagogical theories provide a valuable framework for the consideration of how wearables and the Internet of Things may facilitate learning. These theories are: constructivism (see Seel, 2012), experiential learning (e.g., Kolb, 2015), and the cognitive theory of multimedia learning (e.g., Mayer, 1997, 2001, 2002, 2014a). A fourth theory, connectivism (Siemens, 2005), suggests a networked perspective of learning that provides an insightful theoretical framework to consider the impact of the IoT in particular.

Constructivism is an educational and epistemological theory that explains how people learn. This theory has developed thanks to several prominent educational thinkers and cognitive psychologists of the 20th century, including John Dewey, Jean Piaget, Lev Vygotsky, Jerame Bruner, Maria Montessori, and others (Seel, 2012). While there are different models of constructivism (such as social constructivism and cognitive constructivism) that emphasize different processes, a constructivist perspective generally includes the notion that knowledge is constructed by learners as they make meaning out of new information and attempt to integrate new knowledge with their existing knowledge (Brooks and Brooks, 1999; Krahenbuhl, 2016; Seel, 2012). Rather than viewing knowledge as something that is transmitted from a source to a receiver (e.g., teacher to student), this perspective emphasizes the active role that learners must assume for learning to take place.

Constructivist pedagogy emphasizes social interaction with peers and the instructor, guided student practice, and it encourages students to take an active lead in their own learning (Fosnot, 2005; Fosnot and Perry, 2005; Seel, 2012). Constructivism reflects principles of what is now commonly identified as "student-centered learning" wherein students are provided with more opportunities to actively engage with course content as opposed to sitting passively for a lecture (e.g., Weimer, 2002; Wright, 2011). The renowned American educational theorist John Dewey (1859–1952) is often cited as an influential figure in constructivism (Vanderstraeten, 2002); however, it is Dewey's work regarding the role of experience in learning—a perspective that became a hallmark of the progressive education movement of the early 20th century—that established his standing in the educational community. Dewey's (1938) work emphasized the importance of experience for facilitating learning (as opposed to rote memorization associated with "traditional" pedagogy) and it laid the groundwork for experiential learning theory (Kolb, 2015), a pedagogical theory which privileges experience as essential to learning. Experiential learning theory also explains how new technology, like wearables and the IoT, can help students learn.

Experiential learning theory places experience at the center of education. While experiential learning owes its intellectual legacy, in part, to constructivism, subsequent educational theorists have refined ideas about how experience can best be structured and leveraged to facilitate learning. In particular, Kolb (2015) has articulated a theoretical model of experiential learning that integrates experience, reflection, and practice as pathways to more effective learning.

Kolb (2015) describes a dynamic process of experiential learning in which "knowledge is created through the transformation of experience" (p. 49). Kolb (2015) articulates a learning cycle that consists of both taking in new experiences or "grasping experiences" and interpreting or acting on those experiences—what the authors calls "transforming experience" (p. 51). Together, grasping and transforming experience creates a learning cycle that is described as a recursive and dialectical process, in which learners take in information through concrete experience (CE) and abstract conceptualization (AC)—and then they transform the experience through reflective observation (RO) and active experimentation (AE), which subsequently influences their concrete experiences. Thus, in this model, experiences are central to learning.

Like constructivism, experiential learning theory privileges a student-centered approach, and, together, these theories provide frameworks for understanding how wearables and the IoT can facilitate learning. These theories suggest that integrating new technologies into the classroom can provide students with opportunities to construct new knowledge based on the experiences these technologies provide, particularly in regards to technologies like virtual and augmented reality goggles. Consistent with these theories, Mayer's (e.g., 1997, 2001, 2002, 2014a, 2014b) cognitive theory of multimedia learning also privileges active learning, while examining, in detail, the role that multimedia play in facilitating learning.

Mayer's (2002, 2014a, 2014b) research is anchored in a knowledge construction paradigm wherein learners actively construct knowledge, with varying outcomes, based on the format in which content is communicated. Thus, multimedia platforms are not simply information transmission systems, but are "venues for fostering the process of sense making by learners" (Mayer, 2002, p. 100). Mayer (1997, 2002) has compared how learners construct knowledge when content is presented in different formats, such as verbal only versus verbal and pictorial (i.e., multimedia) explanations, and he has found consistent support for a multimedia effect: learners learn more deeply when they receive information in words and pictures, as opposed to words alone (Mayer, 2014b).

Mayer (2002, 2014a) provides an explanation for a multimedia effect that relies on three assumptions about how people learn: (1) the dual channel assumption; (2) the limited channel capacity assumption; and (3) the active processing assumption. The dual channel assumption suggests that individuals have separate processing systems for visual and auditory/verbal material. Individuals also have a limited amount of information they can process in any one channel at one time. The limited channel capacity assumption suggests that too much information in any channel can exceed the cognitive load capacity of that channel, resulting in a negative impact on learning. Finally, the active processing assumption suggests that individuals engage in meaningful, deep learning by actively attending to and organizing incoming information.

Mayer's research has focused extensively on how verbal and pictorial representations of information are associated with student learning, particularly in print form; in addition, he and other researchers (see Mayer, 2014c) have also studied the impact of content presented in digital formats, such as computer animation (e.g., Mayer and Moreno, 2002) and computer games (e.g., Tobias, Fletcher, Bediou, Wind, and Chen, 2014), as well as video (e.g., Mayer, Lee, and Peebles, 2014). Within this body of work, researchers have found evidence for a modality effect, indicating the channel of information delivery has an effect on learning (e.g., Mayer and Moreno, 2002). For example, Mayer (2002) found that animation and narration is more effective for learning than animation and on-screen text. He suggests this difference may be attributed to the animation and text exceeding the cognitive capacity of the visual channel, whereas animation and narration does not have such an impact.

The cognitive theory of multimedia learning provides a framework for understanding the potential role of new, "smart" technologies in facilitating learning. Mayer's research (e.g., 1997, 2002) suggests that communicating knowledge through multimedia channels can have a positive impact on learning, with the caveat that too much information cannot be communicated through any one channel at a single time (thus exceeding the processing capacity of individuals). Moreover, information communicated to students should avoid including too much extraneous detail that can distract students from the key concepts that instructors would like them to learn (Mayer, 2002; Mayer and Fiorella, 2014). Many other studies examining multimedia learning have also suggested additional principles for understanding the processes and impacts of learning through multiple communication platforms (see Mayer, 2014c).

The cognitive theory of multimedia learning focuses on the differential impacts of information presented to learners through multiple communication channels. This theory has been used to examine the impact of content communicated across a variety of platforms; consequently, it is pertinent for considering how new technology, such as VR/AR, can be used most effectively to support student learning. Another theory that considers the impact of technology on learning is Siemens' (2005) theory of connectivism, which presents a different theoretical perspective on learning and what it means to be knowledgeable.

Siemens (2005) argues that because knowledge is expanding so rapidly and the "shelf life" of current knowledge is becoming ever shorter, we need a new theory of learning that more effectively understands learning in the "digital age." Rather than assessing learning as something that happens within an individual, or within the interaction between an individual and the environment, Siemens (2005) proposes a networked theory of learning (Duke, Harper, and Johnston, 2013) that recognizes the role of connectivity in facilitating knowledge transfer. Siemens (2005) suggests, "we derive our competence from forming connections" (para. 15).

The theory of connectivism suggests that learning occurs through one's connections to other individuals, activities, groups, information sources, etc. (Siemens, 2005). This theory builds on principles suggested by chaos, network, complexity, and self-organization theories, and suggests new ways of learning that are facilitated by networks comprised of both human and non-human nodes (Siemens, 2005). Learning is not just knowing content, but knowing where to find reliable information when you need it and forming social connections that help facilitate content retrieval. As Siemens (2005) suggests, "the amplification of learning, knowledge and understanding through the extension of a personal network is the epitome of connectivism" (para. 31). This theory may foretell the potential impact of the IoT in education by suggesting that the connectivity facilitated through the IoT will support a new kind of learning that goes beyond a student's own internal processes to also consider how students navigate and negotiate knowledge contained within networks comprised of both human and non-human entities.

The pedagogical theories presented here all share a central assumption: they each position the student as an active participant in the learning process who must be engaged for learning to take place. The integration of new technologies in the classroom that encourage students to be active learners is congruous with these theoretical perspectives that foreground experience, active learning, and sense making as central routes to learning. However, with the adoption of innovations in the classroom, additional opportunities and challenges are inherent.

ADOPTION

The sections above detailed the background of wearable technologies and the IoT, as well as theoretical approaches to learning. Many opportunities and challenges exist relating to widespread adoption of the IoT and wearable technology devices in the college classroom. Though the Internet is an intrinsic aspect of the relationship between the IoT and wearable technology in the classroom, it is worth noting that the focus in this chapter is on learning activities taking place in the traditional face-to-face classroom environment, rather than through a distance education format. As pedagogical applications of IoT and wearable technology devices are relatively new, it would be impossible to predict and describe the full array of potential applications. Specific distance learning applications may currently exist and will likely further develop. However, after defining the current situation regarding IoT and wearable technology in the sections above, this chapter now turns to potential opportunities and challenges in adoption of the IoT and wearable technology in the physical face-to-face (FtF) classroom setting.

Opportunities

Perhaps the most promising opportunity offered through integration of the IoT and wearable technology devices into the classroom is the possibility of bringing the "real world" into the educational experience. Classroom integration of virtual reality (VR) and augmented reality (AR), in particular, allow students to apply knowledge and skills learned in the course material to real world scenarios. Relatedly, these activities could allow instructors to directly assess specific competencies that could be pragmatically and/or ethically impossible outside of VR or AR context. For example, plentiful VR/AR applications exist for health-related courses. VR/AR can be used to help students learn human anatomy (Smith, 2016). Further, VR/AR could allow students in the health sciences to have opportunities for safe practice and assessment by dealing with uncommon but potentially life-threatening situations.

No matter the course and course content, wearables and the IoT present exciting possibilities. In addition to the health and medical VR/AR applications, augmented and virtual reality could enhance student communication skills in simulated settings. Recent research suggests that experiences in virtual environments can influence individuals' ability to consume different perspectives, even after leaving the virtual environment (Ahn et al., 2016). Communication competency-based scenarios could allow students to actively engage and analyze interpersonal interactions, such as workplace conflict situations, and then apply skills they have learned in class in real time.

In addition to real-life skill application, the IoT and integration of wearable technologies may also facilitate experiential learning outside of the VR/AR context. For example, students could track specific health behaviors in order to conduct personalized data analyses. Similar to using a FitBit, students could log nutrition and exercise habits (see Kurzweil and Baker, 2016) on wearable devices throughout the week and then upload the data to a class database to examine and analyze during class time. This type of data analysis presents an opportunity for students to develop health management plans, and potentially interventions, by targeting the attitudes and behaviors of their specific class and/or create data-driven health promotion campaigns that could address wider college student populations on campus.

The opportunities for more engaged instruction go beyond even that of real-life application and experiential learning. In fact, students may experience improvement in course content understanding if interactive activities incorporate wearable devices and the IoT. The notion of perceptual bandwidth (Reeves and Nass, 2000), within the context of user interaction with web sites, suggests that more interactivity leads to greater user engagement with the site content, which can then increase the amount of information that the user processes, and ultimately retains. Further testing of interactivity in web sites by Xu and Sundar (2016) found that users who experience medium and high levels of interactivity were able to better recall and recognize the information they received through the interactivity. Similarly, as described earlier, student-centered and experiential learning theories suggest that experience and activity is essential for student learning (Kolb, 2015). Thus, research suggests that more interactivity opportunities in the FtF classroom itself, made possible through the IoT and wearable technology, could provide similar outcomes in terms of student engagement with the course content.

CHALLENGES

Though the adoption of wearable technologies in the classroom, supported with the development of the IoT, offers a number of positive educational opportunities, there are also challenges that should be considered before implementation. When speaking on the organizational technology environment, Markus (1987) noted that for new technology adoption in an organization to be successful, it must be adopted by all potential users in the community (i.e., "universal adoption"). Within the context of education, this means that for wearable technologies to be universally adopted, all students must: (1) have access to the technology and (2) actually use the technology for its intended purpose. Achieving a "critical mass" (Markus, 1987) in terms of student use could be challenging primarily because of cost/access, classroom integration, and issues of privacy/security.

Financial cost certainly impacts widespread adoption of wearable technology in the classroom. Depending on how the technology is used, and whether the technology is essential to completing course activities and assessments, the financial cost to students could potentially create an access divide. Evidence exists that suggests a digital divide among students in terms of mobile technology use in K–12 education (Zhang, Trussell, Tillman, and Song, 2015). Further, the use of mobile phones to access the Internet appears strongly related to income (Zhang, 2017). Instructors may have more success implementing technologies students already use (e.g., mobile phones), rather than devices that are more expensive and less likely owned by undergraduate students (e.g., the Apple Watch). However, even when mobile technologies are accessible, critics argue that the Internet capabilities of mobile technologies are substantially less than computers (Napoli and Obar, 2014). Therefore, student access, especially due to financial cost, is a primary, if not the primary, challenge with widespread pedagogical integration of the IoT and wearable technology.

Another challenge in adoption is the face-to-face physical classroom integration of the IoT and wearable technology. Classroom integration primarily concerns appropriate student use of the technology for its intended purpose. A challenge for instructors is ensuring that adoption of any new technologies for the purpose of learning add to the classroom experience, rather than generating a distraction for students. Such concerns are especially salient given widespread student use of mobile devices for non-educational reasons in classrooms (Ledbetter and Finn, 2016). The IoT creates an image of a classroom where all devices are connected. However, pre-existing issues, such as students using mobile technology in class for non-educational purposes, may be exacerbated, challenging adoption of wearable technology and the IoT in the classroom.

Student privacy and data security are important areas to consider as wearables become more popular. The use of a device like Google Glass in an educational context would likely come with increased challenges, especially considering legal issues with student confidentiality. Further, if grades, and other personal student data, are captured through Internet-connected wearable technologies in the classroom, questions will undoubtedly arise concerning how the data is used.

The ownership of data is a looming ethical question (Kurzweil and Baker, 2016). In particular, who owns data that is generated as part of classroom activities (i.e., students, instructors, institutions)? Further, does ownership of data differ whether students are directly connected and identifiable (as with graded assessments), rather than indirectly connected through anonymous personal data uploads as part of a class data set? Relatedly, whose responsibility is it to protect the data? With increasing interest in learning analytics in higher education, questions concerning student privacy/confidentiality, as well as data security/ownership, there are significant challenges to adoption of the IoT and wearable technology in the college classroom.

INFLUENCE

Beyond the challenges of adopting these new platforms in the classroom, once adopted, they have the potential to impact the college classroom in new and unforeseen ways. Certainly, these technologies provide innovative methods to facilitate learning, but they also have the potential to profoundly disrupt the classroom culture, the work that instructors and students do, and the role of the instructor. Thus, in considering the potential influence of these new technologies in the classroom, it is important to temper the excitement of new technology with a sober assessment of both its advantages and disadvantages to the classroom learning community.

Building a cohesive classroom community requires that a sense of belonging, which is associated with stronger learning outcomes, is nurtured among students (Saville, Lawrence, and Jakobsen, 2012). While new technologies like wearables have the potential to energize the classroom by bringing to life the off-campus world and providing students with more opportunities for experiential learning, there is a risk that these technologies will also undermine classroom community. Establishing a sense of community among students and the instructor is important to facilitate a learning experience wherein students feel a sense of connection (Frymier and Houser, 2000; Hill 2002). The introduction of these new technologies may weaken classroom community by transporting students—at least intellectually and emotionally—into another "space" and away from their classmates and instructor. Therefore, while these new technologies pull students "away," instructors must work steadily to anchor students in the classroom context by frequently interjecting class discussion and/or lecture into the experiential activities, thus requiring students to share and engage each other in their learning experiences.

The activity that these new technologies bring into the classroom may also present another instructional challenge: students and faculty may focus more on the experiential aspect of learning to the detriment of critical reflection and theorizing. "Doing" in the classroom—engaging in active learning, especially in a high-arousal context—can be appealing to students because of the novelty. However, good instruction pushes students to achieve higher learning outcomes that build on critical reflection (e.g., Bloom, 1956; Kolb, 2015). Therefore, the introduction of new technologies may emphasize "doing" rather than "thinking"—unless instructors are careful to situate the hands-on learning within a strong theoretical and analytical perspective, as Kolb (2015) suggests.

The integration of advanced technologies within the classroom also runs the risk of shifting the instructor's role to that of technician, overseeing and implementing technology, rather than as a facilitator of learning. Inherent within this instructor role is the obvious requirement that educators be technologically proficient. In light of this expectation, the future of education may be one in which instructors must not only be experts in their subject matter and experts in pedagogy, but also experts in technology use and application. Thus, as in other areas of life, the implementation of technology may serve to complicate rather than simplify the learning environment.

While there are always costs associated with implementing new technologies (financial and otherwise), through careful planning and critical reflection, instructors can mitigate the drawbacks and focus on leveraging the strengths of these tools to support and supplement pedagogy, enhance course curriculum, and benefit student learning. In addition, the interconnectivity of wearables and the IoT can be used to create a new sense of community and connectedness among students and between students and the instructor.

Finally, to alleviate increased burdens on instructors and subsequent effects on the quality of their instruction, institutions should maintain ongoing training and support for instructors to learn new technology. Additionally, institutions should provide tangible support to faculty through increased numbers of IT support, educational tech specialists, course designers, and teaching assistants (TAs). As instructors continue to juggle course content, pedagogy, and technology, these additional support resources are essential for supporting faculty enthusiasm for the integration of new technology in the classroom.

CONCLUSION

Nearly 20 years ago, Postman (1998) suggested that "all technological change is a trade-off" (p. 3). In contemplating the use of new technologies in the classroom, there are obvious pedagogical benefits that may result from wearables and the IoT as tools to facilitate learning. However, as Postman (1998) further suggested, the impact of new technology is ecological. Integrating new technology into the classroom is not a simple, discrete change, rather its impact is broader and more comprehensive. New technologies, and thus new media, will surely provide exciting learning opportunities, but they will also bring with them unique problems and they may ultimately change the culture, community, and student work that occurs in the classroom, in both positive and more challenging ways. However, with technology increasingly integrated into higher education, it is important for instructors to recognize the opportunities that technology provides and consider how they can leverage these tools to support effective pedagogy. Technology is, after all, only a tool and its impact in the classroom should be predicated upon the instructors' imagination and thoughtful planning.

REFERENCES

Abbate, J. (2000). *Inventing the internet.* Cambridge, MA: MIT Press.

Ahn, S. J. G., Bostick, J., Ogle, E., Nowak, K. L., McGillicuddy, K. T., and Bailenson, J. N. (2016). Experiencing nature: Embodying animals in immersive virtual environments increases inclusion of nature in self and involvement with nature. *Journal of Computer-Mediated Communication.* doi: 10.1111/jcc4.12173.

Anderson, L. W., and Krathwohl, D. R. (2001). *A taxonomy for learning, teaching, and assessing: A revision of Bloom's taxonomy of educational objectives*. New York: Longman.

Ashton, K. (2009, June 22). That "Internet of Things" thing. *RFID Journal.* Retrieved from http://www.rfidjournal.com/articles/view?4986.

Atkinson, S., and Curtin, R. (2016, August 8). Connected campus experiences in the age of IoT. *Educause Review.* Retrieved from http://er.educause.edu/articles/2016/8/connected-campus-experiences-in-the-age-of-iot.

Bilton. (2015, February 4). Why Google Glass broke. *The New York Times.* Retrieved from http://www.nytimes.com/2015/02/05/style/why-google-glass-broke.html?_r=1.

Bloom, B. S. (Ed.), Engelhart, M. D., Furst, E. J., Hill, W. H., Krathwohl, D. R. (1956). Taxonomy of educational objectives, Handbook I: *The cognitive domain.* New York: David McKay Co.

Brooks, J. G., and Brooks, M. G. (1999). *The case for constructivist classrooms.* Virginia: Association for Supervision and Curriculum Development.

Dewey. J. (1938). *Experience and education.* New York: Collier Books.

Duke, B., Harper, G., and Johnston, M. (2013). Connectivism as a digital age learning theory. In E. Petrova (Ed.), *The International HETL Review Special Issue, 2013* (pp. 4–13). New York: The International HETL Review.

El-Amrawy, F., and Nounou, M. I. (2015). Are currently available wearable devices for activity tracking and heart rate monitoring accurate, precise, and medically beneficial? *Healthcare Informatics Research, 21*, 315–320. doi: 10.4258/hir.2015.21.4.315.

Fidalgo-Blanco, A. L., Sein-Echaluce, M. L., García-Peñalvo, F. J., and Conde, M. A. (2015). Using Learning Analytics to improve teamwork assessment. *Computers in Human Behavior,* 47,149–156. doi: 10.1016/j.chb.2014.11.050.

Fosnot, C. T. (2005). Preface. In C. T. Fosnot (Ed.), *Constructivism: Theory, perspectives, and practice* (pp. ix–xii). New York: Teachers College Press.

Fosnot, C. T., and Perry, R. S. (2005). Constructivism: A psychological theory of learning. In C. T. Fosnot (Ed.), *Constructivism: Theory, perspectives, and practice* (pp. 8–38). New York: Teachers College Press.

Frymier, A. B., and Houser, M. L. (2000). The teacher-student relationship as an interpersonal relationship. *Communication Education 49*, 207–219. doi: 10.1080/03634520009379209.

Glass. (n.d.) Retrieved from https://www.google.com/glass/start.

Hill, J. R. (2002). Overcoming obstacles and creating connections: Community building in web-based learning environments. *Journal of Computing in Higher Education, 14*(67), 1867–1233. doi: 10.1007/bf02940951.

Hook, R. (1665). *Microfagia: Or some physiological descriptions of minute bodies made by magnifying glasses.* London.

Kolb, A. Y., and Kolb, D. A. (2009). The learning way: Metacognitive aspects of experiential learning. *Simulation & Gaming, 40*, 297–327. doi:10.1177/1046878108325713.

Kolb, A. Y., and Kolb, D. A. (2013). *The Kolb learning style inventory 4.0: A comprehensive guide to the theory, psychometrics, research on validity and educational applications.* Boston, MA: Hay Resources Direct.

Kolb, D. A. (2015). *Experiential learning: Experience as the source of learning and development.* New Jersey: Pearson Education, Inc.

Krahenbuhl, K. S. (2016) Student-centered education and constructivism: Challenges, concerns, and clarity for teachers. *The Clearing House: A Journal of Educational Strategies, Issues and Ideas, 89*, 97–105. doi:10.1080/00098655.2016.1191311.

Krathwohl, D. R., Bloom, B. S., and Masia, B. B. (1964). Taxonomy of educational objectives. The classification of educational goals, Handbook II: Affective domain. New York: David McKay Co.

Kurzweil, D., and Baker, S. (2016, August 8). The Internet of Things for educators and learners. *Educause Review.* Retrieved from http://er.educause.edu/articles/2016/8/the-internet-of-things-for-educators-and-learners.

Ledbetter, A. M., and Finn, A. N. (2016). Why do students use mobile technology for social purposes during class? Modeling teacher credibility, learner empowerment, and online communication attitude as predictors. *Communication Education, 65*, 1–23. doi: 10.1080/03634523.2015.1064145.

Leslie, J. (2016, July 22). Wearable tech sales explored: Just how many devices have been sold? *Wearable: Tech for your connected self.* Retrieved from http://www.wareable.com/wearable-tech/how-many-apple-watches-sold-2016.

Make fitness a lifestyle with flex. (n.d.) Retrieve from https://www.fitbit.com/ca/flex.

Markus, M. L. (1987). Toward a "critical mass" theory of interactive media: Universal access, interdependence and diffusion. *Communication Research, 14*, 491–511. doi: 10.1177/009365087014005003.

Mayer, R. E. (1997) Multimedia learning: Are we asking the right questions? *Educational Psychologist, 32*, 1–19. doi: 10.1207/s15326985ep3201_1.

Mayer, R. E. (2001). *Multimedia learning.* New York: Cambridge University Press.

Mayer, R. E. (2002). Multimedia learning. *Psychology of Learning and Motivation, 41*, 85–139. doi: 10.1016/S0079-7421(02)80005-6.

Mayer, R. E. (2014a). Cognitive theory of multimedia learning. In R. E. Mayer (Ed.), *The Cambridge handbook of multimedia learning* (2nd ed.) (pp. 43–71). New York: Cambridge University Press.

Mayer, R. E. (2014b). Introduction to multimedia learning. In R. E. Mayer (Ed.), *The Cambridge handbook of multimedia learning* (2nd ed.) (pp. 1–24). New York: Cambridge University Press.

Mayer, R. E. (Ed.). (2014c). *The Cambridge handbook of multimedia learning* (2nd ed.). New York: Cambridge University Press.

Mayer, R. E., and Fiorella, L. (2014). Principles for reducing extraneous processing in multimedia learning: Coherence, signaling, redundancy, spatial contiguity, and temporal contiguity principles. In R. E. Mayer (Ed.), *The Cambridge handbook of multimedia learning* (2nd ed.) (pp. 279–315). New York: Cambridge University Press.

Mayer, R. E., Lee, H., and Peebles, A. (2014). Multimedia learning in a second language: A cognitive load perspective. *Applied Cognitive Psychology, 28*, 653–660. doi: 10.1002/acp.3050.

Mayer, R. E., and Moreno, R. (2002). Animation as an aid to multimedia learning. *Educational Psychology Review 145*(1), 87–99.

Miller, L., and Spiegel, A. (2015, February 13). Can a computer change the essence of who you are? *NPR.* Retrieved from http://www.npr.org/sections/health-shots/2015/02/13/385205570/can-a-computer-change-the-essence-of-who-you-are.

Napoli, P. M., and Obar, J. A. (2014). The emerging mobile internet underclass: A critique of mobile internet access. *The Information Society, 30*, 323–334. doi: 10.1080/01972243.2014.944726.

Postman, N. (1998). Five things we need to know about technological change. Address to New Tech98 Conference, Denver, CO, March 27, 1998. Reproduced in P. De Palma (Ed.), *Technologies, social media, and society 12/13* (18th ed.) (pp. 3–6). New York: McGraw Hill.

Reeves, B., and Nass, C. (2000). Perceptual user interfaces: Perceptual bandwidth. *Communications of the ACM, 43*, 65–70. doi: 10.1145/330534.330542.

Rhodes, B. (n.d.). A brief history of wearable computing. Retrieved from http://www.media.mit.edu/wearables/lizzy/timeline.html#1993d.

Rodriguez, J. I., Plax, T. G., and Kearney, P. (1996). Clarifying the relationship between teacher nonverbal immediacy and student cognitive learning: Affective learning as the central cause mediator. *Communication Education 45*, 293–305. doi: 10.1080/03634529609379059.

Saville, B. K., Lawrence, N. K., and Jakobsen, K. V. (2012). Creating learning communities in the classroom. *New Directions for Teaching and Learning, 132*(Winter 2012), 57–69. doi:10.1002/tl.20036.

Schraw, G. (1998). Promoting general metacognitive awareness. *Instructional Science, 26* 113–125. doi: 10.1007/978-94-017-2243-8_1.

Seel, N. M. (Ed.). (2012). Constructivist learning. In *Encyclopedia of the learning sciences*. (pp. 783–786). Boston, MA: Springer US. doi: 10.1007/978-1-4419-1428-6_2096.

Shepherd, K. (2008). Higher education for sustainability: Seeking affective learning outcomes. *International Journal of Sustainability in Higher Education, 9*(1): 87–98. doi: 10.1108/14676370810842201.

Siemens, G. (2005, January). Connectivism: A learning theory for the digital age. *International Journal of Instructional Technology & Distance Learning*. Retrieved from http://www.itdl.org/Journal/Jan_05/article01.htm.

Smith, D. F. (2016, April 18). Could HoloLens' augmented reality change how we study the human body? *EdTech Magazine*. Retrieved from http://www.edtechmagazine.com/higher/article/2016/04/university-testing-limits-hololens-augmented-reality.

Step into the rift. (2015, June 11). Retrieved from https://www3.oculus.com/en-us/blog/the-oculus-rift-oculus-touch-and-vr-games-at-e3/.

Stevens, T. (2013, May 22). Wearable-technology pioneer Thad Starner on how Google Glass could augment our realities and memories. *Engadget*. Retrieved from https://www.engadget.com/2013/05/22/thad-starner-on-google-glass/.

Tobias, S., Fletcher, J. D., Bediou, B., Wind, A. P., Chen, F. (2014). Multimedia learning with computer games. In R. E. Mayer (Ed.), *The Cambridge handbook of multimedia learning* (2nd ed.) (pp. 762–784). New York: Cambridge University Press.

UW Internet of Things Lab. (2016). Internet of Things Lab, University of Wisconsin Madison. Retrieved from http://www.iotlab.wisc.edu/.

Vanderstraeten, R. (2002). Dewey's transactional constructivism. *Journal of Philosophy of Education, 36*(2), 233–246. doi: 10.1111/1467-9752.00272.

Veenman, M. V. J., Van Hout-Wolters, B. H. A. M., and Afflerbach, T. (2006). Metacognition and learning: Conceptual and methodological considerations. *Metacognition and Learning, 1*, 3–14. doi: 10.1007/s11409-006-6893-0 .

Watch: Series 1. (n.d.). Retrieved from http://www.apple.com/apple-watch-series-1/.

Weimer, M. (2002). Learner-centered teaching: Five key changes to practice. San Francisco, CA: Jossey-Bass.

Wright, G. B. (2011). Student-centered learning in higher education. *International Journal of Teaching and Learning in Higher Education, 23*(3), 92–97.

Xu, Q., and Sundar, S. S. (2016). Interactivity and memory: Information processing of interactive versus non-interactive content. *Computer in Human Behavior, 63*, 620–629. doi: 10.1016/j.chb.2016.05.046.

Zhang, M., Trussell, R. P., Tillman, D. A., and Song, A. A. (2015). Tracking the rise of web information needs for mobile education and an emerging trend of digital divide. *Computers in the Schools, 32*, 83–104. doi: 10.1080/07380569.2015.1030531.

Zhang, X. (2017). Exploring the patterns and determinants of the global mobile divide. *Telematics and Informatics, 34*, 438–449. doi: 10.1016/j.tele.2016.06.010.

Chapter Nine

Current Tools and Trends of New Media, Digital Pedagogy, and Instructional Technology

Renee Kaufmann, Nicholas T. Tatum, and T. Kody Frey

TECHNOLOGY USE IN THE CLASSROOM

Exploring the vast options of current tools and technology trends in the educational context not only provides instructors and education professionals the opportunity to reach their students in innovative ways, it also allows for conversation about best practices. Currently, technology for instructional purposes is abundant, but deciding which to use may be overwhelming. Researchers in the fields of instructional communication and education have explored how these technologies not only enhance or hinder the educational experience, but also how these instructional technologies may impact instructor credibility (Schrodt and Witt, 2006), learning outcomes (Young, Klemz, and Murphy, 2003), and even motivation (Weimer, 2001).

Technology may serve as a means for furthering explanation regarding course content and concepts. Buzzard, Crittenden, Crittenden, and McCarty (2011) note that while students may report being satisfied with traditional instructional technologies (e.g., Internet, email), they are also willing to try out new technologies in the classroom. Buzzard and colleagues do caution instructors to not assume students are aware of the tool or even knowledgeable on its appropriate use when experimenting with new technologies and tools. They encourage educators to have a conversation concerning technological support with students and to then create teachable moments with the use of the technology and tools. Therefore, fostering an environment of acceptance and support with technology may help with the adoption of the technology in the classroom.

More recently, Johnson, Jacovina, Russell, and Soto (2016) claim that technology use in the classroom is one of the most prevalent factors in how educators shape the educational experiences for their students, stating that while there are many benefits for technology in the classroom, this charge is not to be met without challenges. They clarify that there are barriers that exist in order for technology use and integration to be successful for both the students and the instructor. Echoing Buzzard and colleagues, Johnson et al. note that support can be a major constraint to whether or not a student uses technology successfully. Further, they note that access and training are equally as constraining to a student's success with technology. Thus, if a student does not understand the technology or have the means necessary to use the technology, then this could impede on the student's learning experience.

Further, Langan et al. (2016) note technology use and integration in the classroom may be a product of the students' expectations to use personal technologies in their learning experience. The assumption that students who are "digital natives" should and could handle all the technologies and tools instructors present them is false; instructors still may need to "educate students on basic digital literacy skills needed at university level" (Leonard, Mokewele, Siebrits, and Stoltenkamp, 2016, p. 33). Otherwise, as Johnson and colleagues suggest, students may not be successful at achieving the goals or outcomes set forth by the instructor.

The use of technologies and tools in the classroom is growing. Creating opportunities for research and discussion regarding appropriate use and implementation of instructional technology as tools for learning is warranted. Thus, this chapter will be an accumulation of the work conducted to explore and test the application of technologies and tools to the classroom. Further, this chapter will discuss the emergence of technology and tools in the classroom as well as review theoretical frameworks for understanding this phenomenon. Finally, this chapter will provide an evaluation of numerous applications of instructional technology.

CURRENT TOOLS AND TRENDS: EMERGENCE AND RESEARCH

Emergence of Technology into the Classroom

Technology is constantly evolving, and as new technologies emerge, educators and researchers alike work to find the balance for use and implementation. While the introduction of technology into the classroom is not a new or novel concept (Strommen and Lincoln, 1992), the quickly emerging possibilities for technological use may hinder educators from learning and implementing strategies that would ensure best practice and application if more time were warranted.

The historical movement of technology as tools in the classroom can be seen as early as 1945 (Saettler, 1968). Some would argue the existence of technologies in the classroom emerged even earlier, claiming "the first educational technology endeavors started at the end of the 1800s with the school museums," and that "technology widely started being used after film, radio and television entered in the vision around the 1920s" (Tozoglu and Varank, 2001, p. 463). At that time, the adoption of radio/audio/visual instruction was due in part to a technological boom in the United States, and from 1945 to 1965, the implementation of instructional technology within the classroom sought to teach and train those for using technology in the workforce (Saettler, 1968). The movement to incorporate technology in the classroom only grew when "in 1994, a challenge was brought to the nation's educators: connect all of your schools to the Internet by the year 2000" (Ezarik, 2001, p. 1). Subsequently, with the integration of technology into schools and universities, also came the expectation that educators would have knowledge regarding appropriate use of instructional technologies, and that they would also instruct students on how to use the technologies (Kim and Bonk, 2006). Further, this expectation was embraced by most, but was not met without caution and confusion by many (Kim and Bonk, 2006).

Currently, technology used in the classroom may serve as an example for future technology use for students. Reiser (1987) explains that in general, technologies and tools are typically viewed in one of two ways: (1) audiovisual or as (2) a "systems approach process," which lends itself to an "individualized instruction" model to aid in instruction (p. 12). Examples of current technology and tool use trends explored in research examine use of video (e.g., web-conferencing; Kaufmann and Frisby, 2013), audio (e.g., podcasts), and blogs (Courts and Tucker, 2012), as well as social media (Frisby, Kaufmann, and Beck, 2016). Learning management systems (LMS) are also considered a technological tool that is used within traditional and mediated classrooms. As noted, technology continues to transform the way instructors deliver content. As this happens, making connections to what we know regarding technology use is vital for the success of the instructor and students.

However, the evolution of technological learning tools in the classroom is more than just a change from using chalkboards to whiteboards to smart boards, it also encompasses how educators access the technology and provide their students with skills necessary for digital literacy. As more technologies enter the classroom, the way educators choose and use technology seems to become more convoluted (Foulger, Buss, Wetzel, and Lindsey, 2015). In fact, Hooper and Rieber (1995) state that too often "in education we have failed to find the right blend of technologies" (p. 160). Thus, relying on theoretical frameworks and research to better understand best practices and implementation of technologies is key.

Theoretical Understandings

Instructional communication and educational scholars have long been interested in understanding the phenomenon of learning coinciding with technology use. Whether it is exploring what enhances or hinders the learning experience or developing models that outline the process of learning with technology, these explanations, from both fields, provide clarification, implications for use, and a trajectory for future research directions. Alavi and Leidner (2001) call for more research that continues to examine how technology and learning outcomes impact course design and even training or support for instructors.

Currently, those who are interested in examining use of technology and tools in the classroom rely on some of the following popular theoretical lens and models as guides: Technological Pedagogical Content Knowledge (TPCK; Koehler, Mishra, and Yahya, 2007), Instructional Beliefs Model (Weber, Martin, and Myers, 2011), and Social Cognitive Theory (Bandura, 1977).

In educational literature, Shulman (1986, 1987) developed a widely used framework for understanding how pedagogy and content coincide, defined as having pedagogical content knowledge (PCK). More recently, instructional technologies and tools have been conceptualized as another construct of knowledge within the classroom for this model (Koehler et al., 2007). This framework, Technological Pedagogical Content Knowledge (TPCK; Koehler et al., 2007), builds upon the constructs presented by Shulman and purported a relationship between knowledge, "content, pedagogy, and technology," further stating that "good teaching with technology requires understanding the mutually reinforcing relationships between all three elements taken together to develop appropriate, context-specific, strategies and representations" (p. 741). The inclusion of technology knowledge into the framework clarifies how technology interacts with content and pedagogy to ensure optimal teaching practice and learning experiences (Mishra and Koehler, 2006). Thompson (2008) coined the term "TPACK"; both TPCK and TPACK represent the same model purported by Mishra and Koehler.

The Information and Communication Technologies–Technological Pedagogical Content Knowledge (ICT–TPCK; Angeli and Valamnides, 2009) extension was created to fill a gap in understandings towards the knowledge of ICT, students or learners, and context to the TPCK framework. The ICT–TPCK serves as an extension to the TPCK framework developed by Koehler et al. (2007), and is a "unique body of knowledge that makes a teacher competent to design technology-enhanced learning," further noting that the ICT–TPCK highlights "the view that technology is not a delivery vehicle that simply delivers information, but a cognitive partner that amplifies or augments student learning" (p. 158). Graham (2011) argues that all the TPCK frameworks still need further building regarding definitions for constructs and encourages researchers to unpack the conflated technology terms (e.g., integration and knowledge).

There is a plethora of research incorporating the TPCK or ICT–TPCK framework. For example, these studies have sought to develop measures (Schmidt et al., 2009) as well as explore teacher knowledge (Cox and Grahman, 2009); incorporation of technology and tools into the classroom (Roblyer, Edwards, and Havriluk, 2002); online learning in K–12 (Archambault and Crippen, 2009); instructor self-efficacy (Graham et al., 2009; Lee and Tsai, 2010); pre-service teacher preparation (Chai, Koh, and Tsai, 2010; Lei, 2009); and wiki technology (Hazari, North, and Moreland, 2009). These studies serve to build on knowledge for how educators should approach implementing technology in the class to impact learning outcomes.

In instructional communication literature, the Instructional Beliefs Model (IBM; Weber, Martin, and Myers, 2011) posits three first-order variables (i.e., instructor behaviors, student characteristics, course-specific structural issues) that contribute to the student's instructional belief (e.g., academic self-efficacy), which in turn impacts the student's perception of certain learning outcomes (e.g., affective and cognitive). This "holistic view" for examining the classroom context has been tested in both the face-to-face (i.e., traditional) and online classroom (Weber et al., 2016, p. 68). Of those studies using IBM, two currently address the use of technology in the classroom context. Kaufmann et al. (2016) explored the online classroom climate using IBM as a theoretical framework, and created a scale that examined what factors contributed to the perception of online climate. Wombacher et al. (2016) examined computer-mediated communication anxiety and its impact on the online learning experience.

Social Cognitive Theory (SCT; Bandura, 1977) helps to explain how certain educational behaviors are adopted and modeled. One of the components of SCT, Bandura explains, is self-efficacy. Bandura defines self-efficacy as the "capability in which cognitive, social and behavioral sub-skills must be organized into integrated courses of action to serve innumerable purpose" (Bandura, 1982, p. 391); simply, self-efficacy is how one views his or her own belief or ability in accomplishing a behavior. Studies that use SCT as a theoretical framework tend to explore the impact of one's perception of ability with technology. For example, topics range from technology acceptance from instructors (Gu, Zhu, and Guo, 2013); technology acceptance from students (Goh, Tang, and Lim, 2016); technology rejection (Rosen, 2005); integration of social media (Westerman, Daniel, and Bowman, 2016); technology integration (Hur, Shannon, and Wolf, 2016; Weber and

Waxman, 2015); and students' reactions towards technology (Chung, and Ackerman, 2015). These studies provide deeper understanding regarding instructors' and students' beliefs for technology in the classroom.

Notably, other theories such as social presence theory (Short, Williams, and Christie, 1976) have explored how technology helps to foster presence in mediated contexts (Gunawardena, 1995), media richness theory (Daft and Lengel, 1986) to explore student interactions and technology acceptance (Balaji and Chakrabarti, 2010; Liu, Liao, and Pratt, 2009), and theory of planned behavior (Ajzen, 1991) to explore technology adoption and use by instructors (Salleh, 2016). All in all, these theoretical frameworks have served as lenses for investigating technology and tool use in classroom contexts.

Theory and Research Informing Trends

The theories and research outlined above provide a framework for understanding how technological tool trends may impact certain outcomes for students and instructors. Currently, instructional communication and education are investigating how these technologies and tools impact outcomes like technology adoption, learning content, affect for course or instructor, credibility, and even motivation. Based on the theories discussed, the next section of this chapter will summarize selected studies and will provide the implications for practical use for the classroom.

CURRENT TOOLS AND TRENDS: APPLICATION AND INFLUENCE

Before reviewing current tools and trends in new media, digital pedagogy, and instructional technology, two important clarifications must be made. First, when incorporating new technology into the instructional process, it is not the tool itself, but rather the instructional rationale necessitating the tool, that should drive adoption (Frisby, Kaufmann, and Beck, 2016). Technology for technology's sake is futile, but utilizing technology to reach instructional goals is vital. Thus, when considering incorporating tools as suggested below, the authors encourage readers to evaluate tools based on potential instructional outcomes, not simply on novelty. Second, the lifespan of any given tool is short; what may be innovative and effective today may quickly become archaic and inadequate tomorrow. Because of this, the content herein offers a snapshot of technology commonly used in today's classrooms, as the relevant longevity or future usefulness of these technologies is unknown. Four major instructional technology tools are explored: mobile technology, social media, learning management systems, and gaming. For each, considerations for incorporating each technology, along with possible classroom applications, are elucidated.

Mobile Technology

Advances in wireless Internet services over the past two decades have allowed mobile technologies to permeate everyday settings (Lu, Yao, and Yu, 2005), including the classroom. It is not the capacity to connect to the Internet that makes the influence of mobile technology powerful, but rather the "everywhere and at any time" communication capabilities they enable (Liccope, 2004, p. 152). The proliferation of mobile technology provides numerous opportunities to support learning both inside and outside the classroom. However, it is important to first draw a distinction between students' non-instructional and instructional use of technology.

Non-instructional technology use describes utilization of mobile technology for purposes outside a classroom's academic goals, and is often seen as a form of student incivility (Bjorklund and Rehling, 2009; Feldmann, 2001). This is often, but not always, socially motivated (Ledbetter and Finn, 2016; Smith, Rainie, and Zickuhr, 2011). Non-instructional technology use has garnered increased attention, as such use may distract students from fully engaging in the learning environment, resulting in lower levels of cognitive learning or reduced final course grades (Kraushaar and Novak, 2010; Kuznekoff and Titsworth, 2013; Kuznekoff, Munz, and Titsworth, 2015; Wei, Wang, and Klausner, 2012). As such, researchers and instructors alike are concerned with the role that classroom technology policies play in curbing this potentially detrimental behavior (Finn and Ledbetter, 2013; Ledbetter and Finn, 2013, 2016).

Contrarily, *instructional* technology use describes students' utilization of mobile technology for instructional, learning-oriented purposes, and is either self-motivated (i.e., independently using mobile technology to further learning) or instructor directed (i.e., using mobile technology as directed by the instructor; e.g., Gulek and Demirtas, 2005). For instance, students may use their devices to take notes, search the Internet for relevant information, or access their course's learning management system (Mandinach and Jackson, 2012).

Instructional Considerations

Before choosing to incorporate mobile technology into the classroom for instructional purposes, several considerations must be highlighted. First, it is naive to assume all students have regular access to various forms of mobile technology. Thus, by requiring the use of particular mobile technologies within the classroom, some students may be disadvantaged or embarrassed. Because of this, before choosing to incorporate mobile technology into the classroom, (a) ensure all students have access to mobile devices or (b) provide mobile devices for all students to use. Second, utilizing various software or platforms for mobile technology integration is relatively ineffectual unless compatible across multiple operating systems; because the mobile technology market is growing exponentially diverse, students may enter the classroom with an array of devices with varying capabilities. With this in mind, ensure your desired utilization of mobile technology works on a variety of operating systems (e.g., IOS, Android OS, BlackBerry OS). Third, because it is difficult, if not impossible, to fully monitor student's activity on personal devices, incorporating mobile technology into instruction further enables students to utilize that time for non-instructional purposes, introducing more possibility for digital distraction. Finally, the effective use of any wireless technology, particularly mobile technology, is dependent on secure, reliable Internet connection. While this is a practical barrier, poor connectivity is often mentioned as a source of concern when utilizing mobile technology for instructional purposes (Stowell, Tanner, and Tomasino, 2015).

Classroom Application

Mobile technology has increasingly been used in place of "clickers" to gain real-time student responses during class (Stowell, 2015). In fact, recent research suggests students prefer mobile devices over clickers for engaging with their instructor during class (Koppen et al., 2013; Tao et al., 2010). Using mobile phones as a student response system has shown to cultivate instructor-student interactivity, improve academic performance, and increase student engagement (for a review, see Aljaloud, Gromik, Billingsley, and Kwan, 2015). However, unlike clickers, using mobile technology for polling is relatively inexpensive, allows for more open-ended responses, and can be used by multiple instructors simultaneously (Stowell, 2015). These inherent advantages, along with the increasingly ubiquitous and affordable nature of this technology, forecast that using mobile technology to elicit real-time student responses during class will continue to surpass, if not potentially abolish, the use of clickers in instruction.

The pedagogical embracement of "here and now learning" is largely attributed to the ubiquity of mobile technology. Here and now learning occurs when learners have access to information anytime and anywhere to engage in authentic activities to promote learning in specific contexts (Martin and Ertzberger, 2013). Centered on the idea that learning occurs naturally through activities, contexts, and cultures (Lave, 1988), mobile technology enables students to be in the context of learning while simultaneously having access to information related to what they are experiencing. For instance, when visiting a museum, students could employ mobile technology to find relevant, supplemental information about works of art to further enrich their experience (e.g., Martin and Ertzberger, 2013). Or, students may utilize mobile technology as a just-in-time research and organization tool when engaging new concepts in a science classroom (e.g., Looi et al., 2014). Evidence from these examples, along with others, suggest here and now learning enabled by mobile technology helps cultivate students' engagement and agency, but may distract learners if the novelty of usage is too unexpected.

Finally, practitioners suggest mobile technology plays an increasingly important function in language acquisition. Importantly, research suggests non-native speakers often prefer utilizing mobile technology over other forms of technology when acquiring a new language because of their familiarity with the platform (Thornton and Houser, 2003), the manageability of content due to screen size (Chen and Hsieh, 2008), and the relatively inexpensive, but powerful, capabilities offered (Chinnery, 2006). Reinders (2010) offered a succinct summary of potential uses for mobile phones in the language classroom. Several notable classroom applications include using the picture function to capture foreign text in everyday settings, using memo features to record language from everyday conversations or from media outlets, or using mobile technology to connect with native speakers to improve fluency. Moreover, mobile technology and social media deem to be two popular choices for technology use in the classroom by instructors and students.

Social Media

The exponential growth of social media is unprecedented (Lenhart, Purcell, Smith, and Zickuhr, 2010). Broadly, social media is defined as any number of technological systems related to collaboration and community (Joosten, 2012), and is often best described through enumeration. As Tess (2013) explained, "the task of defining social media is made more challenging by the fact that it is constantly in a state of change" (p. A61), as new platforms emerge regularly and functionality of current platforms is constantly adapting. While seemingly commonplace in everyday life, social media, and subsequent research investigating its usage, has invaded educational settings. Each social media platform offers varying features and tools. These individualities have been described as technological affordances (e.g., Idris and Wang, 2009), or unique technological capabilities, and these affordances shape how and why various types of social media may be used in the classroom.

When using social media in the classroom, one should consider the purpose for implementing the tool. Selwyn (2010) forwarded three major purposes for incorporating social media use into classroom settings. First, today's students are often highly connected, collective, and creative, and social media provides an appropriate outlet to meet these needs. The technologically dependent culture college students inhabit necessitates avenues to allow students to continuously stay in contact with one's social network (Hall and Baym, 2012). Second, as institutions have begun to deemphasize institutionally driven learning to accentuate user-driven education, social media provides an appropriate outlet for real-world application of knowledge. Third, today's students have a changing relationship with knowledge construction, consumption, and learning, perhaps largely fueled by their habitual use of technology from a young age (Buckingham, 2013).

Instructional Considerations

When choosing to incorporate social media into instruction, several factors should be considered. First, providing a social media platform for free student expression of opinions and ideas is not for the faint at heart (Young, 2010). The familiarity of students with these platforms often mixed with some level of anonymity may embolden students to provide shocking opinions, off-topic responses, or simply too much personal information. Second, as using social media is inherently a social endeavor, instructors should be aware of the potential relational impacts their interaction can have on student's perceptions of teaching, especially because students may have access to instructors' private information (i.e., self-disclosure; Mazer, Murphy, and Simonds, 2007). Third, while students may use social media in their personal lives, one must consider this may not necessarily mean they enjoy or expect these platforms to be utilized for pedagogical purposes. Finally, Flanigan and Babchuk (2015) equated students' use of social media to academic quicksand, such that its usage by students during instruction may cause diminished learning outcomes or lessened classroom engagement. As such, instructors should incorporate social media into the classroom warily given students' magnetic connection to using various platforms for non-instructional, distracting purposes (Fewkes and McCabe, 2012).

Classroom Applications

The possible applications for social media in the classroom are numerous and diverse. Particularly, an instructor may choose to implement social media if it has a direct connection to the content of a specific course. For instance, incorporating LinkedIn's professional social media platform into a business or professional communication class may offer direct connections to relevant course outcomes. LinkedIn has proven essential in developing student skills related to cultivating professional presence (Slone and Gaffney, 2016) or implementing personal or corporate branding techniques (McCorkle and McCorkle, 2012). Similarly, incorporating social media platforms that regularly disseminate up-to-date news (e.g., Twitter; see Kwak, Lee, Park, and Moon, 2010) relates well to courses pertaining to broadcasting and current events. Particularly, Twitter is an effective platform for exploring how various news outlets may present stories using different angles or with different agendas (Frey, Tatum, and Beck, In Press).

Because of the inherent connectivity afforded by social media, various platforms also promote effective group work among students. Facebook often serves as a formal (e.g., facilitate group project meetings) or informal (e.g., plan study sessions) avenue for students to engage in collaborative classroom activities (Lampe, Wohn, Vitak, Ellison, and Wash, 2011). Recently, Frisby, Kaufmann, and Beck (2016) longitudinally examined the influences of video chatting, Twitter, and Facebook on group development. While their findings supported the critical role that these tools played in enhancing a group's relational connections, these tools proved less helpful in aiding students in accomplishing assigned tasks. Additional research confirms this finding, advising instructors to be wary of student non-productivity on this platform, as student report that Facebook often becomes "more for socializing and talking to friends about work than for actually doing work" (Madge, Meek, Wellens, and Hooley, 2009, p. 141). So, in these instances, while Facebook may have improved students' perceptions of classroom connectedness (Dwyer et al., 2004) or even online classroom climate (Kaufmann, Sellnow, and Frisby, 2015), the platform itself may not have directly impacted student learning outcomes.

Finally, social media is useful in reinforcing classroom content in a relevant way. Outside of the classroom, instructors often use social media platforms to remind students of pertinent topics related to class (Manzo, 2009). For example, Blessing, Blessing, and Fleck (2012) utilized Twitter to broadcast informative "tweets" to students on a regular basis related to course content. As a result, students reported increased memory and performance concerned with this content in test situations. Supplementing course curriculum with social media in this way likely increases content relevance, thus enhancing students' motivation to engage in the endeavor of the learning (Frymier and Shulman, 1995).

Learning Management Systems

Lonn and Teasley (2009) define Learning Management Systems (LMS) as "web-based systems [that] allow instructors and students to share instructional materials, make class announcements, submit and return course assignments, and communicate with each other online" (p. 686). While the development of new technology and resources has since added more affordances of various LMS, the nature of the technology remains the same: the LMS is the integrative framework that facilitates all aspects of the learning process (Watson and Watson, 2007). LMS are used at universities across the globe and serve an integral role in supporting the teaching and learning process (Coates, James, and Baldwin, 2005). In response to this sweeping trend, it is important that scholars practically consider the advantages and disadvantages of integrating complex LMS frameworks into existing learning structures.

Numerous research studies have emerged analyzing the adoption and use of LMS by university faculty and administrators. For example, Walker, Lindner, Murphrey, and Dooley (2016) collected open-ended responses from faculty members regarding the benefits and hindrances of using LMS to supplement teaching. The results suggested that faculty perceived an equal number of negative features as they did positive features in their newly adopted LMS. Furthermore, Weaver, Spratt, and Nair (2008) found that 70 percent of academic staff participating in a survey experienced problems with the university's LMS. Clearly, the rapid growth and adoption of such technology may be clouded by the persistence of faculty resistance to technology and issues with seamless integration by university staff.

Aside from faculty perceptions, research on LMS have also considered student perceptions of similar systems. Based on behavioral documentation from the actual LMS, Lonn and Teasley (2009) concluded students associated more value with document and communication management tools of LMS (e.g., announcement, assignments, modules) in comparison to interactive tools and features (e.g., discussion boards, chat, group pages). McGill and Klobas (2009) highlighted other potential benefits of LMS for students, claiming that perceptions of task-technology fit, or "the ability of the LMS to support students in the range of learning activities they engage in, whilst accommodating the variety of student abilities," played an important role in students' perceived utilization and success of LMS (p. 497). LMS may even play an important role in future assessment and analyzation of student behaviors and characteristics at the administrative level. Young (2016) suggested that the companies supporting and developing LMS software (e.g., Blackboard) may be using data obtained through various platforms to obtain large-scale data sets related to student learning, engagement, and behavior. While these results depict only a slice of the research concerning LMS in higher education, there are clear implications for both faculty and students that warrant strategies for integrating LMS successfully into the classroom context.

Instructional Considerations

Ultimately, the instructional considerations in the context of an LMS depend on the affordances offered by a particular platform. Salter (2016) outlines five general tips for facilitating a student-centered approach to the utilization of LMS across various programs: (1) Include a guide for use, (2) Use LMS sections consistently, (3) Be careful of redundancy, (4) Watch for relics of past semesters, and (5) Consider suggesting a schedule, even for flexible material. Moreover, Marshall, Mandiangu, and Venter (2015) offer an integrative framework for evaluating the type of LMS best suited for specific learning tasks. It is also imperative for instructors to ensure that their students become involved in using LMS as a supplement to learning. Klobas and McGill (2010) found that increased student involvement led to increased perceived benefits of LMS use for students; however, instructors' involvement within the LMS played an essential role in persuading students to engage with the system appropriately.

Classroom Application

Clearly, LMS serve various purposes and allow for a multiplicity of pedagogical functions in an instructional context. Some LMS platforms now include integrative technology that links to outside features or software, highlighting the malleability of LMS in the current higher educational context. As such, LMS are constantly changing and presenting new opportunities for application. For instance, Azmi and Singh (2015) used Microsoft SharePoint technology to introduce game-based concepts into their LMS system, providing students with auxiliary rewards for engagement with the technology. Wang, Woo, Quek, Yang, and Liu (2012) adopted Facebook as an LMS, reiterating the loose definition of the concept and dependence on technological affordances for organization and facilitation. Even as more and more LMS begin to hit the market, there will be room for new features that shape the process of classroom instruction to an even greater extent. Thus, researchers in fields like communication, information technology, and social psychology should concentrate on research concerning LMS to ensure that both students and faculty remained engaged, informed, and satisfied with their respective platforms.

Gaming

Scholars of both education and instruction have demonstrated an increased interest in using games as a form of pedagogy (Backlund and Hendrix, 2013). In fact, Sellnow et al. (2015) argued that "understanding how games can be used effectively in the teaching and learning process will be a key area of research for years to come" (p. 425). However, due to conflicting findings and methodological limitations of game-based research (Hainey, Connolly, Boyle, Wilson, and Razak, 2016; Ke, 2009), researchers should turn their attention towards more theory-guided approaches that illuminate the effects of gaming on cognitive processes (Limperos, Downs, Ivory, and Bowman, 2013).

In a review of the foundations of game-based learning, Plass, Homer, and Kinzer (2015) introduced four theoretically grounded areas that point to the effectiveness of games within learning environments. First, games possess an inherent motivational function that may lead students to enjoy prolonged engagement with specific features (Gee, 2003). Second, the design characteristics within certain games allow for students to engage themselves with learning content in a variety of ways. Third, the existing research on *gamification* suggests that games can be developed or adapted to meet students' learning needs (Azevedo, Cromley, Moos, Greene, and Winters, 2011). Fourth, gaming may enhance the learning environment through *graceful failure.* The lower consequences of failure in game-based learning encourage risk taking and self-regulated learning; students who fail may be driven to play until they achieve success within a comfortable, non-threatening learning context (Hoffman and Nadelson, 2010). Because empirical evidence for each perspective is still scarce (Plass et al., 2015), instructors should practically evaluate the design of their games through specific theoretical frameworks before making the decision to integrate games into their pedagogy.

Instructional Considerations

Echeverría et al. (2011) forwarded a two-dimensional framework guiding the development and integration of games into the classroom setting. Essentially, game-based pedagogy centers on *educational* and *ludic* dimensions. Within the educational dimension, game designers should consider the learning outcomes associated with the knowledge and cognitive process dimensions of Bloom's Revised Taxonomy (Anderson, Krathwohl, Bloom, 2001). Specific game mechanics designed to stimulate the cognitive process categories may include repetitive tasks with supplementary rewards, observations of desired processes, or activities allowing students to modify or correct existing objects (Echeverría et al., 2011). At the same time, additional characteristics of the game geared towards the knowledge dimension must have the appearance of explicit facts as content to be visualized, forced exploration of procedures associated with the desired knowledge, and long-term strategies for reoccurring action (Echeverría et al., 2011). Second, while the educational dimension defines the pedagogical structure within the game (Echeverría et al., 2011), the ludic dimension is concerned with the actual elements of the game itself. The researchers draw upon Schell's (2008) suggestion that four elements comprise this dimension: mechanics, story, aesthetics, and technology. Game designers must take extra caution to evaluate the constraints placed on the game design elements by the overarching pedagogical goals. Ultimately, through applied theoretical frameworks such as the one presented herein, the research on the effects of gaming in the classroom continues.

Classroom Application

An immense variety of educationally based games have been applied to the classroom setting across communication, social psychology, education, and health research. From teaching geriatric house calls to medical students (Duque, Fung, Mallet, Posel, and Fleiszer, 2008), to learning about United States constitutional amendments (Lee, Heeter, Magerko, and Medler, 2012), games clearly serve a variety of pedagogical purposes. For example, *Second Life* is one of the most popular virtual reality games available, and has been used extensively as a tool for classroom pedagogy (Wang and Burton, 2012; Warburton, 2009). *Second Life* allows students to virtually immerse themselves in a shared space with multiple users, embody the physical persona through an avatar, and experience real-time interactions over lengthy geographic distances (Smart, Cascio, and Paffendor, 2007). Moreover, Wang and Burton (2013) provide an extensive review of the various approaches researchers have undertaken in developing *Second Life* as a pedagogical tool, including the potential for supporting learning and example courses taught through the system. Clearly, as the game-based learning industry continues to grow and evolve, more nuanced, parsimonious technologies should eventually develop, making game-based learning a viable area of research for the future.

CONCLUSION

Using technology in the classroom has its benefits and challenges. We caution instructors and education professionals to consider the following questions based on research and theory presented in this chapter. Posing these questions to oneself should take place before the technology is adopted and implemented into the course.

First, consider audience. Is the technology something that will need to be taught to your specific audience? Is the technology readily accessible to your specific audience? Second, consider time. Will this technology require more time on behalf of me or my students? Is that time toward the technology use appropriate and efficient? Finally, consider overall impact: How will using the technology hinder or enhance the learning of the content for my specific audience? Does using this technology clarify the content? Does this technology encourage engagement? Asking yourself these questions and considering what we know based on research can help provide a stronger argument for which technologies should be implemented in the classroom. This will also provide a rationale to students regarding why and how you decide to use instructional technology.

REFERENCES

Ajzen, I. (1991). The theory of planned behavior. *Organizational Behavior and Human Decision Processes, 50*, 179–211. doi:10.1016/0749-5978(91)90020-T.

Alavi, M., and Leidner, D. E. (2001). Research commentary: Technology-mediated learning—A call for greater depth and breadth of research. *Information Systems Research*, *12*(1), 1–10. doi:10.1287/isre.12.1.1.9720.

Aljaloud, A., Gromik, N., Billingsley, W., and Kwan, P. (2015). Research trends in student response systems: A literature review. *International Journal of Learning Technology*, *10*, 313–325. doi:10.1504/IJLT.2015.074073.

Anderson, L. W., Krathwohl, D. R., Bloom, B. S. (2001). *A taxonomy for learning, teaching, and assessing: A revision of Bloom's taxonomy of educational objectives*. New York, NY: Longman.

Archambault, L., and Crippen, K. (2009). Examining TPACK among K-12 online distance educators in the United States. *Contemporary Issues in Technology and Teacher Education*, *9*, 71–88.

Azevedo, R., Cromley, J. G., Moos, D. C., Greene, J. A., and Winters, F. I. (2011). Adaptive content and process scaffolding: A key to facilitating students' self-regulated learning with hypermedia. *Psychological Testing and Assessment Modeling*, *53*, 106–140.

Azmi, M. A., and Singh, D. (2015). Schoolcube: Gamification for learning management system through Microsoft Sharepoint. *International Journal of Computer Games Technology*, *2015*, 1–5. doi:10.1155/2015/589180.

Backlund, P., and Hendrix, M. (2013, September). *Educational games—Are they worth the effort?: A literature survey of the effectiveness of serious games*. Paper presented at the Games and Virtual Worlds for Serious Applications Conference, Poole, England.

Balaji, M. S., and Chakrabarti, D. (2010). Student interactions in online discussion forum: Empirical research from "media richness theory" perspective. *Journal of Interactive Online Learning*, *9*(1), 1–22.

Bjorklund, W. L., and Rehling, D. L. (2009). Student perceptions of classroom incivility. *College Teaching*, *58*, 15–18. doi:10.1080/87567550903252801.

Blessing, S. B., Blessing, J. S., and Fleck, B. K. (2012). Using Twitter to reinforce classroom concepts. *Teaching of Psychology*, *39*(4), 268–271. doi:10.1177/0098628312461484.

Buckingham, D. (2013). *Beyond technology: Children's learning in the age of digital culture*. Malden, MA: Polity.

Buzzard, C., Crittenden, V. L., Crittenden, W. F., and McCarty, P. (2011). The use of digital technologies in the classroom: A teaching and learning perspective. *Journal of Marketing Education*, *33*(2), 131–139. doi:10.1177/0273475311410845.

Chai, C. S., Koh, J. H. L., and Tsai, C. C. (2010). Facilitating preservice teachers' development of technological, pedagogical, and content knowledge (TPACK). *Educational Technology & Society*, *13*, 63–73.

Chen, N. S., and Hsieh, S. W. (2008). Effects of short-term memory and content representation type on mobile language learning. *Language Learning and Technology*, *12*(3), 93–113.

Chinnery, G. M. (2006). Emerging technologies: Going to the MALL (Mobile Assisted Language Learning). *Language Learning and Technology*, *10*(1), 9–16. doi:10.1080/03634523.2012.72513.

Chung, C., and Ackerman, D. (2015). Student reactions to classroom management technology: Learning styles and attitudes toward Moodle. *Journal of Education for Business*, *90*, 217–223. doi:10.1080/08832323.2015.1019818.

Coates, H., James, R., and Baldwin, G. (2005). A critical examination of the effects of learning management systems on university teaching and learning. *Tertiary Education and Management*, *11*, 19–36. doi:10.1007/s11233-004-3567-9.

Courts, B., and Tucker, J. (2012). Using technology to create a dynamic classroom experience. *Journal of College Teaching & Learning*, *9*, 121–127.

Cox, S., and Graham, C. R. (2009). Using an elaborated model of the TPACK framework to analyze and depict teacher knowledge. *TechTrends*, *53*(5), 60–69. doi:10.5176/2251-2195_CSEIT15.31.

Daft, R. L., and Lengel, R. H. (1986). Organizational information requirements, media richness, and structural design. *Management Science*, *32*, 554–571. doi:10.1287/mnsc.32.5.554.

Duque, G., Fung, S., Mallet, L., Posel, N., and Fleiszer, D. (2008). Learning while having fun: The use of video gaming to teach geriatric house calls to medical students. *Journal of the American Geriatrics Society*, *56*, 1328–1332. doi:10.1111/j.1532-5415.2008.01759.x.

Dwyer, K. K., Bingham, S. G., Carlson, R. E., Prisbell, M., Cruz, A. M., and Fus, D. A. (2004). Communication and connectedness in the classroom: Development of the connected classroom climate inventory. *Communication Research Reports, 21*, 264–272. doi: 10.1080/08824090409359988.

Echeverría, A., García-Campo, C., Nussbaum, M., Gil, F., Villalta, M., Améstica, M., and Echeverría, S. (2011). A framework for the design and integration of collaborative classroom games. *Computers & Education, 57*, 1127–1136. doi: 10.1016/j.compedu.2010.12.010.

Ezarik, M. (2001). Charting the technology explosion. *Curriculum Administrator, 37*, 36–41.

Feldmann, L. J. (2001). Classroom civility is another of our instructor responsibilities. *College Teaching, 49*, 137–140. doi:10.1080/87567555.2001.10844595.

Fewkes, A. M., and McCabe, M. (2012). Facebook: Learning tool or distraction? *Journal of Digital Learning in Teacher Education, 28*(3), 92–98. doi: 10.1080/21532974.2012.10784686.

Finn, A. N., and Ledbetter, A. M. (2013). Teacher power mediates the effects of technology policies on teacher credibility. *Communication Education, 62*, 26–47. doi: 10.1080/03634523.2012.725132.

Finn, A. N., and Ledbetter, A. M. (2014). Teacher verbal aggressiveness and credibility mediate the relationship between teacher technology policies and perceived student learning. *Communication Education, 63*, 210–234. doi:10.1080/03634523.2014.919009.

Flanigan, A. E., and Babchuk, W. A. (2015). Social media as academic quicksand: A phenomenological study of student experiences in and out of the classroom. *Learning and Individual Differences, 44*, 40–45. doi:10.1016/j.lindif.2015.11.003.

Foulger, T. S., Buss, R. R., Wetzel, K., and Lindsey, L. (2015). Instructors' growth in TPACK: Teaching technology-infused methods courses to preservice teachers. *Journal of Digital Learning in Teacher Education, 31*(4), 134–147. doi: 10.1080/21532974.2015.1055010.

Frey, T. K., Tatum, N. T., and Beck, A. C. (In Press). Is it really JUST Twitter!?: Agenda setting in social media. *G.I.F.T.S. Collection*. Bedford/St. Martin.

Frisby, B. N., Kaufmann, R., and Beck, A. C. (2016). Mediated group development and dynamics: An examination of video chatting, Twitter, and Facebook in group assignments. *Communication Teacher, 30*, 215–227. doi:10.1080/17404622.2016.1219038.

Frymier, A. B., and Shulman, G. M. (1995). "What's in it for me?": Increasing content relevance to enhance students' motivation. *Communication Education, 44*, 40–50. doi: 10.1080/03634529509378996.

Gee, J. P. (2003). *What video games have to teach us about learning and literacy*. New York, NY: Palgrave Macmillan.

Goh, W. W., Tang, S. F., and Lim, C. L. (2016). Assessing factors affecting students' acceptance and usage of X-Space based on UTAUT2 model. In S. F. Tang and L. Logonnathan (Eds.), *Assessment for learning within and beyond the classroom: Taylor's 8th Teaching and Learning Conference 2015 proceedings* (pp. 61–70). Singapore: Springer Singapore.

Graham, C. R. (2011). Theoretical considerations for understanding technological pedagogical content knowledge (TPACK). *Computers & Education, 57*, 1953–1960. doi: 10.1016/j.compedu.2011.04.010.

Graham, R. C., Burgoyne, N., Cantrell, P., Smith, L., St Clair, L., and Harris, R. (2009). Measuring the TPACK confidence of inservice science teachers. *TechTrends, 53*, 70–79.

Gu, X., Zhu, Y., and Guo, X. (2013). Meeting the "digital natives": Understanding the acceptance of technology in classrooms. *Educational Technology & Society, 16*(1), 392–402.

Gulek, J. C., and Demirtas, H. (2005). Learning with technology: The impact of laptop use on student achievement. *The Journal of Technology, Learning and Assessment, 3*(2), 4–38.

Gunawardena, C. N. (1995). Social presence theory and implications for interaction collaborative learning in computer conferences. *International Journal of Educational Telecommunications, 1*(2/3), 147–166.

Hainey, T., Connolly, T. M., Boyle, E. A., Wilson, A., and Razak, A. (2016). A systematic literature review of games-based learning empirical evidence in primary education. *Computers & Education, 102*, 202–223. doi:10.1016/j.compedu.2016.09.001.

Hall, J. A., and Baym, N. K. (2012). Calling and texting (too much): Mobile maintenance expectations, (over)dependence, entrapment, and friendship satisfaction. *New Media & Society, 14*, 316–331. doi:10.1177/1461444811415047.

Hazari, S., North, A., and Moreland, D. (2009). Investigating pedagogical value of wiki technology. *Journal of Information Systems Education*, *20*(2), 187–198.

Hoffman, B., and Nadelson, L. (2010). Motivational engagement and video gaming: A mixed methods study. *Educational Technology Research and Development*, *58*, 245–270. doi:10.1007/s11423-009-9134-9.

Hooper, S., and Rieber, L. P. (1995). Teaching with technology. In A. C. Ornstein (Ed.), *Teaching: Theory into practice* (pp. 154–170). Needham Heights, MA: Allyn and Bacon.

Hur, J. W., Shannon, D., and Wolf, S. (2016). An investigation of relationships between internal and external factors affecting technology integration in classrooms. *Journal of Digital Learning in Teacher Education*, *32*(3), 105–114. doi:10.1080/21532974.2016.1169959.

Idris, Y., and Wang, Q. (2009). Affordances of Facebook for learning. *International Journal of Continuing Engineering Education and Life Long Learning*, *19*(2–3), 247–255.

Johnson, A. M., Jacovina, M. E., Russell, D. G., and Soto, C. M. (2016). Challenges and solutions when using technologies in the classroom. In S. A. Crossley and D. S. McNamara (Eds.), *Adaptive educational technologies for literacy instruction* (pp. 13–30). New York, NY: Routledge.

Joosten, T. (2012). *Social media for educators: Strategies and best practices*. Hoboken, NJ: Jossey-Bass.

Kaufman, R., and Frisby, B. N. (2013). Let's connect: Using Adobe Connect to foster group collaboration. *Communication Teacher*, *27*, 230–234.

Kaufmann, R., Sellnow, D. D., and Frisby, B. N. (2016). The development and validation of the online learning climate scale (OLCS). *Communication Education*, *65*(3), 307–321.

Ke, F. (2009). A qualitative meta-analysis of computer game as learning tools. In R. E. Ferdig (Ed.). *Handbook of research on effective electronic gaming in education* (Vol. 4, pp. 1–32). New York, NY: IGI Global.

Kim, K. J., and Bonk, C. J. (2006). The future of online teaching and learning in higher education. *Educause quarterly*, *29*(4), 22–30.

Klobas, J. E., and McGill, T. J. (2010). The role of involvement in learning management system success. *Journal of Computing in Higher Education*, *22*, 114–134. doi:10.1007/s12528-010-9032-5.

Koehler, M. J., Mishra P., and Yahya, K. (2007). Tracing the development of teacher knowledge in a design seminar: Integrating content, pedagogy, and technology. *Computers & Education*, *49*, 740–762. doi:10.1016/j.compedu.2005.11.012.

Koppen, E., Langie, G., and Bergervoet, B. (2013). Replacement of a clicker system by a mobile device audience response system. In *Proceeding of the 41st SEFI Conference*, Leuven, Belgium. Retrieved from http://www.kuleuven.be/communicatie/congresbureau/congres/sefi2013/eproceedings/28.pdf.

Kraushaar, J. M., and Novak, D. C. (2010). Examining the effects of student multitasking with laptops during the lecture. *Journal of Information Systems Education*, *21*, 241–251.

Kuznekoff, J. H., and Titsworth, S. (2013). The impact of mobile phone usage on student learning. *Communication Education*, *62*, 233–252. doi:10.1080/03634523.2013.767917.

Kuznekoff, J. H., Munz, S., and Titsworth, S. (2015). Mobile phones in the classroom: Examining the effects of texting, twitter, and message content on student learning. *Communication Education*, *64*, 344–365. doi:10.1080/03634523.2015.1038727.

Kwak, H., Lee, C., Park, H., and Moon, S. (2010, April). What is Twitter, a social network or a news media? In *Proceedings of the 19th World-Wide Web (WWW) Conference*, Raleigh, North Carolina.

Lampe, C., Wohn, D. Y., Vitak, J., Ellison, N. B., and Wash, R. (2011). Student use of Facebook for organizing collaborative classroom activities. *International Journal of Computer-Supported Collaborative Learning*, *6*, 329–347. doi:10.1007/s11412-011-9115-y.

Langan, D., Schott, N., Wykes, T., Szeto, J., Kolpin, S., Lopez, C., and Smith, N. (2016). Students' use of personal technologies in the university classroom: Analyzing the perceptions of the digital generation. *Technology, Pedagogy and Education, 25*(1), 101–117. doi:10.1080/1475939X.2015.1120684.

Lave, J. (1988). *Cognition in practice: Mind, mathematics and culture in everyday life*. New York, NY: Cambridge University Press.

Ledbetter, A. M., and Finn, A. N. (2013). Teacher technology policies and online communication apprehension as predictors of learner empowerment. *Communication Education, 62*, 301–317. doi:10.1080/03634523.2013.794386.

Ledbetter, A. M., and Finn, A. N. (2016). Why do students use mobile technology for social purposes during class? Modeling teacher credibility, learner empowerment, and online communication attitude as predictors. *Communication Education, 65*, 1–23. doi: 10.1080/03634523.2015.1064145.

Lee, M. H., and Tsai, C. C. (2010). Exploring teachers' perceived self-efficacy and technological pedagogical content knowledge with respect to educational use of the World Wide Web. *Instructional Science, 38*(1), 1–21. doi:10.1007/s11251-008-9075-4.

Lee, Y. H., Heeter, C., Magerko, B., and Medler, B. (2012). Gaming mindsets: Implicit theories in serious game learning. *Cyberpsychology, Behavior, and Social Networking, 15*, 190–194. doi:10.1089/cyber.2011.0328.

Lei, J. (2009). Digital natives as preservice teachers: What technology preparation is needed? *Journal of Computing in Teacher Education, 25*(3), 87–97.

Lenhart, A., Purcell, K., Smith, A., and Zickuhr, K. (2010). *Social media and young adults*. Washington, DC: Pew Internet and American Life Project. Retrieved from http://www.pewinternet.org/files/oldmedia/Files/Reports/2010/PIP_Social_Media_and_Young_Adults_Report_Final_with_toplines.pdf.

Leonard, L., Mokwele, T., Siebrits, A., and Stoltenkamp, J. (2016). "Digital natives" require basic digital literacy skills. In *The IAFOR International Conference on Technology in the Classroom Official Conference Proceedings* (pp. 19–35). Retrieved from http://repository.uwc.ac.za/bitstream/handle/10566/2372/Leonard_Digital_2016.pdf?sequence=5&isAllowed=y.

Liccope, C. (2004). "Connected" presence: The emergence of a new repertoire for managing social relationships in a changing communication technoscape. *Environment and Planning D: Society and Space, 22*, 135–156. doi:10.1068/d323t.

Limperos, A. M., Downs, E., Ivory, J. D., and Bowman, N. D. (2013). Leveling up: A review of emerging trends and suggestions for the next generation of communication research investigating video games' effects. *Communication Yearbook, 37*, 348–377. doi:10.1080/23808985.2013.11679155.

Liu, S. H., Liao, H. L., and Pratt, J. A. (2009). Impact of media richness and flow on e-learning technology acceptance. *Computers & Education, 52*, 599–607. doi:10.1016/j.compedu.2008.11.002.

Lonn, S., and Teasley, S. D. (2009). Saving time or innovating practice: Investigating perceptions and uses of learning management systems. *Computers & Education, 53*, 686–694. doi:10.1016/j.compedu.2009.04.008.

Looi, C. K., Sun, D., Wu, L., Seow, P., Chia, G., Wong, L. H., Soloway, E., and Norris, C. (2014). Implementing mobile learning curricula in a grade level: Empirical study of learning effectiveness at scale. *Computers & Education, 77*, 101–115. doi:10.1016/j.compedu.2014.04.011.

Lu, J., Yao, J. E., and Yu, C. S. (2005). Personal innovativeness, social influences and adoption of wireless Internet services via mobile technology. *The Journal of Strategic Information Systems, 14*, 245–268. doi:10.1016/j.jsis.2005.07.003.

Madge, C., Meek, J., Wellens, J., and Hooley, T. (2009). Facebook, social integration and informal learning at university: "It is more for socialising and talking to friends about work than for actually doing work." *Learning, Media and Technology, 34*, 141–155. doi: 10.1080/17439880902923606.

Mandinach, E. B., and Jackson, S. S. (2012). *Transforming teaching and learning through data-driven decision making*. Thousand Oaks, CA: Corwin Press.

Manzo, K. K. (2009). Twitter lessons in 140 characters or less. *Education Week, 29*(8), 1–14.

Marshall, L., Mandiangu, E. K., Venter, J. (2015). A methodology for comparing and identification of the best suited learning management system for modules. In *Proceedings of the 6th*

Annual International Conference on Computer Science Education (pp. 134–142). Singapore, Singapore.

Martin, F., and Ertzberger, J. (2013). Here and now mobile learning: An experimental study on the use of mobile technology. *Computers & Education*, *68*, 76–85. doi:10.1016/j.compedu.2013.04.021.

Mazer, J. P., Murphy, R. E., and Simonds, C. J. (2007). I'll see you on "Facebook": The effects of computer-mediated teacher self-disclosure on student motivation, affective learning, and classroom climate. *Communication Education*, *56*, 1–17. doi: 10.1080/03634520601009710.

McCorkle, D. E., and McCorkle, Y. L. (2012). Using LinkedIn in the marketing classroom: Exploratory insights and recommendations for teaching social media/networking. *Marketing Education Review*, *22*, 157–166.

McGill, T. J., and Klobas, J. E. (2009). A task–technology fit view of learning management system impact. *Computers & Education*, *52*, 496–508. doi: 10.1016/j.compedu.2008.10.002.

Plass, J. L., Homer, B. D., and Kinzer, C. K. (2015) Foundations of game-based learning. *Education Psychologist*, *50*, 258–283. doi:10.1080/00461520.2015.1122533.

Reinders, H. (2010). Twenty ideas for using mobile phones in the language classroom. *English Teaching Forum*, *48*(3), 20–33.

Reiser, R. A. (1987). Instructional technology: A history. In R Gagne (Ed.), *Instructional technology: Foundations* (pp. 1–34). New Jersey, NJ: Lawrence Erlbaum.

Roblyer, M. D., Edwards, J., and Havriluk, M. A. (2002). *Integrating educational technology into teaching* (3rd ed.). Columbus, Ohio: Prentice Hall.

Rosen, P. 2005. Acceptance and rejection: Two sides of the same coin, or two different coins? *DIGIT 2005 Proceedings*. Retrieved from http://aisel.aisnet.org/digit2005/2.

Saettler, P. (1968). A history of instructional technology. New York, NY: McGraw-Hill.

Salleh, S. (2016). Examining the influence of teachers' beliefs towards technology integration in classroom. *The International Journal of Information and Learning Technology*, *33*(1), 17–35. doi:10.1108/IJILT-10-2015-0032.

Salter, A. (2016, August 22). Student-centered design within an LMS. *Chronicle of Higher Education*. Retrieved from http://www.chronicle.com.

Schell, J. (2008). *The art of game design: A book of lenses*. Burlington, MA: Morgan Kaufman.

Schmidt, D. A., Baran, E., Thompson, A. D., Mishra, P., Koehler, M. J., and Shin, T. S. (2009). Technological pedagogical content knowledge (TPACK): The development and validation of an assessment instrument for preservice teachers. *Journal of Research on Technology in Education*, *42*, 123–149.

Schrodt, P., and Witt, P. L. (2006). Students' attributions of instructor credibility as a function of students' expectations of instructional technology use and nonverbal immediacy, *Communication Education*, *55*, 1–20. doi:10.1080/03634520500343335.

Sellnow, D. D., Limperos, A., Frisby, B. N., Sellnow, T. L., Spence, P. R., and Downs, E. (2015). Expanding the scope of instructional communication research: Looking beyond classroom contexts. *Communication Studies*, *66*, 417–432. doi:10.1080/10510974.2015.1057750.

Selwyn, N. (2010). Looking beyond learning: Notes towards the critical study of educational technology. *Journal of Computer Assisted Learning*, *26*(1), 65–73. doi:10.1111/j.1365-2729.2009.00338.x.

Short, J., Williams, E., and Christie, B. (1976). *The social psychology of telecommunications*. London: John Wiley.

Slone, A. R., and Housley Gaffney, A. L. (2016). Assessing students' use of LinkedIn in a business and professional communication course. *Communication Teacher*, *30*, 206–214. doi:10.1080/17404622.2016.1219043.

Smart, J., Cascio, J., and Paffendor, J. (2007). *Metaverse roadmap: Pathways to the 3D web*. Retrieved from http://metaverseroadmap.org/MetaverseRoadmapOverview.pdf.

Smith, A., Rainie, L., and Zickuhr, K. (2011). *College students and technology*. Washington, DC: Pew Internet and American Life Project. Retrieved from http://pewinternet.org/Reports/2011/College-students-andtechnology/Report.aspx.

Stowell, J. R., Tanner, J., and Tomasino, E. (2015). Harnessing mobile technology for student assessment. In *Encyclopedia of Mobile Phone Behavior* (pp. 479–489). IGI Global.

Strommen, E. F., and Lincoln, B. (1992). Constructivism, technology, and the future of classroom learning. *Education and Urban Society, 24*, 466–476. doi:10.1177/0013124592024004004.

Tao, J., Clark, J., Gwyn, G., and Lim, D. (2010). Hand-held clickers vs. virtual clickers: What do our students think? *Journal of Interactive Instruction Development, 21*(4), 17–23.

Tess, P. A. (2013). The role of social media in higher education classes (real and virtual)—A literature review. *Computers in Human Behavior, 29*, A60–A68. doi:10.1016/j.chb.2012.12.032.

Thornton, P., and Houser, C. (2003). Using mobile web and video phones in English language teaching: Projects with Japanese college students. In B. Morrison, C. Green, and G. Motteram (Eds.), *Directions in CALL: Experience, experiments & evaluation* (pp. 207–224). Hong Kong, China: Hong Kong Polytechnic University.

Tozoglu, D., and Varank, I. (2001, November). Technology explosion and its impact on education. Paper presented at the National Convention of the Association for Educational Communications and Technology, Atlanta, GA. (ERIC Reproduction Service No. ED470179). Retrieved August 8, 2005, from http://www.eric.ed.gov.

Walker, D. S., Lindner, J. R., Murphrey, T. P., and Dooley, K. (2016). Learning management system usage: Perspectives from university instructors. *Quarterly Review of Distance Education, 17*, 41–50.

Wang, F., and Burton, J. K. (2012). Second Life in education: A review of publications from its launch to 2011. *British Journal of Educational Technology, 44*, 357–371. doi:10.1111/j.1467-8535.2012.01334.x.

Wang, Q., Woo, H. L., Quek, C. L., Yang, Y., and Liu, M. (2012). Using the Facebook group as a learning management system: An exploratory study. *British Journal of Educational Technology, 43*, 428–438. doi: 10.1111/j.1467-8535.2011.01195.x.

Warburton, S. (2009). Second Life in higher education: Assessing the potential for and the barriers to deploying virtual worlds in learning and teaching. *British Journal of Educational Technology, 40*, 414–426. doi: 10.1111/j.1467-8535.2009.00952.x.

Watson, W. R., and Watson, S. L. (2007). An argument for clarity: What are learning management systems, what are they not, and what should they become? *Tech Trends, 51*, 28–34.

Weaver, D., Spratt, C., and Nair, C. S. (2008). Academic and student use of a learning management system: Implications for quality. *Australasian Journal of Educational Technology, 24*, 30–41.

Weber, N. D., and Waxman, H. C. (2015). *The impact of classroom technology availability on novice teacher and student use*. In D. Rutledge and D. Slykhuis (Eds.), *Proceedings of Society for Information Technology & Teacher Education International Conference 2015* (pp. 3500–3506). Chesapeake, VA: Association for the Advancement of Computing in Education (AACE).

Wei, F. Y. F., Wang, T. K., and Klausner, M. (2012). Rethinking college students' self-regulation and sustained attention: Does text messaging during class influence cognitive learning? *Communication Education, 61*, 185–204. doi:10.1080/03634523.2012.672755.

Weimer M. J. (2001) *The influence of technology such as smart board interactive whiteboard on student motivation in the classroom*. Retrieved from http://www.smarterkids.org/research/paper7.asp.

Westerman, D., Daniel, E. S., and Bowman, N. D. (2016). Learned risks and experienced rewards: Exploring the potential sources of students' attitudes toward social media and face-to-face communication. *The Internet and Higher Education, 31*, 52–57. doi:10.1016/j.iheduc.2016.06.004.

Wombacher, K. A., Harris, C. J., Buckner, M. M., Frisby, B., and Limperos, A. M. (2016). The effects of computer-mediated communication anxiety on student perceptions of instructor behaviors, perceived learning, and quiz performance. *Communication Education*, 1–14. doi:10.1080/03634523.2016.1221511.

Young, J. R. (2010). Teaching with Twitter: Not for the faint of heart. *Education Digest, 75*, 9–12.

Young, J. R. (2016, September 7). What clicks from 70,000 courses reveal about student learning. *Chronicle of Higher Education*. Retrieved from http://www.chronicle.com.

Young, M. R., Klemz, B. R., and Murphy, J. W. (2003). Enhancing learning outcomes: The effects of instructional technology, learning styles, instructional methods, and student behavior. *Journal of Marketing Education, 25*(2), 130–142. doi:10.1177/0273475303254004.

Chapter Ten

The Next Phase

New Media and the Inevitable Transition

Shawn Apostel

BACKGROUND AND HISTORICAL CONTEXT

Twenty years ago (1997) a state-of-the-art library was constructed in a small, private university in a southern city. The 70,000-square-foot library housed the computer network that supported campus computing and featured 400 outlets to access the Internet and online journals, a satellite classroom that allowed students to connect via video to people in another location, a listening-viewing room, and a technology lab with 18 desktop computers. Furthermore, students were given a free email address (Hotmail was only a year old at the time) and access to a 24-hour computer lab. Faculty were provided with a virtual bulletin board (the university's first learning management system, or LMS) to share information outside of class. And, like many of today's libraries, the facility offered study carrels, research rooms, and spaces for study groups. At the time this library was considered state of the art. However, first and foremost, "the guiding principle throughout [the construction of the library] was that technology should be designed to support teaching, learning and communication" (Hall, 1999, p. 34).

Technology has changed over the last twenty years, but the fundamentals of education needs are still relevant today. By looking at what the library provided then—access to technology (email and Internet) and the ability to connect with others (in different buildings, faculty and students, classrooms to the world)—we can understand what role technology has played and continues to play in a university setting. We can then project what changes may take place in the future.

Many of the technologies we take for granted today were expensive and space consuming twenty years ago. First, access was a major concern. While computers in 1997 were generally as expensive as a typical, high-performing computer today, having the space for a computer (e.g., *large* monitors) and Internet connection was still relatively difficult for the novice users. Computers were on the verge of becoming mainstream; America OnLine (or AOL) was about two years old, and previously, Internet connection was only offered by colleges and universities. Microsoft had just released Windows 95, the first software that actually pushed Disk Operating System (or DOS) commands away from view, meaning one could now use a graphic user interface (and no coding) to operate a computer. However, these new features were still catching on in many homes, and the university was the first place many users were introduced to the concept of surfing and communicating via email. For perspective, consider that several popular sites in 2017 were not in existence when the library was built: Facebook began in 2004; YouTube began in 2005; and Twitter began in 2006.

This brings us to a second observation from the technology offered in the 1997 library, and that is one of connectivity. Owning or providing a computer is one thing, but connecting computers and users was still state of the art. Thus, the library had the challenge of creating quite a few connections. One, it connected buildings. Two, it connected faculty and students. Three, it connected classrooms to the world. And fourth, it connected students and faculty to the international academic community. The institutional response to these connectivity challenges was, at the time, groundbreaking. The library answered the first challenge by housing the main networking computer and connecting buildings via fiber optic lines. This allowed faculty in one building to post and retrieve information from a central location. By providing this access, students and faculty did not have to leave their buildings to locate and download information. Computer labs were constructed throughout campus, and the second concern (connecting faculty and students) was addressed via an online bulletin board. Using this tool, faculty could make announcements, post assignments and study guides, and answer student questions—all outside of the classroom. For this tool to work, however, students needed access to computers, so the 24-hour computer lab in the library was a welcomed space for those unable to wait in line for their turn at the computer. The third concern had to do with classroom experiences. The satellite classroom was designed with that connection in mind. Now faculty could reserve a space and connect with another class or researcher using similar technology—an experience that was very cost-prohibitive at the time for the average home user. And finally, connecting the student and faculty to online resources opened up new levels of research. The library used the initiative to offer, for the first time, online journal articles and reference materials to the entire campus community. This was an important tool because searching for information online was still in its infancy. For perspective, note that Yahoo, the first popular search engine, was only about a year old. Finding reputable online information was difficult, and the library took on the task to help the academic community during that time of transition.

Having access to this new technology did not come without problems. A quick look at the student newspaper from that time reveals several concerns students and faculty had with the technology of the day. First, professors lamented that students were becoming so hooked on "surfing the web" they weren't able to complete assignments on time. Second, students were constantly warned that the computer lab had become infected with viruses. And third, faculty were accidently posting things publicly on the online bulletin board LMS when they thought they were posting messages privately.

Sound familiar? Unfortunately, we continue to see these same concerns today as we use technology to communicate and create content online. But today, students are so connected to their phone screens that they don't pay attention in class. Viruses, fake news, and hacking still plagues our online environments. And messages we felt were private, like political emails, become hacked and published for the world to read.

Recently, the same twenty-year-old, state-of-the-art library was renovated, and, like its original construction, the focus of the redesign was to support the teaching, learning, and communication initiatives of the university community. Based on what has changed, we can begin to make inferences about the way technology will shape the future of education. First, what's the same? Students still receive a free email account, and faculty still can use a university-provided LMS to connect with students. There are still computers available in the library, both desktop and laptop. However, there are a few notable differences. For example, the library provides excellent Wi-Fi to any connected device, many of the computers feature wireless mice and keyboards, large screens are available to connect (both via wire or wirelessly) to a wide range of devices, and many books have been moved into storage to facilitate more collaborative learning environments.

Other services are enhanced as well. For example, in addition to emails, students receive a much broader range of communication tools via technology; take the LMS as an example. One specific LMS, Moodle, provides an online platform for faculty to communicate with students, similar to the online bulletin board. Moodle also provides a place for students to turn in assignments, take quizzes, watch videos from faculty and fellow students, interact with each other on discussion boards, and the list goes on. Furthermore, while emails are still a dominate form of communication for faculty, students have expanded their communication resources and seem more inclined to text or use social media for information rather than check their email, and the university has responded by incorporating social media and text messaging into their announcement cycles.

THEORETICAL UNDERSTANDING

In 1999, Dr. Sugata Mitra installed a computer inside a wall facing a street in the slums around his company in India. He was amazed at how quickly the children there learned how to use the computer to play games and look up information. He thought one of the software engineers he worked with taught the children how to use the device, so he conducted another experiment further away to see how children could learn without a teacher; he got the same results. What Mitra learned was that given enough time and motivation, people can teach themselves. Teachers are not always necessary. In fact, he argues, if teachers can be replaced by a computer, they should be (Mitra, 2007). One of the biggest challenges for educators in the next twenty years will be the integration of available learning modules with classroom activities. Take children born in the last seven years as an example. For all of their lives, they've been able to look up information using Siri, a voice-assistant program which is now standard on an iPhone and commonly used in the United States. After working with Siri for so many years, a typical one-hour, half-hearted university lecture on a topic that is thoroughly explored online will have little value to them, and rightly so. The computer can teach them more effectively because it provides information when and where it's needed. Educators have less than ten years to figure this out if they want to reach the minds of our next generation. Indeed, even today, students are less likely to communicate with each other using written words as they increasingly utilize multimodal communication tools because these tools/apps are free and commonly found on their smartphones (Apostel and Apostel, 2017).

The speed and efficiency of "modern" devices are impressive. Moore's Law (basically, that computer-processing speeds will double every two years) has been amazingly true. It's been so true that today processing speeds are no longer an issue for the typical person's current technology needs. In fact, smartphones created today have enough technology to be reused as satellites. Currently, developers and designers are focused on the size of the device and technology's most pernicious problem: the advancement of battery technology. Lithium ion has taken us far, but a new type of energy storage is needed to truly make the majority of our devices useable for more than a day at a time between charges.

As computers continue to get smaller, lighter, and longer lasting, the next concern for educators is how, and in what way, students and educators should interact with these devices inside and outside of the classroom. Should educators focus on providing an immersive learning environment, one in which students embed themselves in the information? Or should students have multiple displays of information, which facilitate the widest range of learning styles? In their 1999 book *Remediation: Understanding New Media*, authors Bolter and Grusin make a compelling argument that there are two major ways we interact with technology: Hypermediacy and Immediacy. These concepts can be helpful as we consider ways to adapt technology into a learning environment.

Hypermediacy is the integration of multiple sources of information. Think ESPN. As you watch the game, you hear announcers and see relevant information along the bottom of the page. When something important happens, the announcers explain what happens by writing on the screen or showing the same play in slow motion. This all happens in real time. While the game is on, viewers can find information through a wide range of media on one screen, and they can participate by connecting with other fans or even with ESPN through hashtags and message forums. Hypermediacy is also common on many web sites, even those used for shopping. In this case, the display integrates multiple sources of information to engage with the user. When the viewer clicks on one item, similar items appear. Comments are displayed to persuade or dissuade a purchase. Related items appear on the side of the screen. For a final example, consider the online, live-cast web site Twitch. On this site, viewers watch a person completing a task (cooking a dish, tattooing a person, playing a video game) while a live chat stream section along the side of the screen populates comments from viewers from around the world. As the show goes on, the performer engages with the audience—doing a "Dap" for tipping, offering a shout-out to popular viewers, and answering questions that seem pertinent.

In contrast to Hypermediacy, Immediacy is total immersion in the computer's simulated environment. We see this taking place when people interact with virtual reality devices like Google Cardboard or Oculus Rift. In this case, the users place a device in front of their eyes, and they can see and interact with a completely different environment, a virtual environment, by turning their heads and moving their hands. This total immersion is currently being used to aid those suffering from speech anxiety. The users wear the device and see an audience of recorded people watching them. Users can choose a small audience or large audience to practice a speech. Furthermore, students can learn by virtually visiting locations like museums, world heritage sites, even the Great Barrier Reef.

Combining these two approaches to interact with technology, we have augmented reality; this technology has the ability of becoming a real game changer for education. With augmented reality, we are given information via a transparent screen as we interact with the world around us. Information is offered to the user when it is needed. This information can be delivered to a user without the knowledge of other people in the area. In traditional skill-and-drill environments, augmented reality will present a major challenge. Why? Because students will argue (and indeed they already do) that the need to memorize information available on their connected devices is outdated. Information is readily accessible at lightning speed. To ensure educational integrity on tests and quizzes, we can remove student phones before a test. Imagine checking everyone's glasses and ear buds (and eventually contact lenses). That day will be here faster than you think.

So here's the question. Do we continue to design new testing protocols to make sure students don't cheat on their tests (e.g., dead zones with no connectivity)? Or do we design tests that require an integration of current knowledge with the ability to find viable solutions, new insights, and re-imagined possibilities? The latter is more sustainable. About the time that the state-of-the-art library mentioned earlier was constructed, a collection of scholars called the New London Group (1996) argued that writing has changed. No longer, they argued, should we see writing as words on paper; computers allow educators to easily integrate visual communication practices in the forms of graphics, images, and videos into what was once a traditional, five-page-essay assignment. Computers have only become more advanced since then, and we are slowly seeing more multimedia assignments incorporated into learning modules; however, educators have a long journey ahead, and the time is short. Augmented reality will be mainstream soon, so instructors must move beyond being just content distributors; they must be experience facilitators.

While multimedia assignments offer one approach, gamification is also a growing approach to education challenges. We can already see this approach being taken with popular online learning platforms like Khan Academy, Code Academy, and the language learning software DuoLingo. All are free platforms that turn the rather mundane learning of math, coding, and language into a rewards-based social environment. The more you do, the more points you get. You can compete with others and show your results to your friends and followers. You can collect badges and upgrade characters. Gamification enables students to be motivated through acquiring social capital (as Bourdieu, 1986, would argue) instead of merely avoiding a poor grade. Proper gamification makes the motivation to learn intrinsic instead of extrinsic (as is most commonly the case today).

With the advancements made in technology since the opening of the state-of-the-art library twenty years ago, we can see that the main goals of the building are still goals we strive for in our integration of technology and education: "technology should be designed to support teaching, learning and communication" (Hall, 1999, p. 34). Our challenge, as educators, is to continue seeing technology as a "support" and not a hindrance to learning. Considering Mitra's (2007) statement at the beginning of this section, be sure to integrate these new tools. Don't find yourself teaching in a way that a computer can do better.

ADOPTION

Twenty years ago, rooms in the library were specially outfitted with technology and designed to help students connect with the world. Now students and instructors have the ability to connect with people via low-cost, connected devices and free programs like Skype, Google Hangout, and FaceTime. Soon, connecting with virtual reality (VR) will be a mainstream option. Today, it's easy to purchase a cheap cardboard VR device, download an app, and insert your phone to enjoy a virtual reality experience. Of course, this is only the first wave of usage. One can easily imagine using the device to meet and collaborate with others in different locations. Like Skyping a meeting today, a virtual meeting is a logical next step in our ability to connect with people who are not geographically near us. Virtual student field trips are another logical progression of this technology. But virtual reality is only one application of these types of devices. Augmented reality can benefit from this technology as well. While we already see the beginnings of computer-assisted translation services provided via lenses and ear buds, the next steps are easy to imagine. Students can participate in a virtual chemistry lab to save money on chemicals. They can also dissect virtual cadavers to understand the human body. They can learn the names of plants as they walk through a forest. The potential is limited only by our imagination.

Looking back again at the progress the library has made in the past 20 years, we see that computers were connected to the Internet to help students find information for research. Now we can connect via Wi-Fi or cell phone signal. These connections are available throughout campus and should get faster as technology progresses. However, artificial intelligence will eventually be used to help us filter vast amounts of data produced by the academic community. In his 1981 book *Critical Path*, R. Buckminster Fuller looks back at human development and argues that the doubling of human knowledge increases exponentially throughout time. While it used to take 100 years for knowledge to double, today, technology leaders estimate that human knowledge doubles every 13 months, and the prediction is that the time for a "Knowledge Doubling Curve" will continue to decrease. As knowledge increases at increasingly rapid rates, searches for information will be facilitated by computers. Artificial intelligence (AI) will be the only way we'll be able to navigate this abundance of knowledge. Imagine asking a virtual assistant to pull up any peer-reviewed journal that mentions a scholar's use of a certain term in a particular circumstance. As AI becomes more mainstream, we'll have access to a system that can understand, process, and filter trillions of pages in microseconds. Think Google on steroids.

By offering computers 20 years ago, the library enabled students with the ability to type their papers on a screen via a keyboard, so students no longer needed typewriters, ink ribbons, and whiteout to correct mistakes. This also gave students the ability to easily rewrite and revise papers. Today, we can easily add illustrations, photographs, and tables to our written works. Multimedia composition has never been easier or less expensive. In the future, we may see the reduction of academic texts and a surge of academic video and image files, especially as smart paper and flexible, energy-efficient tablets become more affordable and advanced.

THE INFLUENCE OF TECHNOLOGY ON THE UNIVERSITY

Consider the, arguably, first university, begun by Plato in ancient Greece. Unlike his predecessors, Plato embraced writing technology, much to the chagrin of Socrates. Ironically, the only reason we know Socrates existed is because Plato wrote about him. Socrates was afraid that writing would ruin human memory. He also felt that one-on-one communication was superior to written communication because a person can be questioned and interrogated when they are in front of you; it's impossible to ask a scroll what a written phrase means. Despite the hesitations of Socrates, the academic community has continued to embrace writing technology since that time. Over the years, new technologies have reshaped the way we teach. Because of writing, instructors were able to work with more than one person at a time and lectures became more common. Students would write down solutions to problems on their clay (later slate) tablets, and the teacher could walk around and inspect student work. This took a bit of time because a teacher had to say the instructions out loud, then walk around and make sure students wrote things correctly, then a revolution occurred. About 200 years ago, the chalkboard was invented in Scotland. Suddenly, a teacher could write something on the board and be relatively assured that students could make an exact copy on their slate tablets. Since then, we have seen modern iterations of the chalkboard concept. For instance, PowerPoint has only been around 30 years, and that technology has totally changed the way many instructors and students interact. Today, it's common for a professor to post PowerPoint slides online for students to print out and bring to class. As tablets become more affordable, students may feel more comfortable downloading PowerPoints and using a stylus or keyboard to write notes on their electronic devices.

The point is, technology is the reason why we have universities to begin with. Writing enabled one instructor to work with many students at the same time, and today's technology is really no different. While chalkboards enabled instructors to remain at the front of a classroom during a lecture, PowerPoint and clicker technology allow instructors to move about the room once again. As students and instructors become more accustomed to learning and teaching in digital environments, physical environments will enable students to interact with each other, conduct collaborative research, prototype and test possible solutions, and propose creative solutions to the problems the instructors provide. Incorporating augmented and virtual reality into those learning situations will require instructors to venture from the traditional lecture and skill-and-drill instruction and weave online modules with classroom and virtual learning experiences. As instruction changes, so will tests. With the ability to constantly communicate with artificial intelligence, memorization will be less important than creative problem solving. Universities that successfully navigate technological innovations will move beyond being a content distributor; they will be an experience facilitator—offering students a safe place to reach their full creative potential.

We began this chapter with a look back at the opening of a new, state-of-the-art library in 1997—a library designed to facilitate teaching, learning, and communication. Twenty years later, the same library has been updated to incorporate new technology, addressing the technological and space requirements for today's academic community. Twenty years from now, in 2037, we can only imagine how technology will continue to bring instructors closer to their students, students closer to the course curriculum, and scholars closer to each other. Collaboration between peers, students, and artificial intelligence will create the potential for creative problem solving and innovation at a level we are only beginning to imagine.

REFERENCES

Apostel, S., and Apostel, K. (2017). The flexible center: Embracing technology, open spaces, and online pedagogy. In M. Kim and R. Carpenter (Eds.), *Writing studio pedagogy: Space, place, and rhetoric in collaborative environments*. Lanham, MD: Rowman & Littlefield.

Bourdieu, P. (1986). The forms of capital. In J. Richardson (Ed.), *Handbook of theory and research for the sociology of education*. New York: Greenwood, 241–258.

Hall, W. (1999). *High upon a hill: A history of Bellarmine College*. Louisville: Bellarmine College Press.

Mitra, S. (2007). Kids can teach themselves. Ted Talk. Retrieved from https://www.ted.com/talks/sugata_mitra_shows_how_kids_teach_themselves.

The New London Group. (1996). A pedagogy of multiliteracies. *Harvard Educational Review* 66, 1.

Index

About the Editor and Contributors

Shawn Apostel, PhD, is an assistant professor of communication and instructional technology specialist at Bellarmine University where he provides support to faculty and IT to facilitate online and classroom instruction that incorporates technology. He teaches multimedia communication, data visualization, digital portfolio, and technical communication. His research interests include teaching with technology, digital ethos, e-waste reduction, learning space design, and technical and visual communication. His work is published by IGI Global, CCDigital Press, Lexington Books, New Forums Press, *Kairos: A Journal of Rhetoric, Technology, and Pedagogy*, and Computers and Composition Online. He co-edited *Online Credibility and Digital Ethos: Evaluating Computer-Mediated Communication* and co-authored *Teaching Creative Thinking: A New Pedagogy for the 21st Century*. His latest project, a co-edited collection entitled *Establishing and Evaluating Digital Ethos and Online Credibility*, was published by IGI Global in 2016.

Marjorie M. Buckner (PhD, University of Kentucky, 2015) is an assistant professor in the Department of Communication Studies, College of Media and Communication at Texas Tech University. She researches organizational and instructional communication, focused particularly on antecedents and outcomes related to expressed dissent in various contexts. With regards to new media pedagogy, Marjorie is particularly interested in learning outcomes related to the use of social media platforms and synchronous computer-mediated communication in college instruction.

Russell Carpenter, PhD, is executive director of the Noel Studio for Academic Creativity and associate professor of English at Eastern Kentucky University. Recent books include *Sustainable Learning Spaces: Design,*

Infrastructure, and Technology and *The Routledge Reader on Writing Centers and New Media.* He is editor of the *Journal of Faculty Development*.

Beth Case is the program manager for Digital, Emerging, and Assistive Technologies at the Delphi Center for Teaching and Learning at the University of Louisville. She has two master's degrees, one in clinical psychology and one in instructional technology. She is also completing her dissertation for a doctoral degree in instructional technology from Texas Tech University. Prior to returning to graduate school, Beth worked in postsecondary disability services for thirteen years, specializing in online accessibility. Her background in both disability services and instructional technology prepares her for helping faculty make online courses accessible to students with disabilities. She stays on top of emerging trends in using technology in education and enjoys sharing that knowledge with others.

Andrew W. Cole received a PhD in communication from the University of Wisconsin–Milwaukee. His research interests focus on communication and technology, particularly in educational and health contexts. He has work experience in online and hybrid/blended course design, and development in competency-based curriculum. He has taught courses in public speaking, interpersonal communication, conflict resolution, and business and professional communication.

Clay Ewing is an assistant professor at the University of Miami. His research focuses on serious games, implementing game mechanics into real-world applications, and social justice. As an award-winning game designer and developer, Professor Ewing's games have tackled issues such as vector-borne diseases, the cost of health care, social safety nets, and labor practices. His most recent game, Unsavory, is the winner of a special emphasis award at the Serious Games Showcase and Challenge for its use of social media crowdsourcing for peer learning. Clay has worked with numerous non-profits including Red Cross Red Crescent, Open Society Foundations, ROC United, Oxfam, and the AIDS & Rights Alliance for Southern Africa. His projects have been covered by The Huffington Post, NPR, *Forbes*, and *The Consumerist*. He also is the creator of Queso, an open-source learning management for gamifying the classroom.

T. Kody Frey (MA, Illinois State University, 2015) is a doctoral student in the College of Communication and Information at the University of Kentucky. His research interests investigate the potential uses of technology as a means of enhancing the basic communication course classroom. Additionally, he concentrates on pedagogical innovation, assessment, and training as potential mechanisms to improve the general education experience for both students and instructors. Kody has published in both *Communication Education* and *The Basic Communication Course Annual*, in addition to presentations at numerous regional and national conferences.

Nigel Haarstad (PhD, University of Kentucky, 2016) is the online learning & LMS specialist in the University of Mary Washington's Division of Teaching & Learning Technologies. There, he collaborates with faculty to develop their digital pedagogies and experiment with new instructional technologies. He also administers the school's learning management system and offers guidance to departments and administration to support the development of effective online courses and programs. His research has focused on the impact of technology on instructional communication, particularly in emergency and risk communication settings.

Heather J. Hether, PhD, is a faculty member in the Department of Communication at the University of California, Davis. Her research interests focus on digital media in the health and education contexts, effective pedagogy, and health communication. Dr. Hether teaches courses in public relations and health communication. She earned her PhD at the Annenberg School for Communication and Journalism at the University of Southern California.

Renee Kaufmann (PhD, University of Kentucky, 2014) is an assistant professor in the College of Communication and Information, School of Information Science at the University of Kentucky. Her research lines examine online learning in higher education and the use of communication technologies for educational and relational outcomes. More specifically, she focuses on how instructors can enhance the learning experience for their online students, as well as how communication on social media platforms can enhance or hinder learning and relationships. Renee has published her research in *Computers and Education*, *Communication Education*, *Communication Teacher*, and *Computers in Human Behavior*.

Jason M. Martin, PhD, is an assistant professor in the Department of Communication Studies at the University of Missouri–Kansas City where he teaches persuasion, intercultural communication, and the department's capstone class. He received his PhD in communication from the University of Kentucky, his MA in journalism and communication from the Ohio State University, and his bachelor degrees in communication and business administration from the University of Kentucky. His work has been presented at regional, national, and international conferences and published in various academic journals and educational books.

Joe C. Martin is a faculty lecturer in instructional communication and research at the University of Kentucky. He earned his MDiv (2010) and his ThM (2012) from the Southern Baptist Theological Seminary, and is currently pursuing a PhD in instructional communication at the University of Kentucky. His primary research interests include instructional communication, instructional technology, and the biology of human communication.

Mary S. Norman (MA, Baylor University, 2007) is a doctoral student in media and communication, College of Media and Communication at Texas Tech University. She researches gender depictions in children's programming and advertising and is interested in children's implicit attitudes towards gender. Mary is interested in incorporating new media typically employed in online courses in face-to-face class sessions as a means of increasing active learning.

Crystal Simons is an MA candidate in the School of Communication at Bellarmine University. Crystal's research interests include environmentalism and journalism. After receiving her MA, Crystal plans to pursue a position with the US Peace Corps and eventual PhD studies.

Michael G. Strawser, PhD, is an assistant professor in the School of Communication at Bellarmine University where he also serves as the director of Graduate Programs. He received his PhD in communication from the University of Kentucky and he specializes in instructional and organizational communication. Michael has published his research in *Communication Education*, *Communication Teacher*, and the *Basic Communication Course Annual*.

Nicholas T. Tatum (MA, Abilene Christian University) is an instructor and PhD student in the College of Communication and Information at the University of Kentucky. He primarily studies instructional communication. His interests include scale development, quantitative methods, communication technology, and training and development, with research presented at numerous state, regional, and national conferences. In addition to actively pursuing research in the field, much of Nicholas' past and current professional experience in higher education, production management, and non-profit administration informs his academic pursuits.

Phillip E. Wagner (PhD, University of Kansas) is the director of General Education, chair of the Chancellor's Council on Diversity, Equity, and Inclusion, and a faculty member of Communication Studies at the University of South Florida Sarasota–Manatee. Phillip's research explores the technological intersections of identity, health, and communication. His work has been featured in journals such as *The International Journal of Men's Health*, *The Journal of Applied Communication Research*, *Communication Quarterly*, and *Women and Language*. Phillip's work has also been featured on the stages of TED at Tampa Bay's TEDx 2016 event. In his spare time, Phillip enjoys soaking up the sun on Florida's beaches with his family.

Jason Zahrndt works as a digital media consultant for the Delphi Center for Teaching and Learning at the University of Louisville. He holds a master's degree in library science and in English. He provides faculty development sessions on the creation and instruction of new media assignments and the role of technology in the classroom.

www.ingramcontent.com/pod-product-compliance
Lightning Source LLC
Chambersburg PA
CBHW021142070326
40689CB00043B/984

* 9 7 8 1 4 9 8 5 4 8 5 3 3 *